Beyond the Outback

Beyond the Outback

Gulf Women of Remote North West Queensland

Edited by

BRONWYN BLAKE

hachette
AUSTRALIA

Published in Australia and New Zealand in 2019
by Hachette Australia
(an imprint of Hachette Australia Pty Limited)
Level 17, 207 Kent Street, Sydney NSW 2000

www.hachette.com.au

10 9 8 7 6 5 4 3 2 1

Introduction and selection © Bronwyn Blake 2019

Individual stories © retained by the authors, who assert their rights to be known as the author of
their work.

A catalogue record for this
book is available from the
NATIONAL LIBRARY OF AUSTRALIA   National Library of Australia

ISBN: 978 0 7336 4220 3 (paperback)

Cover design by Christabella Designs
Cover photographs courtesy of Tanya Arnold (Miranda Downs Station Qld) and Toni Tapp Coutts
Inside cover photograph courtesy of Alamy
Typeset in Sabon LT Std by Kirby Jones
Printed and bound in Great Britain by Clays Ltd, Elcograf S.p.A.

The paper this book is printed on is certified against the
Forest Stewardship Council® Standards. McPherson's Printing Group
holds FSC® chain of custody certification SA-COC-005379. FSC®
promotes environmentally responsible, socially beneficial and
economically viable management of the world's forests.

CONTENTS

INTRODUCTION

Bronwyn Blake

Mustering twenty Gulf women!

I FIRST MET THE GREGORY DOWNS COMMUNITY THROUGH an evening with the Royal Flying Doctor Service (RFDS) in 2015 and at each subsequent gathering was more impressed with the responsibility these people took for each other and for their tiny dot of a community. So, at an initial meeting with the women in November 2015, I offered to create a writing anthology for the benefit of the Gregory and Gulf communities in North West Queensland. It was agreed that all contributions to the anthology would be voluntary and proceeds would be used to support community projects.

To look at, Gregory is a crossroad, a collection of dusty, weather-beaten buildings, the RFDS clinic, the sportsground and the famous Gregory Pub. It is 400 kilometres from

Mount Isa, its closest major town, and 120 kilometres from the small town of Burketown on the Gulf of Carpentaria. You would be making a terrible error to judge this place on the way it looks from the highway. The heart of Gregory is in its people, people who are self-sufficient, generous and cope with almost anything that life and the environment throws at them – floods, drought, sickness, emergencies and all the difficulties that come with running a business and family far from anywhere. They are forthright, outspoken and don't take kindly to being told by outsiders what they can and cannot do, should or shouldn't think.

In March 2016, I gave five workshops and talks at Gregory, Burketown and Doomadgee with copious notes on 'How to write your piece'. As work began to flow in, email support and mentoring became vital (despite often terrible internet access) and the year-long process of editing, rewriting and polishing began (as well as the laughing, bossing, encouraging, questioning and suffering the dreaded red pen).

The project grew and grew until many women were contributing, the book doubling its initial intended size. The contributing authors' excitement and anticipation was tangible, with many expressing their joy at writing their piece both as a contemporary Gulf narrative and as the basis for a family memoir.

It is not often that a person is fortunate enough to be told the story of another's life – warts, joys, terrors and all – but that is exactly what has been happening at my desk. I feel as if many friends have told me long and intriguing stories and, as I opened each one, it became my favourite.

So then, why would any sane editor want to wring the necks of these extraordinary and skilful women? My defence? Because as each was asked to contribute, the answers coming back, with few exceptions, were almost identical: 'I'm just ordinary, it's just life', 'There's nothing to write about', 'I can't write, I haven't written anything since school' and finally, reluctantly, 'Well okay, I'll give it a go, but it'll be boring,' or 'a dog's dinner', or 'unprintable', 'You'll have to fluff it all up,' 'You'll be sorry, I'm warning you!'

'Extraordinary', 'skilful', 'modest', 'pragmatic' and the ability to 'just do it' should have been added in bucketloads.

There are women in remote areas managing stations, bush hospitals and tourist ventures; new mothers on properties inaccessible in the wet season; women giving birth at home helped by a neighbour, rearing families and educating their children through Mount Isa School of the Air; women spending years fishing in the Gulf in sometimes unimaginable conditions, and so on ...

And then there are those wild and woolly Gulf kids! For toughness, capability, courtesy and independence – there are none quite like them. Reading about Dallas Daley's childhood, I wonder how any of them survive!

Nothing to write about, really. So ordinary. Just what you do. Just life.

As you will read, permanent roads are relatively new to Gregory. Mobile coverage is patchy (if it works at all). 'It's too far!' is a common excuse for anything (such as mains electricity) that doesn't arrive. For many years I lived in what was the remote and isolated town of Fairbanks, Alaska. There are remarkable similarities between the two towns and their people, from the extremes in temperature, plus or minus forty-five, to the swarms of seasonal biting insects and the flocks of tourists from down south: 'outsiders from the lower forty-eight states', or 'Mexicans' from Victoria and New South Wales. Alaskans also call their wilderness the bush. And I too grew to think that minus fifty and a measly two hours of twilight was a bit much, but ordinary in winter, and reading a paper by sunlight at midnight with visiting bear or moose was what you expected of summer. Newcomers often arrived up north with romantic ideas of the country. If they got over that and stayed, they often stayed for years, decades or forever. And if they had to leave, having drunk the Chena (or the Gregory), part of their heart always remained. Fifty years after leaving Fairbanks the smell of birch leaves in autumn or new spruce in spring still lifts me to that place, as the smell of the earth after the Wet will to those who have lived in the Gulf.

So, my road to the Gulf Country has been, as for many others in this book, a winding one, full of chances and sudden swerves into new tracks – a bit like driving after the ice Break-up or in the Wet. As their editor, I feel closely connected with these women writers who trusted me with very personal details. Through conversations and writing they gave me a window into their lives, so different from most of ours. They can, of course, all write. Some easily, some with difficulty, but all of them have the wonderful ability to tell a good yarn straight, the way things happened, with no fancy words or slick phrases, nothing 'fluffing them up'. I, the greedy editor constantly begging for more, more, more, have tried very hard to preserve these individual voices. They are the essence of these hardworking, no-nonsense people who deeply love their land and sea.

When I conceived the idea for this anthology I had two goals in mind. The first was to preserve the histories of Gulf women of the early twenty-first century, the second was that we could create an income for the women of Gregory to fund their community projects, including support for the RFDS clinic. Another positive outcome emerged as we progressed from writing workshops and mentoring to the back-and-forth work of editing and rewriting – the value the women placed on their writing for themselves and their families, and for the connectivity that the anthology was bringing to a very widespread community.

The writers and I are very proud that our original book is now being published by Hachette, that the stories of these remarkable women will travel well beyond North Queensland, and that this book will answer, to some degree, a friend's comment: 'Driving along these outback roads, you always wonder what goes on behind the gates.'

I had no idea when we began what a rich vein of gold we were tapping into. As the collector, collator and wielder of the dreaded red pen, I've been very lucky. I hope in writing their stories, these women see in black and white, for all time, just how extraordinary they are and how proud we are of them.

Map of the region

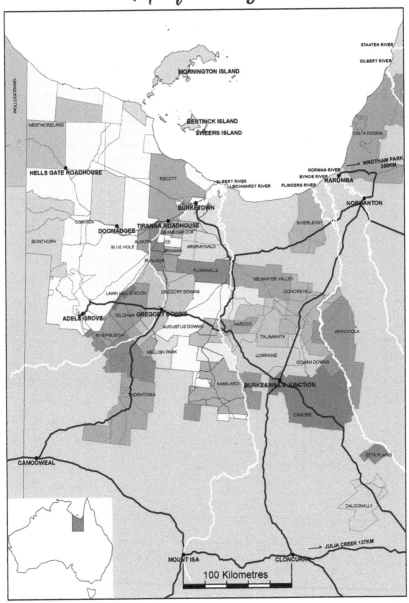

Map was created by Shari Rankin, Southern Gulf Natural Resource Management, Mount Isa.

Iconic Gulf cattle stations

Tess Arnold

Tess Arnold was born and raised in Cairns, north Queensland but spent a lot of her young life in Chillagoe, 300 kilometres to the west, where she developed a healthy love of the outdoors and the outback. Tess is a strong supporter of rural communities and appreciates the great work of the Royal Flying Doctor Service in rural and remote areas. For all their married life, Tess and her husband of thirty-four years, David, have lived on and managed Gulf cattle properties for Australian Agricultural Company and, more recently, for the past fourteen years, Paraway Pastoral Company at Gregory Downs Station. They have raised five children and currently have six grandchildren and counting.

REPTILES TO ROYALTY

Tess Arnold

SOMETHING ABOUT THE TONE OF VOICE SHOUTED 'URGENT' at me, even though she was whispering. I was not quite awake; the voice spoke a little louder and more urgently.

'Mum, Mum, quick! Jessica has been bitten by a snake. It looked like a king brown.'

That worked. I hit the floor at a run. The words were still being processed in my sluggish and sleepy brain. 'Jessica' and 'snake' were two words trying to reconcile themselves in my head, while another part of my brain thought, *Of course it's Jessica. Who else would get themselves into this predicament?*

Wondoola was renowned for its number of snakes. I knew it was more than probable it was a king brown, if indeed she had been bitten. I guess I should have thanked

God it was Jessica, as she is the calmest and most laid-back in our family. She is the second of our five children and is often described as a 'character'. Jess achieved her pilot's licence at sixteen years, and tandem skydived when not much older. Not yet seventeen, she had been bungee jumping and swimming with dolphins, and now here she was taking on a king brown in the middle of the night on a remote cattle property in North West Queensland.

Added to that, it was raining cats and dogs, and Wondoola Station is in the middle of 2700 square kilometres of black soil clay. Meaning, of course, there was no way for the Royal Flying Doctor Service (RFDS) to land on the gravel strip that had just had over twenty-five millimetres dumped on it.

All this ran through my brain while I grabbed bandages and shot questions at poor Kimberley, our eldest daughter, who alerted me to Jessica's plight – against Jess and her younger sister Hannah's wishes, as they were not supposed to be outside in the middle of the night.

My name is Tess Arnold. I have lived and worked on remote cattle stations in north Queensland since 1979. I was born and raised in Cairns with my two brothers, but as Dad came from Chillagoe, about three hundred kilometres west of Cairns, we spent most of our childhood camping in and exploring that area.

As soon as we left school, all three of us headed out and scored jobs on the stations west of Chillagoe. I started on

Highbury Station, which at the time was an outstation of Wrotham Park. During the off, or wet, season when there was no work on the stations, I went back to Cairns to see my parents and usually got volunteer jobs at local youth groups or childcare facilities until it was time to head west again.

In 1982 I spent some time working at Drumduff and Gamboola Stations, which were part of the bigger Wrotham Park (better known to locals as 'The Park'). That is where I met and married my husband, David, who worked as a helicopter pilot for the four stations. His father, the late Gordon Arnold, had managed Wrotham Park since 1963. David and I were married in July 1983 and Kimberley, our eldest daughter, was born in April 1984. We stayed on at Wrotham Park and David took over management when his mother and father retired in January 1989. Jessica came along in March 1987 then Hannah in 1988, followed by Rachel in 1990. We were blessed with our son, Gordon, in 1993. So we had five children in nine years.

At that time we were still quite remote. Satellite television was introduced in 1988; however, the phones didn't come to Wrotham Park until 1992 and we relied on the high frequency (HF) radio for everything. The bitumen road ended at Dimbulah, so there was nearly three hundred kilometres of gravel road to Wrotham Park.

During this time we worked very closely with the RFDS and Cairns School of the Air. There were quite a lot of children at Wrotham Park – sixteen at one stage – so health and education were paramount in the minds of the young mothers on the station.

We had a monthly doctor's clinic through RFDS that was an all-day event. People from the surrounding stations came to access the GP and child health services. David's parents were strong RFDS supporters and we continued the tradition, raising quite a lot of money over the years for this worthwhile cause.

We built up a close relationship with the staff and doctors, and it was Sister Carmel Bannon who, after lots of time with the mothers and children, identified the need for a remote-area first-aid procedure course. From little boys falling into septic tanks to premature labours, dislocated wrists, and chicken pox ... we dealt with it all, as do most remote-area mums. We'd always dealt with accidents and injuries on the station and also from the highway that runs near the station carrying traffic from Cairns in the east to Kowanyama in the west. Although the highway was graded every year, it was all gravel and noticeably claiming a higher number of accidents annually as more and more tourists came to explore the outback. This was my first taste of formal first-aid training and I enjoyed being part of the consultation team that started the first remote area course at Wrotham Park. Since then, trainers and presenters have coached the staff every year in remote-area first aid and it has paid off many times over the years. However, while it has been exceptionally valuable, with so many staff and visitors coming and going to and from the station every year, I originally wanted the children to learn first aid and what to do in an emergency. I must say, though, that with all this concern and preparation it was only twice that any of our own children caused us enough concern that we wanted to evacuate them – and guess what? Both times it was Jessica!

Getting back to the snake bite. We wrapped and immobilised Jessica's leg and called the RFDS. Unfortunately, through no fault of theirs, there was no way they could evacuate her with the rain coming down. They now have an emergency helicopter in Mount Isa, but back then the closest one was 500 kilometres away in Townsville, and that couldn't leave until morning anyway. I have only praise for the Mount Isa RFDS doctor who rang every fifteen minutes for an update on her condition. Jessica's leg went as hard as cement and there were a few other symptoms, such as nausea and pain. Dave and I were determined we weren't going to let six feet of wriggling reptile beat us, but secretly I was absolutely terrified and remember praying several times to God, Jesus, Mary, Mother of God and whoever else might have been listening. It was one of the longest nights of my life, and one I will never forget as it was also Christmas Eve. Jess got through it, all smiles, and wondered what on earth all the fuss was about.

The second time the RFDS retrieved our adventurous daughter was when she ran to shut a gate in the yards. The ringers had just yarded up a large mob and there was a lot of dust, so she couldn't see much. Jessica was shutting the gate when a mob of cows came back and hit it, knocking her flying and unconscious to the ground. Jessica's mates in the yard saw it happen and came to her rescue, pulling her out of the way of the thundering mob. I was called and accessed the helicopter to attend to her faster. Hannah, our third daughter, stayed at home to ring the RFDS and I relayed the necessary information through the ultra high frequency (UHF) radio.

Everyone was very subdued and anxious, especially after we loaded Jessica onto the Toyota via the scoop stretcher and secured her head to stabilise her for the very slow trip in. When we lost her pulse, it was all hands on deck. I've never seen men draw so deeply on cigarettes as when we regained a pulse and continued our journey. I guess adrenaline kicks in because it wasn't until the RFDS plane landed – only forty minutes from the first call – and I could hand her over to much more qualified people, that I started to shake and it all became real. The doctor and nurses were ready for it, though, and were amazing in the way they handled everybody. Jess stayed unconscious for four hours and we were never so grateful as when she came to, recognised me immediately and said my name. I think I cried more then! Through the grace of God and the RFDS, she came through and is now a photographer and the mother of three beautiful children. Karma!

Raising five children in remote western Queensland means a lot of ups and downs. Our kids are all primary graduates of the Cairns School of the Air and we had a lot to do with that facility. My husband David's family has a long history with them. His sister, Fiona, was the first student ever enrolled, and my mother-in-law, Nell Arnold, the first Parents and Citizens president. Our family was enrolled when they changed their name from School of the Air to Cairns School of Distance Education in 1990, and we were also there when they changed from the HF radio lessons to phones. The last radio broadcast was quite nostalgic and was performed by the late Peg Shephard, who was with the school when it still operated out of the RFDS base pre-1990. Mrs Shephard, sadly, was killed in an accident while helping raise money for the school on their coast-to-coast bike ride.

The Cairns School of the Air initiated a school band, which was quite unique in that all students learned their instruments over the phone. This, of course, was before the days of Skype or Facetime. The students got together four times a year at camps and usually performed somewhere – in old people's homes or shopping centres – so you can imagine our amazement when the Queen of England requested that the school band play for her when she came to Cairns to christen the new RFDS plane. It was in February, the middle of the north's wet season – and Rachel, our fourth daughter, was playing trumpet. We lived at Wondoola Station at the time, having transferred from Wrotham Park in 1997. The rivers were flooded, so the road to Cairns was unusable. Rachel and I set forth – we were not going to let the band down! The normal nine-to-ten-hour trip took two days as we had to travel from near Normanton down to Cloncurry, across to Charters Towers and then up to Cairns. I kept pinching myself to remind myself it was real. Our shy, quiet, beautiful little country girl was sitting in front of thousands of people ready to play in a band at the request of Queen Elizabeth II.

I remember the noise being so loud: the emcee giving last-minute direction and cues to those involved in the ceremony; the roar of the jet engines; the static of the security men's radios along with the band rehearsing, all inside the RFDS hangar. The sweltering heat that was Cairns in February, combined with the nervous tension of the parents of the band members, and the kids watching the crowds gathering for the 11.00 a.m. arrival of The Queen's plane, meant the butterflies fluttered in more than one stomach and most of us were very restless and fidgety.

This was all mixed with the nervousness in the music teacher's face. Had they practised enough? Would they get scared? Would they remember to watch him as conductor of the band? What was I thinking! Twenty-four bush kids learning music over the phone and now being watched by the public. And not just local media: this was being transmitted around the globe! There were encouraging nods from the expectant parents, the mayor introduced The Queen and she actually mentioned the Cairns School of Distance Education band in her speech! The band struck up their first song while Her Majesty announced the name of the newest plane in the Cairns RFDS fleet. Prince Philip went over and chatted to the band members while The Queen met the distinguished guests. He was very encouraging to them all and spoke for quite a time with them.

Now, whether you are a monarchist or not, the pride in every parent's face was a sight to see, but everything fell into perspective when the school principal, Mr Ian Mckay, presented all band members with a special certificate and told them how proud he was.

Rachel came running over at the end of it, and I said, 'Sweetheart, you played for The Queen!'

Her reply was, 'Yeah, but guess what – Mr Mckay gave us an award!'

It brought home that they weren't worried about The Queen at all: they were more worried about what Mr Mckay was going to say.

The band members received a letter from The Queen, thanking them for their performance. That is really something to tell the grandchildren.

Sending our kids to boarding school was one of the hardest things we ever had to do. We were worried, but we put on a happy face and waved goodbye. Luckily, our kids did really well. I was told it got easier with each child, but

I'm here to tell you it doesn't – it just gets easier to hide the fact that you miss them like crazy. Not that you would ever let them know – never give teenagers an edge!

All five kids attended Columba Catholic College in Charters Towers for their high school years. That was when the travelling really did start and I averaged about sixty thousand kilometres per year travelling to Cairns for School of the Air and Charters Towers for Columba. It was worth it, though, and I am so glad I had the opportunity to attend many of the school events that a lot of other parents couldn't make. Our kids did well at boarding school, with Kimberley and Hannah making school captain, and all of them doing well academically and in the sporting field. Gordon made the firsts rugby league team when he was only in Year Nine! So we didn't need to worry, and we discovered that most kids who completed School of the Air succeeded: they already knew how to research and access any information because they had been doing it for years.

We transferred from Wondoola to Gregory Downs Station in 2005. Gregory Downs is a 2747.6 square-kilometre (266 425-hectare) 'jewel', situated on the banks of the Gregory River, one hundred kilometres south of Burketown in the Gulf of Carpentaria. The Gregory River flows all year round and runs right through the full length of the property. Gregory Downs runs about 35 000 head of Brahman cattle and we currently have sixteen permanent staff. The river has beautiful, clear running water and is a very popular spot for tourists, although we worry that with more and more estuarine crocodiles coming into the fresh waters of the Gulf, people are not heeding the warnings given. We have a very strong little community with everyone pitching in during events such as campdrafts and races, and anything else we have a mind to organise.

Our kids are now all grown, with the baby, Gordon, married in 2016. Two of our girls have married and the weddings were both wonderful events, surrounded by family and friends. One wedding was here on the station, making it even more special. That was another great story, as eight weeks before the wedding the Gregory River flooded and came through the houses and lawns. We washed mud off the lawns and planted flower gardens as the river went down.

David and I have been married for thirty-four years, have raised five very wonderful children, and now have six healthy grandchildren of whom we are eternally proud. We feel extremely lucky to be part of the wonderful community that makes up the Gregory Downs area.

Megan Munchenberg

Megan Munchenberg was born in Sydney in 1980 and was raised there by great parents with her four older brothers. Even though Megan grew up in a big city, she spent her last three years of high school in a country boarding school.

Megan first moved to North West Queensland when she was eighteen, first working for a private farming family near Rockhampton before moving further north to work on larger cattle stations in the Gulf of Carpentaria. Megan's love of horses was the initial driver behind her move.

As well as currently working on Gregory Downs Station, Megan also works part time as a grazing land management consultant around the region, and is currently the Chair of the local Natural Resource Management Group, Southern Gulf NRM.

For the past fifteen years Megan has lived and worked on Gregory Downs Station with her husband and children. She says that it truly has been a joy to live and work on Gregory Downs Station and she feels privileged to have become a part of the local community.

A LIFE I CHOSE

Megan Munchenberg

GROWING UP IN SYDNEY, I HAD A GOOD CHILDHOOD. MY parents were great parents, I had a relatively carefree childhood, and I was blessed to have that experience given I grew up in a big city. But after spending my last three years of high school in a country boarding school, I knew that after I finished Year Twelve, Sydney was no place for me.

It is always easy to make bad decisions in life, and I made a few in those early days after high school, I'll admit. But the easiest decision for me was knowing I had a future elsewhere and that we lived in a huge country full of opportunities. I just had to find out where my future began.

I managed to get a job quickly on a private cattle station near Rockhampton, near a town called Biloela, so I bought a bus ticket and said bon voyage to Sydney. I felt no regret at leaving, only anticipation. When one is eighteen everything is new, and I still recall the excitement at what potentially lay in front of me. I still feel the pang of guilt though, thinking back, as I looked out the window of the bus to see my mum wiping away her silent tears as she farewelled her last born of five children – the baby – to some remote location in Queensland. I was quite adamant at the time I wasn't going to be sad about leaving but, of course, there was a sense of a loss, or an ending era.

After a few days of travelling in a bus with people getting on and off, I finally arrived at my destination. I expected the landscape to be a red desert and was surprised and dismayed when I realised I wasn't going to the remote central part of Queensland; but I did, however, enjoy the landscape that greeted me. I recall on that last day of travel, a lady entered the bus. I remember vividly her tanned, strong arms and lined face, and thinking, this woman has probably lived a hard but exciting outdoor life and would have a few good stories to tell. Lines etched in her face could tell a hundred funny tales, and a few sad stories. I wanted that sort of life. I knew then I was maybe, finally, heading in the right direction – away from the distractions of Sydney, the crowds and the sense of confusion that living with too many interferences and options can give a young person. I wanted to simplify my life, and I thought I was probably going the right way. I felt great about it.

My first couple of years in Queensland were hard, fun and challenging. I worked on a few different properties and attended a six-month course at the Longreach Pastoral College. I grew up riding horses, and Longreach College provided me with a new perspective on horsemanship. It was here I developed a newer and deeper love and respect for horses beyond anything I'd ever had as a child and teenager. Not easy animals to work with, I found out what I was and wasn't made of after being flung from young breaker colts left, right and centre, every other day for about four months! But when at the end of your six months your bones are still intact and, amazingly, so is your pride, you ride that young breaker out and you know, for better or worse, you made it just the way it was.

I was hooked. Hooked on horses and the musty and familiar smell of horse sweat, hooked on the challenge that riding a young horse every day brings you, and I knew I had to find a life working with them somehow.

Before I left Longreach, though, I found my first baby. An old man was sitting on the main street and in front of him was a washing basket full of black-and-white puppies. Me being me, I just couldn't resist a look. And when I asked about them, he told me the mother died and this, sadly, was a last-ditch effort to rehome them. I took one. A little black-and-white male pup. He was three weeks old approximately, and I handfed him for the next couple of weeks. I named him Clue 'cos I didn't have a clue what to call him. I hid him in my college bedroom for the last month of college, and on my return each afternoon would find him sleeping in my washing basket. I found in him a friend and loyal companion that I haven't ever quite been able to replicate since. He was by my side for the next fourteen years of my life.

After Longreach I returned to New South Wales for twelve months and again attempted university. I wasn't ready for uni and I certainly wasn't finished with Queensland. I knew I needed to be back on a property. I soon met a nice fellow (who happens to be my husband now) and a year later we moved to Dalgonally station in the Gulf of Carpentaria owned by the Australian Agricultural Company. He became the station mechanic and bore man (who checks stock waters) and I had a job in the stock camp with my horses.

We worked for a lovely couple who were the managers and became firm friends over the years. My head stockman was a cheeky lad. You knew if you made a mistake with him. He'd put you right pretty quickly and tell you where you went wrong. He was old-school and taught us some of the old ways to work with the cattle. But he knew how to have fun too. Some of the best days of my early twenties were spent sweating and labouring while back-legging on the weaner cradle for hours on end, listening to the jokes fly from our jokester head stockman. A weaner cradle is the branding cradle where the weaners are caught and held while they are dehorned and castrated. Working the back leg, you must hang on to prevent the person working at the front or back of the animal being kicked. Some weaners were big, sappy fellows that came from the thick scrub further north in the Cape, and holding the leg of one of these young mickey bulls (cleanskin bulls) could wear you out fast.

I worked in a stock camp full of young fellows who ranged in age from seventeen to about twenty-one. The only other female was the manager's wife. The boys always tried to get a rise out of me but only succeeded sometimes. I grew up with four older brothers, so I came well prepared to work in this man's world. Laughs were many over the three years there, along with many silent tears of frustration at times. The work was tough but satisfying, and for a young girl from Sydney it was damn frightening too.

I was comfortable around the horses; I'd been around them nearly all my life. The cattle, on the other hand, were fairly imposing in those first few months when I started working on stations. Dalgonally was a steer and bullock depot where young male steers are fattened to a certain weight or size before being sold. I'd previously worked on another bullock depot down in McKinley at Toolebuc Station and they had some huge old bullocks too, but some of these ones at Dalgonally were old, huge *and* cranky that they were finally caught. We'd muster them from the gidgee and they'd know about that too. They would hear the choppers and the bikes coming and lie down while we mustered everything around them – they were certainly cunning. But some would get flushed out to the main mob and there would appear these goliaths who made the regular steers look like calves again. We'd be hiding our horses in the gidgee scrub not far from the main mob so that they wouldn't spook at our horses, and these big fellows would come in hot and cranky. All day we watched them closely so they didn't get out of the coacher mob – that's the mob the ringers will walk along with to coax along the other cattle the motorbikes and the helicopters bring in. Some of these bullocks were ten to fifteen years old. That's old for a bullock these days. The head stockman's stress levels would be high during mustering as we all struggled to hold the coacher mob together while keeping an eye on these old bullocks who only wanted to escape. Those cunning fellows knew too that once they were in the gidgee there was not much chance of us getting them back again.

Working them in the yards made me feel like a tiny mouse. I always tried to avoid the old 'one foot on the bottom rail' trick as it will usually only end with you getting hurt or the head stockman yelling at you. Putting one foot on the rail usually means you're just half leaning on the fence, and it only slows you down as it gives a false sense of security that you can get out of the way in a hurry from a cranky bullock or steer. I was taught to either get down off the rail and move around the beast, or get all the way over the rails if you're not quick enough on your feet. But these huge cattle had me thinking to jump over every time they even looked my way. Most of those big old fellows weren't too bad once they were in the yards, though. They certainly had your measure.

The channels on Dalgonally were mostly made up of river systems from the Cloncurry River and the Gilliat Channels, while the gidgee country was mostly red stone. Dalgonally had plenty of beautiful stretches of open downs and a lot of hot days were spent in the saddle looking at the same landmark for hours, which never seemed to get closer. The Gulf Country is by no means as large and open as the Barkly Tablelands in terms of distances between waters and length of walks, but it wasn't unusual to walk a mob of steers up to twenty to thirty kilometres in a day between paddocks. The steers were good walkers overall, and Brahman steers are even better for a long walk once they get going.

While at Dalgonally I was given a plant of horses – my own small team of mustering horses. One of them became a firm favourite. His name was Penthouse. He was a small Galloway, a stocky bay Australian Stock Horse with a wall eye (blue eye). He was a little spooky around me at first but soon became a trusting little fellow. I didn't break him in; I was given him to use as an older, going horse. He was smart and very capable. Penthouse had a big heart: I could ride him all day and he would still summon up the energy to keep going after a long day mustering cattle through the gidgee or the channels. He was certainly no reliable kid's pony, though. That's for sure.

On a few instances the ringers made bets about who would be first to get bucked off the fresh horses after the wet season. During the wet season the horses have a three-to-four-month spell while they rest and recuperate in readiness for the dry-season mustering. Some of the horses came in a little full of themselves. Penthouse was no exception. I think in my second year at Dalgonally some of the boys won some money on me being the first. I had a few unexpected busters off him ... but he didn't always lift me.

I recall a day when we were mustering the meatworks fats (fat bullocks) for trucking out. I chased a large one on Penthouse, trying to get him to bend back into the main mob. The helicopter assisted, as this one was sure he didn't want to join up. I rode hard and fast to keep up with him and we fairly leaned against his shoulder. I reached over and slapped the bullock on the rump in a frustrated moment as I cantered fast alongside him, only to have Penthouse decide the slapping noise was a bit frightening. He dropped his head and grunted like a good old bronco next to that bullock. The UHF radio I wore on my chest began making noises at me as the chopper pilot above started laughing and hollering at my predicament, encouraging me to stick to him. I did manage to stick to him without falling off and we even wheeled the bullock back into the mob eventually. I was probably a little rattled, though.

Penthouse helped to make those first years up in the Gulf so much fun and so very rewarding. I often think back with fond memories of those early days, mustering and campdrafting on him, and how privileged I was to be able to have him in my plant. He was also the horse I reluctantly and heartbreakingly said goodbye to late in the dry season during the 2015 drought while living at Gregory Downs. It was just too damn hot and dry for this old fellow to keep going. Some horses make an impression like no human ever will, or can, on your life and in your heart. Penthouse was one of these for me – he took a piece of my heart with him the day I had to say goodbye to him.

Another horse in my plant while at Dalgonally was a bit of a challenge. Her name was Fern, a chestnut mare, and to this day I can never look at a chestnut mare the same as others. Fern was quite young but had been broken in for a while before being turned out for another twelve months due to an injury. I was the 'lucky' one privileged enough to get her when she returned. Fern took some riding in those first few weeks; she had a bit of a buck to her but didn't seem too serious about it, so I took her out mustering after giving her a bit of work at the station compound. Well, it was nice and early in the morning the first time she showed me what she was made of.

Some horses feel a bit fresh in the mornings and might give you a bit of a wake-up buck or pig-root and, if you're expecting it, you can usually ride them through. Fern was a sneaky bugger. She was well behaved all morning. I felt good on her and probably let my guard down prematurely. I had to indicate a steer in the mob to one of the jackaroos, and I stuck my arm out and pointed. At the same moment, Fern decided it was time to boogie. She bucked and bucked and bucked like a good bronco should and a station mustering horse just shouldn't! I hit the dirt quickly and hard on my bum. I must admit I was in a bit of shock, thinking, *Where did that outburst come from?* Not to mention the tailbone agony. And that mare just turned on a dime and took off flat gallop towards home. I was feeling sore and a little bit of pride cracked for the day too.

My head stockman tied his horse up, picked me up in the car and we drove a few kilometres and chased her down. Yep, we had to drive to catch up to her. She was on a mission to get away from us and home in a hurry. Eventually we caught up and managed to catch her. I had to get back on. That was no easy mental task. It is always very hard to get back on something that completely beat you the way she did. But I did, and then I cantered that mare all the way back to the mob without a rest stop. I worked her hard all day – she was sweaty and tired by the end of the day and yet she still tried to buck me off again late in the afternoon. I was ready for her this time, though, and she never threw me again, although Fern always tested you out. She was the kind of horse you just never relaxed on. If she sensed it, she took her opportunity and gave you a bit of a wake-up. She turned out to be an okay mustering mare, but it's funny how I've been put off chestnut mares ever since my time riding her!

* * *

After three great years at Dalgonally Station our managers moved on and so did we. We moved to Gregory Downs Station further north in the Gulf, to the old original homestead, which is now its outstation. I worked in the stock camp and Jason (also known as Munch) worked as the mechanic/handyman for the station. In 2004, Jason and I were married.

Gregory Downs is a breeding station with a Brahman herd. This was new for me as I had only ever worked with steers and bullocks on growing-out places. I enjoyed the slower pace of working with the cows and calves. At the end of the day's mustering or working in the yards I enjoyed watching the calves and the cows mothering up to them. A Brahman mother is surely one not to mess with if her calf is around – most Brahman cows are pretty maternal overall.

An older set of yards was on the property into which we always seemed to muster up the old cows. The older cows were generally on their last weaner before heading off to the meatworks. Rough, I know, but that is just the way of it. It was almost like they knew it was nearly their end. They came in really, really bad tempered and just mad! These old yards weren't the best and some of the cable around the rails sank when you tried to climb up it. You'd often spend half the day scrabbling up the rails to get away from these old girls, only to find you were still nearly touching the ground. Anyway, coming away unscathed was pretty much a testament to your level of fitness and ability to move fast on your feet.

I recall I walked through the corner of a yard one time, to cut through to the back yard. I walked past a mob of baby calves just lying in the shade. One mother was nearby but she wasn't paying much attention to the calves, or so I thought. Just as I was about to climb up over the rails into the next yard I heard a 'whoosh' of breath at my back and a heavy thudding on the ground and there behind me, pushing her head painfully into my back, was a large and touchy Brahman cow. I remember her grey head and her body being a darker grey all over. I don't know how I saw, as I was being corkscrewed into the loose cables on the rail. She was cranky at me for walking past the baby calves. A good maternal mother that one! Shame about me, though – I was jammed tight like a pig on a spit. I felt my face pressing into the steel post as she kept rubbing me hard with her head. She stopped momentarily once, which allowed me to get halfway through the loose old cables and, thank goodness, they were loose enough for me to squeeze myself through, away from her cranky mass. Once I was through I turned and she was still standing there glaring at me, pawing up dust with her front hoof. I decided I might go a different way next time when I needed to move across the yards and avoid walking near the baby calves. I didn't feel like doing the cable tango with her again. I knew she would probably win.

I remember one day I was riding a reliable old mare called Mindy – built like an artillery tank, all broad across the shoulders with a huge chest and a big sway back. She was a chestnut mare, and despite my general dislike of chestnut mares she grew on me and became one of my most reliable mustering horses. I was still able to ride her mustering when I was pregnant with my first child, that was how reliable and safe you felt on old Mindy. Anyway, one day we were finishing off mustering. Sometimes, at the end of the muster when you are yarding up, the young weaners get a little spooked and try to break free of the tail end of the mob. Some managed to do that on this day, so a few of us went off to try and bring them back in. One weaner was giving a couple of the fellows a particularly hard time, to the point where they started arguing and yelling at each other about how best to get it back! By this stage the weaner was just trotting around, not sure what to do with itself, while the two fellas were going red in the face and swearing and yelling. I decided to try and have a go at bringing it back in, and thought that maybe they would appreciate some help, given the situation we were in. The weaner saw me coming and started fleeing away further. I was riding old Mindy, but as we bent the weaner around back towards the mob, it put its foot in a hole and tripped over in front of my horse. Unfortunately for me and Mindy, and the weaner as it turned out, big Mindy couldn't pull up in time and down we all went together. Big Mindy rolled over that

35

poor sappy weaner, with me still on her. I managed to twist away from her mammoth weight and only got my knee pinned under her as she fell. The next few days I was sore and lame. But that weaner just sat there looking stunned afterwards. Mindy, thankfully, was unhurt – she was a bit of a tank, after all – and the weaner simply stood up and started heading in the right direction, with a little guidance from the chestnut tank. The two ringers put a hold on their arguing to come and see if I was alive. I figured there were probably better ways to stop an argument, but whatever works, I guess.

We eventually had two children while living here – a boy, Aidan, and a younger girl, Ayla. Both kids have only known this place as their home and do school through Mount Isa School of the Air. Gregory Downs is certainly a one-in-a-million place to be able to call home; we've had some great times living here. The community around us is made up of some unique and interesting people, and the ability for everyone to pitch in when needed, or for anything at all really, makes it a great community to live in. Although we have some challenges living where we live, we make the best of it. I suppose we have the option of being able to move somewhere else if times get tough or if we need to. We don't own the property. But why would we wish to move? We have everything we need here and more.

When Aidan was born, it was a nice and easy pregnancy and I was a nice relaxed first-time mum. Of course, we all have the usual challenges of being a new mum. When I was pregnant with Ayla, I was flown out early at about thirty-three weeks with a premature labour. Thankfully, the RFDS gave me some magic pills that stopped the labour and Ayla was born a few weeks later in Cairns. Unfortunately, she needed some early surgery down in Brisbane and it is times like this you realise just how isolated we are. Luckily for us we have a wonderful family and a community around us who supported us through the tough times. The RFDS have been a lifesaver on more than a few occasions and this time was no exception. I don't think we could live out here without the RFDS to support us in times such as this one.

I admire the pioneers and the longstanding families of this region; it is hot, harsh and far from anywhere and anyone, but with modernisation and improving technologies, we have most of the mod cons of city people. My family, some of whom live in Sydney and some overseas, think I live an alternative lifestyle to other people. I don't see it that way. If anything, sometimes our lives feel perfectly simple and authentic compared to people living in cities today. I see what we have and think sometimes going to a movie or a café would be nice, but having a barbecue down on the Gregory River or attending a campdraft for the weekend with the horses and the kids sounds more like my kind of fun.

Gregory Downs has been our home for the past fourteen years. We've had our children here and some wonderful experiences. I managed to put myself through a university degree in Applied Science, majoring in Rangelands Management and Animal Production. This allowed me to invest my time into an alternative professional industry once I had the kids. Working stock-camp hours is a little tricky with younger children. Although I miss the time I spend with the livestock, and particularly the rough-and-tumble of the ringer way of life, I guess being a mum changed how available I was for the long hours and long days. I'm in the unique position of living on the station and enjoying the lifestyle while working as a grazing land management consultant, and as a board member of our local Natural Resource Management Group – two jobs I find rewarding that are either directly or indirectly involved with the station and the livestock industry.

Our home is a part of Australian pioneering history, and we feel so privileged to be able to live here and raise our family here. Who knows where we will end up long term? I'm invested in the industry we work in now and hope to remain so in some capacity long term. Our kids are being raised in a wholesome and friendly environment where – although the community is spread out with a neighbour being possibly twenty kilometres away, or a sleepover for the kids happening 120 kilometres or sometimes further away – it is still so rich and full of wonderful people. Not everything is easy, though. Phones sometimes fail, internet is limited and drives are long, but we have such a good supporting network of neighbours from the community that you never really feel isolated. With the high-school years looming closer for our kids, I often wonder if we should move to town or if we will do the boarding school option. There are pros and cons for each. I weight the lifestyle we live now as the best pro overall.

I am often asked why I choose to live out here, so far from anyone, or anywhere. My answer to that is, simply: Why would I live anywhere else?

Sweers Island, Burketown

Lyn Battle

Lyn Battle (née Doyle) was born in Malin Head, Ireland in 1962. In 1986 she travelled to Australia on a working holiday and became Lyn Battle in 1989 when she married her Australian husband Tex and joined him in establishing a tourism venture on Sweers Island in the Gulf of Carpentaria. Sweers Island is thirty kilometres north of Burketown, off the Queensland coast.

MY SWEERS ISLAND HOME

Lyn Battle

WE'D BEEN CAMPING ON THE ISLAND FOR MONTHS, BUT this night felt different. The stars seemed brighter, the water lapping the shore sounded louder, the rustlings outside the tent more ominous. Beside me, my Beloved slept soundly. I heard gentle snoring from the other tent where our two friends were also obviously fast asleep. I lay wide awake, staring through the tent mesh where dark shapes that hadn't been there yesterday loomed just metres away. The tent felt flimsy, barely protecting us from the elements, but as I stared out I smiled in excitement knowing that when the sun came up we would start unpacking those bundles of timber and steel, and start building a proper house to live in. The four of us had pooled our resources and turned all our savings into building materials, which a barge had unloaded onto the beach that afternoon before steaming back to the mainland, leaving the four of us behind. It wasn't just a camping holiday any more. Now we were going to build a home.

I'd always loved the idea of camping. I'd read all the Enid Blyton books and dreamed of being an explorer and having adventures. After three months of living under canvas through a tropical wet season and wearing out three tents, I was definitely now cured of that longing. I can still see the undulating floor as some unknown critter – snake, toad, spider – slithered around beneath me. Then there was the morning I unzipped the tent to be greeted by a rearing brown-coloured snake that hissed and spat at me, so I promptly re-zipped and counted to ten in the hope he'd go away.

And there was the day my Beloved and I had a blazing row and, I confess, if there was a bus back to Ireland I'd have been on it. But, as it was, I stomped off to my room only to get within sight of the tent and realise I could not even slam a door to express my frustration. So, in true revert-to-childhood form, I plonked down in the dirt and bawled my eyes out. It worked, of course. The tent was still there, the frustration waned. The ever-patient Beloved had pottered off to another chore and I was left to reassess my situation, which was clear: I loved him, and I loved this island. It was beginning to feel like home.

I suppose many people dream of being the Swiss Family Robinson for a while, and to live out that dream on a tropical island. I grew up on the windy north coast of Ireland where regular winter gales were as fierce as a category-one cyclone, rainy days were what kept the grass that vibrant shade of green, and occasional blue-sky summer days gave us a tantalising taste of the tropics.

In May 1986, at twenty-three years of age, I quit my job and bought a one-way ticket to Australia.

We learned in school that no part of Ireland is more than one hundred kilometres from the sea. You can drive from one end of the country to the other in a day. Malin Head, County Donegal, where I grew up, lies at the tip of a narrow-necked peninsula so we had salt water all around us. You heard the booming roar of the sea in winter and the clatter of shingle in summer. We breathed salty air.

So, it came as quite a shock when I ended up working as a station cook in the middle of the Barkly Tableland, hundreds of miles from the Gulf coast. I remember going on bore runs with the blokes to check the water supply and climbing up the windmills to gaze northwards. Surely the ocean would be visible on the horizon? Nope. I was flat-out seeing the next windmill, which I duly climbed, ever hopeful of a glimpse of salt water.

It wasn't until my Beloved took me for a flight from Escott Station on New Year's Day 1987 that I finally saw the brown rivers mingle with the blue of the Gulf of Carpentaria. Flat, green islands were surrounded by golden sands. The nearest one was long and narrow, shaped a bit like a dog's bone, with low scrubby trees and purple flowers that looked like Irish heather from the air. No buildings. No runway. I wondered where on earth we were to land. Tex brought the aircraft down smoothly onto a mowed strip of grassland.

'Welcome to Sweers Island!' he grinned.

It is almost flat, but the landscape varies, with golden sandy beaches, rocky mangroves, grassy plains and eucalyptus forests. I looked at the sea just metres away and grinned back. We went for a swim. The water was clear and warm, the bottom sandy. Bliss.

Tex had been flying to the island for camping weekends since the 1970s and, along with friends Ray Atherinos and his wife, Salme, had checked out the possibility of turning their basic campsite into a decent weekender. On investigation, it turned out that there had been a township here during the 1800s and some Crown land was available, the bulk of the island being Aboriginal land. Government policy would not permit a private residence; it would have to be a commercial venture. So the seeds of Sweers Island Fishing Resort were sown.

Exploring the island, Tex showed me the remains of a well the crews of sailing ships dug, sheets of rusty iron from a town built in the 1800s, trees called she-oaks that sighed in the tropical heat, making it sound like there was more wind than actually blew, giving the impression of coolness. Not a coconut palm in sight. This wasn't your typical 'desert island' at all. It had history, and personality;

so many varying landscapes to explore. There was a ghost gum forest, a cave, a hill from the top of which you saw the whole island laid out with the mainland barely visible in the distance, and a small cairn of rocks perhaps the early explorers stacked. Matthew Flinders stood on this very hill in 1802 and named the island for the earlier Dutch explorers of 1644. There were gravestones for early residents. And there were a couple of tents for the new ones.

That was over thirty years ago.

There are no towns along this Gulf coastline, no roads to the coast apart from Karumba in the extreme eastern corner. It is a wilderness of mangrove-lined saltpans cut through by meandering rivers inhabited by crocodiles. Sweers Island is thirty kilometres off the coast. Our nearest town is Burketown, thirty kilometres inland, or sixty kilometres up the winding Albert River. Karumba lies 150 kilometres to the east at the mouth of the Norman River, with Normanton another seventy kilometres upstream. That's it.

One of my Irish friends summed it up when we were driving together from Cairns to the Gulf, repeatedly asking, 'Is this the outback yet?'

Eventually Tex said, 'Yes.'

So he stuck his video camera out the window, panned, and in his best Dublin accent said, 'The great Australian outback. Moiles and moiles of fookin' nuttin'!'

I met Tex in Mount Isa in 1987, on my way to work on the Avon Downs Cattle Station near the Queensland/Northern

Territory border. We kept in touch and romance blossomed. After three months working as station cook, I moved to Mount Isa. During that time, we made numerous trips to the island, enjoying fishing holidays with friends, exploring the island and gradually building up the campsite. Tex and Ray had been visiting the tourist lodge on Escott Station near Burketown regularly since the mid 1970s and were good friends with the owners, Len and Lyn Stolk, who were very supportive of our venture and agreed to be our mainland base where we could store materials and vehicles.

We transported heavy items by boat from Escott, winding forty kilometres down the Gin Arm branch of the Nicholson River, then sixty kilometres across the open sea. The Gulf landscape was so flat that we were out of sight of land until the hill on Sweers rose like a beacon above the horizon.

Other times we flew, with either Tex or Salme piloting us onto that sandy airstrip in their single-engine, four-seater Piper Arrow VH-CJV. Tex and Salme both held private pilot's licences and Salme was one of the earliest female pilots in the Gulf region, and most likely the first woman to land an aircraft on Sweers Island.

When the lease to establish a small fishing lodge was approved in 1987, things got serious. The others sold their homes in Mount Isa. I packed up everything I'd brought from Ireland. Together we packed our bags, chartered the barge from Karumba and loaded it up with building materials. The skipper unloaded everything into a pile on the sand and gave us a wry grin as he backed off and turned for the mainland. We four looked at each other as we contemplated what we had done. Everything we owned lay at the water's edge – and the tide was coming in!

Over the following months, which included the hot and humid Wet, we roped in all the friends we could for building working bees in the mornings, fishing in the afternoons. The main kitchen/bar/dining area was operational by May 1988, along with three small guest cabins. We welcomed our first paying guests that May and they still visit the island every year. We lived in a basic shed for the first year, sleeping on a mattress on the floor, gradually building internal walls and dividing it into rooms. Our initial idea was to make do in the shed for the first couple of years then build a house, but as it grew a verandah, and a couple of extra rooms, floors were tiled and rooms air-conditioned, it became a very comfortable home which we still live in today.

We often say to visitors, 'If we'd known what we were in for, we never would have started.' And Tex sometimes quips, 'It's not all perfect, you know. Some days you could get a flat stubby, or a crook oyster.'

Every day is different. Yesterday morning began with a grassfire, this morning began with a boat dragging anchor and drifting off towards Papua New Guinea, tomorrow morning we expect a TV celebrity guest to arrive. It's certainly never boring on Sweers.

'But what do you DO all day?' people ask, looking around yet seeing so little. We generate our own power with a diesel generator and solar panels, pump our own water from wells we hand dug, and when the monsoon fails we pump water from the sea through a complex desalination system so that we can drink it. The salty air corrodes metal, the termites munch timber, the sun fades paint – there is constant maintenance to be done.

The logistics of living on an island are vast. We must contact mainland shops a week or more ahead to arrange for supplies to be sent by truck from Cairns on the east coast, nearly one thousand kilometres on a twelve-hour drive to the Gulf port of Karumba. Here they are loaded onto a barge that travels nearly two hundred kilometres out to the islands. It's usually a twelve-hour journey, but in very rough seas it has taken them twenty-two hours to get back to the mainland. If we run out of bread we bake our own, but if we run out of flour we must wait another week or more to get it across from the mainland.

When we first came to the island, there was no weekly barge service – we had to fly to the mainland ourselves, or rely on visitors to bring supplies and mail. Communications were virtually non-existent. We borrowed a portable high frequency (HF) radio transceiver from the Stolk family at Escott. It enabled us to keep in contact with our neighbours and we joined daily scheduled radio contacts (scheds) with the Royal Flying Doctor Service (RFDS) base in Mount

Isa, six hundred kilometres to the south. This enabled us to make radiotelephone calls to order supplies and to speak with family and friends. The girls at the base telephoned the shop, explained that they had a call from us, then linked us together – the shop on a telephone handset, us on a radio microphone. I remember joining the queue for the 'traffic list' – we had ten minutes to complete our calls. If not finished, we went back to the end of the list. You can imagine the frustration if there was a new shop girl on the other end of the line, unfamiliar with the system and slow to take the order. Or you waited for hours for the right time difference to ring your mother in Ireland and she was not in! The staff at the RFDS base were terrific. If you had only two or three items to go they let you run over time, but any more than that was unfair to the next person patiently waiting their turn.

These days we have satellite internet for online ordering, which you'd think would be better – but it has limited speed and data limits. It can be painfully slow watching each page load, clicking the item you want, watching it crawl its way into your basket, but the software is unhappy with your slow internet and now the page has frozen so you have to wait, or shut it down and start all over again. It can take up to two hours to place our weekly order online this way so we have reverted to the old system where we simply phone the shop and read out our list!

Nowadays, our phone system is a complex system of circuit boards, solar panels, batteries and antenna. An ultra high frequency (UHF) radio signal beams our voice to another antenna on top of a tower on the next island. That sends a signal across to another tower on the mainland, from there it goes into the normal microwave and fibre optic network. Lots of margin for error there! Most of the time it works well, but when the system fails it can be costly and time consuming to repair. Monsoon rains, lightning strikes, green frogs or snakes can short out the circuit boards at the towers, which are only accessible by helicopter, so we can be without phones or fax for weeks. We are also an official Weather Observation Station for the Bureau of Meteorology and upload daily 'obs' through their laptop system, which connects to head office through the fax line.

Funnily enough, with all that technology, one of my hobbies is amateur 'ham' radio where I use a HF radio and antenna to communicate by voice or Morse code with friends all around the world. At times we have had to resort to my wire antennas to relay information because the telephone and internet were out of action. Ham radio is a great hobby for an islander. Not only does it give me a connection to the outside world, but the whole 'sound over water' thing comes into play, making an island radio station much more effective than the equivalent set-up on the mainland.

Radios play a big part in the lives of all Gulf women, a means of communication between the homestead and the husband working miles away. We operate a marine very high frequency (VHF) radio to keep in contact with our charter boat and dinghies and an aircraft VHF radio to contact incoming aircraft, and keep UHF radios in our vehicles. Staff carry handheld units when away from the main resort buildings. These units have limited range, but are real time savers.

Probably the most important use for radio communications, and the reason we borrowed that first old Flying Doctor radio from Escott, is safety. We are very aware we live in an isolated area and things can – and do – go wrong. Bones get broken, fingers get severed, fish hooks get embedded too deep to extract by ourselves.

One day our skipper, Brett, was out in our charter boat MV *Salomon*. A qualified coxswain, he was helping a guest to unhook his fish when it slipped and next thing the hook was in Brett's foot. He knew it was serious. Two of the treble hooks were deeply embedded in the side of his foot. He called us on the marine VHF, gave his location and ETA back to base, gritted his teeth and drove his passengers back to the island. Meanwhile, Tex phoned the local bush hospital at Burketown and, although there is no doctor, nurse Di Phillips is experienced and excellent and she prepared for her patient. Tex then pushed his two-seater Ultravia Pelican light sports aircraft out of the hangar and by the time Brett reached shore everyone was ready – Brett hobbled off the boat and onto the back of a quad bike, and went straight to the aircraft that took off and flew overhead as his fiancée, Sarah, and I helped the guests ashore and put the boat back on its mooring. The Pelican took less than half an hour to get to Burketown, where the ambulance waited to transport them to the clinic. It was late afternoon and the recreational aircraft is only equipped for daylight flight. Tex explained to Di that they had only half an hour to get back to Sweers before last light.

'Not a chance,' she said, examining the wound.

Tex flew back to Sweers alone, leaving Brett at the clinic. Di cut a couple of small nicks in the skin and Brett pushed the hooks through, while she suggested he might like to start wearing shoes to soften his skin and make it easier for next time!

It just so happened to be Father's Day and Brett's father lived in Burketown at the time, so he had somewhere to stay the night – although he got well teased about the lengths a son will go to in order to spend time with his dad! Next morning, Tex flew across to Burketown and brought him back to the island. The importance of aircraft in isolated areas like the Gulf is critical.

We keep a fully stocked Flying Doctor medical chest at the resort, containing everything from Panadol to Morphine. Each item is numbered and we ring the base for authorisation and instructions: 'Take 172 twice a day for five days.' We also have a defibrillator unit and enough oxygen to supply a patient until the RFDS aircraft can get here – it takes less than an hour for the aircraft to get from Mount Isa to Sweers and the pilots can land day or night.

For around eight years our defibrillator sat on the shelf unused, with occasional replacements of very expensive batteries. Then, in 2017, it paid for itself when a male guest suffered a total cardiac arrest. We had the defib there within minutes, and a team of staff and guests kept up CPR and first aid until the Flying Doctor arrived. It was several hours before they could stabilise him enough to fly, and he suffered another cardiac arrest on the way to Townsville hospital, where he underwent immediate life-saving surgery. He has since recovered completely, and is now assisting the RFDS with their fundraising efforts.

We were surprised and honoured to be nominated for the 2018 RFDS Spirit of John Flynn Award. When accepting the award, Tex commented, 'We feel like a fraud because we owe the Flying Doctor a lot more than they owe us.'

We now have battery lights for night landings, but years ago we just used paint tins three-quarters filled with sand and a litre of petrol lit in each one, giving about an hour's worth of light – enough time for the pilot to locate the airstrip, land and park.

I remember our first night medivac. A young Aboriginal girl on nearby Bentinck Island had severe stomach pains. The family called us on the marine VHF radio. We rang RFDS. Suspecting appendicitis, they decided to fly her out but the airstrip on Bentinck was unlit. Her family put her in a boat and crossed the choppy four-kilometre channel in the dark to Sweers, then transferred her onto the back of the ute for the drive to the airstrip. We had some regular guests here with their young sons. They eagerly helped us to set out the airstrip lights, hopping off the back of the ute to place them in position along the threshold and along the side of the airstrip.

'Hey, Dad!' said eleven-year-old Ben. 'This is my first real drama!'

We watched in awe as the Kingair roared overhead, checking the lights, then it steadily came in to land. RFDS aircraft are kitted out with just about everything you'd find in an emergency ward, so young Nettie was in good hands as they helped her aboard. I think we all felt a little subdued that night, but in a good way, knowing help was at hand when needed. Nettie recovered and returned home a few days later.

Tex has flown a few 'medivacs' himself. We received a call one day on the marine VHF. A prawn trawler needed information on how to get a crew member to Karumba or Cairns for medical treatment. The cook had spiked her hand on a prawn or lionfish in the nets and it became infected. She had a huge blood blister on her finger and was in so much pain she could not sleep or carry out her duties. Trawler cooks don't just spend all day in the galley, they must also pitch in when the nets come on board to help sort the catch. With the cook injured, it was the equivalent of being two crew short.

Tex explained there was a much nearer bush hospital at Burketown that could probably treat the injury and that he could fly the cook across himself. This saved the trawler valuable work time. They steamed towards Sweers – Tex and Brett drove one of our dinghies out to meet them, helped the cook on board and soon she was climbing into the Pelican to fly to Burketown. Di Phillips lanced the wound, drained and cleaned it, and Tex flew the cook back to Sweers. We gave her a bed for the night and dinner – that must have been bliss after weeks of cooking at sea! Next morning, Tex took her back out in the dinghy to rendezvous with the trawler. As she climbed back on board, hands passed down the favourite barter currency in the Gulf – fresh prawns! And bugs and squid. All this freshly caught local seafood had us dining like kings for weeks – more than a fair exchange!

Sometimes the medical emergencies have hit a little close to home. Tex had been complaining of a dull ache in his abdomen. He hoped it was not a recurrence of kidney stone trouble he'd had years earlier. It was. And, true to form, these things always seem to strike in the middle of the night. We rang the Flying Doctor emergency number – they have a doctor on call twenty-four hours a day.

'Renal colic,' the doctor confirmed. 'You'll have to give him some morphine.'

Oh. I'd given needles to other people in the past, but to stick a needle in your own husband? Tex looked at me warily as I held up the needle.

'I think the pain is easing. I think it'll be okay. Don't need the needle.'

So I put it aside and settled down to sleep. Fifteen minutes later he was complaining, 'Ohhhhh!' I got the needle out again. He looked at it and gritted his teeth.

'I think it's easing ...'

This went on for an hour. Our reluctance to stick a needle in him was overcome by the need for both of us to get some sleep. He still reckons I didn't do it properly, but it worked.

Then there was the day that a really rare island came on the ham radio – a group of hams had gone to the uninhabited South Pacific Raoul Island. It was their second-last day and it was our co-worker Mick's birthday. We had no guests so planned a party barbecue on his verandah next door. The radio group started calling for Australian stations.

'Come on, Lyn!' Tex said.

We have sliding doors, and in my haste I failed to notice the door was not fully open. As I pelted through the gap, I caught my right foot on the edge of the door and fell headlong onto the tiled floor. As soon as I fell I knew I'd hurt my foot. You know that cold feeling that runs through you? I looked down, expecting to see blood everywhere, but there wasn't any. Instead, I saw the toe next to the 'pinkie' sticking out sideways. My first thought was, *It's not meant to look like that.* I blinked and looked again but it still looked the same. I called for Tex, but he didn't hear me. Our dog Ella came over, full of sympathy, and tried to lick it better. I didn't know if it was broken or dislocated. I called again and when Tex saw my foot he bolted for the phone and rang the Flying Doctor. Meanwhile, I figured the quicker it went back into place, the better. And best to do it before the pain or swelling set in. I grasped the toe and before I thought about it too much pushed it across until it sat straight again. It looked much better. Tex returned with the doctor's advice – watch for any sign that circulation might be cut off, take two Panadeine Forte and ring him if it got any worse. We bandaged it up, took the medication and hobbled across to Mick and Lee's verandah where the party continued for several hours and several bottles of wine. Something must be in that Panadeine Forte because the next morning I was the only one without a hangover! Oh, and the following afternoon I made it through to the special ham radio group on their final day. I have their confirmation card on the wall with a note – 'Toe Breaker!' Later, X-rays showed the toe was shattered in three places ... Other injuries peculiar to our island location included a scorpion stinging Tex on the palm while we were clearing land to make the new airstrip. The original grass strip was on sand – too soft for heavy aircraft bearing the groups of fishing guests we hoped would visit – so we cleared eleven hundred metres of bush scrub along a well-drained gravel ridge. It was hard work and too hot to tackle until evening, so every day we spent an hour or two pushing over small trees and bushes with a backhoe, then walking along, gathering them into piles and burning them down to ash. We became adept at treating splinters and blisters, but when Tex picked up a branch and red-hot pain flashed through his hand, we knew it was something else. A small brown scorpion had been living under the bark, and although Australian scorpions are not deadly, their sting is very painful.

A few years later he stood on a giant centipede, ten centimetres long. The head and tail ends look very similar. He hoped he was standing on its dangerous end, but it flicked back and struck him on top of the foot. He reckons the scorpion hurt more at the time, but the centipede pain lasted longer. It was the week before our wedding. His foot swelled up quite a lot and I feared he would not fit into his fancy shoes! Fortunately, it was all right on the day and he didn't have to get married in thongs.

We've also had run-ins with snakes, jellyfish, turtles and stingrays. Our nearest neighbours were the Kaiadilt Aboriginal Community on Bentinck Island, four kilometres across the channel. AP, who was for many years the strong man of the Kaiadilt people, was short in stature but tough as nails. He bought and installed a marine VHF radio on Bentinck in the days before a telephone service. He was very protective of his radio and would not allow anyone to chitchat on it (though while he was out hunting the kids occasionally got on and much giggling could be heard).

So one day when we heard a faint call, 'Bentinck to Sweers, Bentinck to Sweers', we answered right away, but there was no response.

Tex called again. 'Is that you, AP?'

Faintly we heard, 'Bentinck to Sweers ...'

Tex tried once more. 'Are you all right AP?'

'Ahhhhh ... stingray ...' was all we could make out.

Tex jumped in the boat and headed across. AP lay beside his beloved radio, everyone standing around worried. His own boat was run up onto the beach. He'd been hunting for stingray around the far side of the island when a ray jammed a ten-centimetre-long venomous barb deep into his wrist. He'd pulled it out, the serrated edges ripping the flesh on the way, and driven his boat back to camp, collapsing with pain on the beach as the others rushed down to help him.

'Call Sweers!' someone yelled, but AP raised his head saying, 'Don't you touch ma radio!' so they had to help him up the beach and stand by in concern and frustration while he tried to relay the situation!

The RFDS was called, and Tex flew him to Mornington Island for treatment. Months later, we would see him rubbing at his wrist. He always had a numbness in it, although he regained full use of his hand.

The islands are surrounded by rocky reefs, with sheltered bays covered in seagrass beds. The reefs provide perfect habitat for fish, including sweetlip, coral trout, nannygai, cod, jewfish and mackerel, and the seagrass beds provide perfect feeding grounds for turtles and dugong. The green flatback (named for the colour of its fat, the shell colour is brown), and olive ridley turtles are often seen in the waters around Sweers Island. Many guests enjoy the tranquillity of a few hours' fishing, when suddenly up pops a big brown head and a loud 'GASP!' breaks the silence, then the splash as a turtle dives back down to the bottom. It is even more startling at night when all you hear is the 'GASP!' Occasionally, we see them come ashore to nest. The tracks on the beach look like tank manoeuvres and often several 'nests' are dug to confuse predators. With no feral animals here, the hundred or so eggs have a reasonable chance of hatching, although then the hatchlings must contend with birds, crabs and sharks.

Dolphins are often seen, sometimes with young, always the cute sea mammal. The dugong misses out on the cute factor, but for us are even more of a treat to see. They too come up for air and can be distinguished from dolphins as they roll through their dive, since they do not have a dorsal fin. Unlike whales, they usually don't raise their tail flukes as they dive, so sometimes all you see is a big, light-brown shape rolling on the surface. Underwater, they are even more graceful than dolphins. I was scuba diving from the boat one day while Tex and his granddaughter Kirsten were on board. I drifted down to the seabed about four metres below, but the water was murky and visibility was poor, so I decided it was pointless to continue the dive. Just as I prepared to surface, a huge shape loomed to my left. My mind must have immediately dismissed 'shark', noticing it was the wrong shape, although indistinct. As it came from behind, gradually filling the view of my dive mask, I was reminded of one of those movies where the space ship appears overhead, filling the sky. I thought to myself, *It's huge! It's a whale!* Then it crossed in front of me and I saw the beautiful undulating movement as it rippled through the water – snub nose, no dorsal fin and the white mark on its back made it instantly recognisable as a dugong that lived in the bay. I waited on the bottom a few minutes more but it didn't return, so I surfaced and saw Tex and Kirsten pointing excitedly a few metres away and calling, 'You just missed seeing the dugong!' I grinned up at them, delighted they had seen it too.

I learned to dive in 2000 and it has been fantastic to explore the sea country as well as the land. Not many people dive around the islands, so every dive was an adventure. The Gulf waters are shallow – most dives are around the five-metre mark. The wind and tides can stir up the bottom so the visibility is not great, averaging two metres, maybe eight on a good day. There is not a lot of coral, but what is there is healthy. There are colourful sponges, live shells, feather stars, nudibranch and lots and lots of fish. One of the most common fish around Sweers is the humble sweetlip. You hear a lot about the dazzling colour-change displays of cuttlefish but fish can change colour too – one of the coolest dives was when I swam around a rock and came face to face with a little sweetlip. We both stopped in our tracks and the normally pale brown fish instantly changed into dark 'fright colours' with an aggressive pattern of darker zigzag stripes. We stared at each other motionlessly for what seemed like ages but was probably less than a minute. It was enough time, though, for this little fish to realise I meant no harm, did not have a baited line with me and was not going to take him home for dinner. As we gazed into each other's eyes, he melted back to pale brown. I drifted backwards, and he turned and slowly swam away. It was a close encounter of the nicest kind!

Another of our most memorable dives was freediving off the north end of the island, where the big Spanish mackerel like to gather. We hung off the anchor line watching dozens of these beautiful navy-and-turquoise fish, over a metre long, zipping through the water around us. Definitely not something you get to do every day!

As well as marine life, there are other treasures beneath the waves. The Dutch mariner Abel Tasman was the first European to sight the island in 1644, but he was too far offshore and thought it was the tip of a mainland peninsula. In 1802 Matthew Flinders landed on the island, naming it after Salomon Sweers, one of the councillors of Batavia who authorised Tasman's voyage. Flinders dug a well and carved the name of his ship, *Investigator*, into a tree. As Flinders had noted Sweers' significance as a safe anchorage and watering place, other vessels and explorers followed. Many also carved their mark on the Investigator Tree, which was damaged during a cyclone in 1887 and removed to the Queensland Museum in Brisbane, where it is housed in a glass case, initials still clearly visible.

By the mid 1860s several cattle properties were established in the Gulf region, including Gregory Downs and Floraville, near Burketown. Robert Towns, after whom Townsville is named, owned several of these properties and established Burketown as a port from which to ship his produce. The emerging pastoral communities throughout the Gulf region were not then connected by road or rail to the east coast. All supplies in, and produce out, had to travel by sea out of the Gulf of Carpentaria and around Cape York to Sydney, or overseas to Java and beyond. The Gulf rivers being shallow, Towns transhipped to larger vessels at Sweers Island where a Bond Store and Customs House was built.

When Gulf Fever devastated Burketown in 1866, magistrate William Landsborough shipped the survivors across to the island, where the township of Carnarvon thrived for the next decade. All this maritime activity has left some treasures on the land and in the sea. Fossicking around the island has turned up old bottles, keys, bullets, even the plunger of a glass syringe. Fossicking the beaches often turns up pieces of crockery, glass, even an old bronze rowlock. Fossicking underwater is not so easy, but can be even more rewarding.

We'd known Robert Towns bought a brig called the *Governor* to act as a store-ship at the island. The four-metre tides and summer storms made a jetty impractical. On 20 August 1868 the two-masted, twenty-two-metre wooden ship was rounding the corner of the island when it ran aground on a reef and could not be refloated. Everyone got off safely and we assume most of the cargo was removed. We studied the eyewitness accounts, considered the time of year and possible weather, then dived the area where the ship most likely sank. We knew the timber frame would have disintegrated and there may not be much left to see. The first day we found nothing.

'Look for piles of ballast rock, metal sheathing, broken bottles,' said Tex as I slipped over the side of the boat again the next day.

I swam along the edge of the reef, scouring the sandy bottom and imagining every lump of rock to be an encrusted sea chest! I swam past a weed-covered rock with a sharp, pointed end, thinking idly, *Now, that one just looks like the bow of a ship*, knowing we would find no such thing.

As I passed, I glanced across again and saw it wasn't the bow of a ship – but the sharp, pointy shape was the fluke of an anchor! A massive anchor! I swam over to it. The shaft was more than twice my length, covered in weed and coral growth, lumpy and irregular but unmistakably an anchor. But something was wrong. I made out the shaft and one of the flukes, and even what looked like a big ring at the end of the shaft, but there was no second fluke opposite the first one. I swam around and checked again but there was just a sandy space where the fluke should have been. It didn't make sense. I surfaced and waved to Tex in the dinghy. 'I found an anchor!'

He motored carefully over, asked a few questions and started to assemble a float to mark the spot. I ducked back down – and it was gone! The current had carried me away and the visibility is never good here, just a few metres at most, so you could be near an object but not see it. I had found and lost an anchor twice the size of me in the space of a few minutes! I swam around for half an hour but with no reference points it was impossible. Unbelievable! But now we knew something was down there. More dives followed. We found chain, pipes which could be the encrusted masts and spars, copper sheathing for the hull with marks identifying the maker, and lots of 'strange shapes' that were obviously not natural rocks. We also found an anchor – with two flukes, but not much longer than me. Everyone thought I must have imagined that massive mysterious one-fluke anchor until several years later, when we found it again. This time we were prepared, with GPS to mark the spot, along with a float and line. It was indeed huge, and it definitely had only one fluke.

We Googled it. Lo and behold, some anchors were specially designed to be permanent moorings. One fluke was bent back along the shaft so it would not foul a mooring chain or damage the hull at low tide. We knew the *Governor* was brought to Sweers to be used as a permanently moored transhipment vessel, so this now made perfect sense. The layout of the chain, which could be traced over and under the sand until it led to the smaller anchor, now seemed to indicate that they tried to kedge the ship off the reef. It was fascinating to piece together all the information and try to visualise what happened nearly 140 years earlier.

One tangible thing that links all us Gulf women together, past and present, far and wide is the Morning Glory cloud. It is a long, cylindrical tube cloud stretching from one side of the horizon to the other. The ultimate panorama photo. It is born from winds that blow onto Cape York Peninsula – each side pushing warm, moist air upwards throughout the day until midnight, when the air cools and collapses, creating a shock wave that ripples westwards across the Gulf of Carpentaria. If conditions are right, cloud forms on the leading edge of this shock wave, dissipating at the rear, so that when it rolls across the Gulf next morning, it looks like a massive tidal wave of cloud rolling towards us, spreading sometimes one thousand kilometres (the full width of the Gulf), and sometimes up to ten rolls in succession.

The Kaiadilt of Bentinck call it *Yehpipi*, meaning 'big wind'; the Lardil of Mornington Island call it *Jargval*; the Gangalidda at Burketown call it *Mabunda*. We're not sure who named it the Morning Glory but, as it usually occurs at daybreak, it seems appropriate.

It rolls over us here on Sweers Island and even after thirty years we never tire of watching. We still stop what we are doing and go outside to see it, as no two are the same.

It rolls over ships at sea. I remember being on a boat when one rolled over, the only cloud in the sky, no other vessel or land in sight. It was stunning.

It rolls inland over Burketown, where glider pilots come from all over the world to surf along the front of this giant sky wave.

It rolls over the cattle properties and Aboriginal communities of the Gulf Country, linking us all together, as women all over the Gulf gaze upward to watch its passing.

Amanda Wilkinson

Amanda Wilkinson was born in the Lilydale Bush Nursing Hospital in the eastern suburbs of Melbourne and grew up in Kilsyth at the foot of Mount Dandenong. After finishing senior school she studied business and then worked in a school office. After ten years there she took long-service leave and eventually moved to Burketown in 1992 with her husband, Paul. They lived in a tin shed for five years until the night a python in their bed bit Amanda on the foot. They started Savannah Aviation in 1992 and then a small accommodation business, Savannah Lodge. Their life in Burketown has gone by in the blink of an eye and they have no intention of ever leaving.

IS IT DANGEROUS YET?

Amanda Wilkinson

WE ARRIVED IN BURKETOWN IN MAY 1992 TO STAY FOR six months and investigate the possibility of moving to town on a permanent basis. We camped very simply along the banks of the Albert River using an old fridge we found up the river as a cupboard, and a blow-up mattress with a hole in it.

After enjoying many weeks there, we decided to head across to Sweers Island. Paul had visited the island many times having flown in with friends, and I had also been there in an aircraft before coming to Burketown.

We packed up our camp complete with our newest addition – an injured fledgling galah called Baby – in a cage we'd built for her from bamboo we collected from Adels Grove some weeks earlier, and wire from the tip. It was

71

actually quite a large cage for a little bird! Anyway, it went on top of everything else – the food, luggage, bedding, camping gear, spare parts, spare motor, fuel – mainly lots of things we didn't require, but we didn't think of that at the time.

It was so exciting! Off we went, feeling like blue-water sailors. I'm not sure if I even wondered or asked Paul how long it would take, or gave fuel or safety equipment a thought. I'm sure we had some of those big, bulky life jackets somewhere on the boat. Ignorance is bliss.

We cast off from the bank of the Albert River in a fourteen-foot V-hull tinny with a twenty-five horsepower outboard motor. With so much weight on board we soon realised our little boat had quite a bit of trouble coping with the load and she couldn't get up to plane. Oh well, isn't this part of the adventure? Ignorance *is* bliss!

We knew we weren't going to make it to Sweers Island that day as we were not making good time at all. That's okay, all part of the fun. We decided to camp a little way down from the mouth of the Albert River. It was a muddy landing, the type of mud that sticks like s**t to a blanket. I remember my leg sinking in up to my knees. I probably thought it was hilarious, not thinking of the potential of being easy croc bait stuck in the mud like that.

We took our gear up onto the top grassy bank quite a way from the water's edge as Paul pointed out that camping on the 'beach' wasn't a good idea because of the potential of crocodiles. Oh, I hadn't thought of that. Ignorance is bliss *and* sometimes dangerous.

We lit our fire and cooked our all-time favourite: two-minute noodles with onions and dried peas and a big splash of tomato sauce. As night fell, all the wonderful noises we heard in the day disappeared and were replaced by creepy, scary sounds you swear are only a few feet away from you. I wondered, was *this* dangerous?

Morning came, and we were back to the terrible mud and into the overloaded little boat.

The mouth of the river is something to see and experience. It reminds me of a birth canal (not that I have a vivid personal memory of that) opening out into a whole new, big world, unprotected from riverbanks, mangroves and calmer waters. I always find it quite dramatic.

So, out we went into that big blue yonder. Up until now, of course, we had no real need for navigational equipment, as the containment of the river banks guided us – although that too can trip you up if you take a wrong turn, but luckily we didn't. At this point we were heading to an island, which we knew was out there somewhere to the north-west of our position. It's a whole new ball game once you lose sight of the land behind you and cannot see land in front. Out came the sophisticated navigation equipment, ha ha! A silver compass – you know, the ones that cubs and scouts are given when going on camp for an orienteering exercise. I, of course, was none the wiser that this piece of plastic wasn't going to take us directly to our destination.

With the boat still not able to plane so just putting along, the conditions getting quite choppy and Paul looking at that compass – that piece of plastic – with hope on his face, I did start to wonder and I asked him, 'Is this dangerous yet?'

I knew that things might be getting a bit hairy when Paul started to talk about throwing things overboard to lighten the load as our fuel consumption was getting a bit critical. OMG, this *IS* dangerous! What would we throw over – the spare motor? But what if the other one failed? The water? No … we might need that too! The food? How about the air mattress with the hole in it? We decided not to throw anything over and keep going for a bit longer.

Surely we must be getting closer to seeing the island ahead. The compass, that piece of plastic, surely wouldn't fail us. I stood on the seat, hand to brow, searching the horizon while trying not to fall out of the boat due to the ever-increasing swell.

Land ahoy! There she was, still quite a way away, but the fact we could see the island made me feel a lot better. We finally made it to Sweers Island, pulled up on the beach very pleased with ourselves and feeling very relieved and excited.

Tex came down to the beach, saying, 'Where the hell have you come from?' and 'You didn't tell us you were coming!' and 'How would we know to come and look for you if we didn't know when you were arriving?' and so on.

Not the reception we thought we would get, but now know it was the reception we well deserved.

We were lucky. We survived our journey and adventure but a whole lot of things could have gone wrong over those two days. We successfully earned the title of 'bloody idiots' for: not telling anyone we were leaving; not telling anyone we were coming; overloading the boat; not having adequate safety and navigational equipment, and mucking around on a muddy beach tempting fate with the crocodiles.

I will never forget this trip and, if we were ever to do it again in a similar-sized boat, we would do it a whole lot differently.

Stockwomen, campdrafts and horses

Dallas Daley

Dallas Daley (née Magoffin) was born in the small north-western town of Julia Creek sixty-eight years ago and remains a diehard lover of outback life and bush people. Along with her parents and three sisters, she lived on a beautiful property called Etta Plains, 75 000 acres of flat, open Mitchell and Flinders grass country, bounded by the Cloncurry River to the west and the Flinders River to the east. Etta Plains originally belonged to her paternal grandfather and was passed on, along with a huge debt, to her father.

LIVING WITH HORSES AND LEARNING THE ROPES

Dallas Daley

Etta Plains Station

ETTA PLAINS IS SITUATED ABOUT 130 KILOMETRES north of Julia Creek on a rough dirt road. The open, sprawling, treeless downs country, which made up about one-third of the property, was used mainly for the sheep Dad ran, ranging from four thousand to ten thousand merinos, depending on the season. The river country, with its channels, waterholes and shaded timber, ran the cattle – usually about two to three thousand head of them. How fortunate we were to be born in a small bush community where we could all run free, climb trees, swim in waterholes, milk the cows, ride horses, work hard, live off the land, look out for each other, but also push each other to the limit and learn independence at an early age. A tremendous way to rear kids.

In those days we would be called 'isolated' (although we never considered it that way), as we were at the end of the mail run. Because money was tight, Dad was always mindful of the cost of fuel – there was never just a quick trip into town. We waited until a car load of necessities was required before we ventured out, and then with much excitement. As it was a dirt road for the 130 kilometres to town (in later years we had the bitumen Beef Road for the eighty kilometres from the Dalgonally turnoff to Julia Creek) we'd always go in the open Land Rover, even if rain was about, even to a ball. We never stayed the night as Dad never drank alcohol and there was always work to do the next day, so it was a long trip home sitting in the back of the Rover trying not to sleep in case we bounced out! I wish I had a photo of that but for some reason I never took one.

I went to boarding school in Julia Creek when I was four. Mum was pregnant with Sarita, and I fretted when my siblings Sharon and Lorena went to board at St Joseph's Convent. I joined them on the understanding there was no turning back once I'd made my decision ... so then I spent the next twelve years rebelling against going back to school. Thank God for sport as I loved playing competitive tennis and basketball on weekends. It provided us with some freedom and made being away from home in a strange city environment more bearable. But in the end, if you live in the bush you don't have a choice about needing to go to boarding school to be educated, so, to look at it in a positive light, being away from home in formative years is character building and it makes kids more independent!

Sharon was my lifesaver when I moved to boarding school in Brisbane, as she looked out for me when I was so homesick and a poor mixer. Kids from the bush – whether black or white – feel totally displaced and lost when they're sent off to boarding school. It was tough for the first twelve months, especially when we were young, as there was no phone at home so we couldn't ring for a talk and mail was only once a week in the dry season. Not like now, when kids have email and iPhones to keep in touch. I eventually found another girl who liked horses as much as I did and her uncle had a farm with horses and cattle on the Gold Coast, so we mated up! We hitched out there on the odd weekend when we were allowed out of school and it was heaven to be back riding horses in the 'bush'.

School did have an adverse effect on me, though, as for years afterwards I couldn't walk into a school ground without being physically sick. That changed when I was asked to teach adults at a copper art workshop in the Cloncurry State School and, maybe because I was the teacher not the student, I could finally walk onto a school ground without being violently ill.

It took all Dad's ingenuity to get us back to school on time after a good wet season, but he managed to do it through hell or high water! Sometimes it involved using the tractor to pull the Land Rover with all our gear plus ourselves stashed in it, and even having to use chains on the Rover. There was a river to cross before we could get to Dalgonally and we'd all be hoping this would stop us and give us more time at home. But if the river was high, Dad swam over and walked the five kilometres up to the homestead, and back. He and the head stockman would come with a boat to ferry us kids and our ports across. We'd then say a tearful farewell to our parents, who made the slow trip home while we were taken on to meet the plane to fly back to school in Brisbane. The nuns never believed the trouble we'd taken to get back to school until they'd seen the photos, but before that we were always in trouble if we were late.

My father always said we needed to see how the other half lived so we could choose whether we wanted to live in the city or bush, and what didn't kill us made us stronger. Lorena and I couldn't get out of the city fast enough once we'd finished school, although we could have had careers in the big smoke. Lorena won a scholarship to the Conservatorium of Music in Sydney, and I wanted to learn more about photography (my other love), but the course I'd been recommended required six years of study in Melbourne. So those careers were knocked on the head. We loved the bush and came home to help on the property and begin the sport of campdrafting, which involved working on our skills with horses.

Dad told us a funny story about Mum helping him in the cattle yards after they'd had some rain. Mum was never an outside person, having been reared in the town, and only learnt to ride after she was married. Early in their married life Dad always had Frank, an Aboriginal stockman, to help him. Later, we kids were old enough to be his offsiders, so Mum's forte was inside the house. However, while we were overseas Mum was Dad's right-hand man and one day they were drafting cattle in the mud in the horse yards at the house. Mum stood in the gateway blocking cattle from going through when one stirry beast decided that gate was his exit. Dad yelled for Mum to get out of the way, but she stood fast and Dad thought she was being very brave, but then she bolted, minus shoes that were stuck fast in the mud! They were both very relieved and had a good laugh afterwards.

Even though in the early days there was no electricity, no phones, kerosene fridges that broke down often, no hot water system apart from bucketing it into the house from the hot flowing bore outside, and a long-drop toilet that housed snakes and redback spiders, we had everything we needed to survive and enjoy life. My childhood was a happy, carefree existence – apart from the twelve years at boarding school.

I was the third daughter and the only one with red hair and fair skin, a throwback to my maternal grandfather (although I always insisted it was strawberry blonde and still do!). A bore drain ran past the house, which ended up in a 'swamp' (a dugout in the bore drain) that was our favourite swimming hole. Sunscreen was never heard of then, so we'd leave the house to walk the kilometre and I would be covered almost completely with a big hat, sunglasses, long-sleeved shirt and shorts while my sisters were in knickers. As soon as I was out of Mum's sight I'd strip off too and very quickly turn red, then blister, then freckle. It was all worth it, though.

We had Frank working for us for fourteen years and he taught us lots of tricks as well as horse riding. He couldn't read or write so he loved to be part of our school when Mum taught my two older sisters – but he'd cause such chaos that she would wave the wooden spoon around then declare school closed for the day, and we'd all happily catch our horses and head out with Frank to track dingoes. I remember Frank asking my sister Lorena and myself to read letters for him even though we could hardly read ourselves. We made up love stories and anything we could think of, so then he'd smell a rat and go and ask Dad to read them to him. When we all went to boarding school in town Frank's three kids went too and came back home with us for the holidays, so it was a very tearful time when we all returned to school.

Horses have always been a huge part of my life, as all the work on the property was done on horseback, and I loved them. From as far back as I can remember I tagged along on a horse whenever anyone saddled up. If we were naughty Frank threatened to leave us at Fred Wilson's grave on the Flinders River so the 'debil debils' could sort us out. Frank was very superstitious and terrified of graves.

Horses were used to check fences right around the boundary (sometimes an extra horse was taken packed with pliers, wire, food and water), to muster, to collect the mail in the wet season when roads were underwater, to check on the bogged sheep when the downs were soggy and waterlogged, and also just ridden for pleasure. Hardly a day went by that Lorena and I didn't go for a ride or catch a young horse to handle. Our two other sisters weren't as keen, though they loved to ride mustering. Because we lived on the open downs there were not many natural jumps around, so Lorena and I threw saddle cloths over the top wire of the fence line and jumped our horses over it. When Dad found out he was not impressed – if our horse slipped it could've caught in the barbed wire, even though we figured it was safely covered with the saddle cloth.

Mum moved out from town as a young eighteen-year-old when she married Dad and started a family soon after. She'd learnt to ride after she moved to live at Etta Plains but was never a confident horsewoman. When Dad or Frank taught us to ride, or we were just playing high jinks on our ponies, Mum shut all the louvres on the verandah so she couldn't see what we were up to as it made her too nervous. She mopped up the blood and cuts when we returned after many busters and would suggest we never ride again, but it was in our blood. One of our favourite pastimes when we were in our early teens was to ride bareback down to the Flinders River six kilometres away with some sandwiches tucked in our shirts, and a gun and knife in our belts, and ride out to hunt pigs as they were a pest. We'd start off so enthusiastically but by the end of the day we'd wish we'd taken saddles ... but we'd do it all again as soon as we had a spare day. Dad introduced us girls as 'his ringers' and hopefully we filled the void of no sons.

There were forty kilometres of dirt road from Etta Plains to Dalgonally and in the wet season the mail always seemed to be able to make it to Dalgonally but no further. After quite a few weeks of no mail Dad would saddle up his big quiet horse, Ned, who my boyfriend, Noel Daley, had given him and, with saddle bags filled with mail to be sent, he'd ride off to bring it home. This usually took a couple of days, depending on how boggy it was, and he'd always deliver the neighbours' mail along the way. It was a big, exciting welcome home when he arrived with lots of reading matter. If the wet season went on for too long (sometimes we'd be stranded for three months), Dad organised a food drop with a friend who flew a chopper or fixed-wing plane and would bring out the main supplies.

We always had poddy lambs and calves, and in the wet season we rode our horses along the bore drain checking the sheep, as they usually stand still when it rains and end up bogged in the black soil. We'd muster up what we could move onto harder ground and take any poddies home. Once it started drying up we'd take the tractor out with a trailer hooked up and bring home any sheep we found bogged. These we put into homemade slings to get their circulation working before releasing them again into the paddocks. We'd have sheep lined up in slings all along the front fence, making it a very grand entrance.

I was always the cowgirl pushing the boundaries, keen on trying my hand at riding buckjumpers and shooting, so when the sheep were bogged I'd stay out there with a gun protecting them from crows or dingoes until they could be collected and carted back to the house. While the sheep were alive and immobilised by the mud, crows would peck holes in their bellies and pick out their eyes, so it was my job not to let this happen. It's hard to shoot a crow, they are so cunning, but I could scare them. It broke my heart if I got there too late and the crows had beaten me and I had to shoot the sheep. They were always so stoic and strong, but I knew it would be a slow death if I didn't put them out of their misery.

After the rain, the sheep regained their strength, but because of the black soil they often had mud balls on their feet that needed to be knocked off with a hammer or something similar. Sometimes the mud balls fell off if the sheep was chased around enough – another job for Lorena and me. We'd take turns driving the ute while the unlucky one not driving hung on for dear life in the back, ready to jump out to grab the sheep that had the mud ball. I was always a speedster. Lorena was more cautious, so she was terrified when I drove as I'd forget she was in the back (even though she'd be yelling) and I'd have the ute ducking and diving after the sheep until it lay down ready to be caught. I'm not so competitive now, but in the early days I didn't like anything to beat me.

My sisters and I loved shearing time. We loved mustering the sheep on horseback and the physical side of drafting thousands of sheep and trying to hurdle the fences. We'd be allowed to join in the shearers' smokos (which were delicious treats) so long as we helped clean up after, and then we'd help the man making the bales to push the wool down. One day I was running late and was racing down to the sheep yards barefoot when I stood on something that hurt. I thought it must've been a piece of glass so had a quick look but couldn't see anything; I limped down then continued to work for the day. Late that afternoon my foot was badly swollen and the next day the ball of my foot was like a balloon and I couldn't walk. When shearing finished, Dad took me in to see the local doc. Remember, we were a long way from town and it cost money to drive there, but this was a bit of an emergency as none of our cures worked. We were shocked when the doctor diagnosed it as a snake bite! He drew all the fluid out then cut the skin away to reveal the bite. I was lucky it wasn't a deadly snake. Shoes were the order of the day for a while, but that novelty soon wore off.

Like most people in the bush we killed our own beef, and that caused much excitement. Frank climbed a tree and we kids mustered the cattle over as close to the tree as we dared. As soon as Frank shot the fattest bullock, Dad brought the knives over in the Land Rover and instructed us to make a fire to cook the rib bones. There were never any left to take home.

I remember it being hot in the house, but the heat never worried us except at night, so sometimes we'd all carry our mattress outside to sleep. It was usually cooler in the open air, but then we'd have the odd poddy lamb or dog annoy us. When I think back I realise how hot our kitchen must have been when Mum cooked on the Aga coke stove. Sometimes she'd have dinner cooked then get sick with a bout of asthma brought on by the heat, so she'd retire to bed with a fan if the batteries were charged enough to run it.

We had a happy household and we all sat down to eat together, then often played ping-pong after dinner or had a music session with everyone on an instrument. The ringers from neighbouring stations, or the bank boys who'd been transferred to Julia Creek and looked for company and home cooked meals, often came out on weekends to dine out on Mum's cooking and play ping-pong.

I remember one night we were all having a 'jam session', with Sharon playing the piano, Lorena on the piano accordion, Dad playing the banjo mandolin, Sarita on the bongo drums, Mum on the shakers and myself on the guitar, when Sharon let out a squeal. She'd felt something moving over her bare foot and, thinking it was the cat, bent down to stroke it – but it was a huge king brown snake! After much pandemonium, Dad removed it outside.

Knowing how much we loved and missed the bush life when we were at school, Dad always organised the cattle muster to be in the school holidays so we could help and join in the fun. Mustering involved camping out under the stars, bathing in the river very quickly as it was usually winter, cooking and eating by an open fire, riding out early to bring in the horses, listening for the horse with the bell tied around its neck so we could find it in the dark, just being part of the team and riding our best horses to bring the cattle to the yards. It was all bronco branding in those days. Frank and another good stockman and family friend, Tiddley, rode a draught horse to rope the calves that were then pulled up to the wooden branding fence to be laid down, earmarked, castrated if needed and branded before being let back in the mob. Sometimes we girls and the young ringers competed to jump on the bigger calves as they were let go and ride them back to the mob.

Poor Mum didn't get to see us much in the May holidays, as we'd camp out in our swags with Frank at the horse paddock on the Cloncurry River near the cattle yards. Sarita was the youngest family member and Frank's favourite, so if she got cold during the night Frank would take a blanket off one of our beds to throw across her.

Men from the neighbouring properties came to attend the muster and take home their cattle that had strayed onto our place. Mum was kept busy filling the cake tins and feeding everybody and we'd all quietly compete to show off our horses' skills cutting out the bullocks on an open camp. This is a dying art but it has led to Australia's own sport of campdrafting.

The rivers played a large part of our life at Etta. We loved watching the fresh water coming down with froth on it and we'd walk at the head of the water poking the froth with long sticks. One day, we girls were walking along in the water and Dad was watching high up on the bank when we heard him call out urgently to get out of the water. We did bolt out as he never wasted words and then we saw the crocodile walking along at the head of the water between us girls. A lot of freshwater crocs were about then but this was a beauty, about six feet long, so we decided to leave him to enjoy it on his own.

When Dad delved the boredrain, sometimes he'd need more weight on the front of the delver, so he'd sit us girls up there. We'd love it but often we'd get so excited about little fish being pushed up onto the delver we'd try to grab them and end up head first in the water. That would never be allowed nowadays with workplace health and safety!

We liked to have a swim in the river after we mustered if we finished early enough, but Mum couldn't swim so it was a general rule that we didn't go in unless Dad was there too. On this occasion – it was in the holidays and Sharon brought a school friend home who was a city girl – we convinced Mum to let us have a quick swim before we went home to do the jobs. The school friend got caught in a whirlpool and Sharon went in to help her, then they were both in trouble and Mum wanted to go in too, but we kept her out. Luckily Lorena thought quickly enough to grab a long branch and we held her arm while she walked out until they could grab hold of it. Between us all they were brought back to safety. Scary time but it was worse when we got home and Dad heard about our close encounter.

When I was only about eight, Dad brought in a couple of men to muster and buy the brumbies running on Etta Plains. They were beautiful horses and we caught and broke in the young ones for our stock work, but the wild horses were also a nuisance on the property as they broke fences, bred into large numbers and ate as much grass as the cattle. We girls were very excited to be allowed to come on the muster as we knew it would be fast and thrilling, but we didn't know how long it would take and how thirsty we would get. We never carried water and it was a known fact you grabbed a quick drink if you passed water because you didn't know how long before you'd get another chance. That day it was hot with lots of galloping as we tried to block and wheel the brumbies, and we began to panic when our tongues started to swell with thirst. Frank came to our rescue again, telling us to suck on stones and gum leaves to get saliva returning to our mouths. Guess we couldn't give him cheek that day!

I'd always admired and wanted desperately to ride Dad's big black gelding, Cavalcade, as he was the fastest walker and a beautiful, smart-looking horse. Dad agreed to let me ride him mustering one day, though Frank didn't think I'd handle him. I thought I was The Queen, stepping out on him, leading everyone. However, things went terribly wrong when I went to block some cattle and Cavalcade took the bit between his teeth and kept going, jumping logs and dodging trees. He probably didn't know there was anything on his back. I galloped until Cavalcade decided he'd had enough and slowed down. I jumped off him, wondering how to get back to find the mob, and started walking, leading my now-tired horse in the general direction of the yards. Thankfully, Frank turned up after following my tracks and after a good dressing-down we swapped horses and he led me back to Dad and the cattle.

I must've been a troublesome, determined child as I remember doing some of the musters bareback to improve my balance. The others thought I was mad, as my butt would be very sore by the end of the day. At another stage I was on a hard-boiled egg diet so would only take hard-boiled eggs for lunch in my saddle bag. When we pulled up to boil the billy for lunch I'd drool over the sandwiches the others had cut for lunch, but luckily Dad knew what would happen so he'd always cut an extra sandwich to share with me.

It was fun when we arrived at the last gate on the way home from a muster. From here was a straight stretch where we'd gallop the racehorses when they were in training for the Sedan Dip races. We'd always been told not to gallop home but thought this was different, as this had a purpose. But Sharon's mare, Arestide, who also doubled as a beautiful, fast racehorse, knew when we arrived at the gate that that was also her starting line for the gallop home – she pranced, danced, and jumped up and down. Mostly my sister gave in and let her go.

In about 1956 a terrible fire ravaged Etta, burning practically the whole place, some of the cattle and most of the horses. It started when a distant neighbour burned his rubbish dump and a wind sprang up, sending sparks into the long grass. The fire spread quickly. Smoke billowed, giving us warning as the fire spread across the property in between us and onto Etta Plains. All the people in the area were out with their firefighting equipment but were not in the race to put the fire out as the wind was increasing. As flames headed for the homestead Mum piled us kids and Grandma into the outside galvanised iron shower rooms thinking that was the safest place if the house went up in flames. Grandma was an English lady not used to the harsh conditions and she only had one leg, so I can't imagine she was in high spirits being locked in a small shower room with four wild kids while a fire raged outside and Mum made sandwiches.

They did eventually put the fire out, but not before our beautiful property was burnt out, most of the sheep and cattle burned, all the fences destroyed and those horses, who initially survived later had to be shot after their hooves fell off after being burnt on the hot ground. Not long before the fire disaster Dad had bought Sharon a new pony, a lovely piebald mare that caused much excitement and envy. After the fire she was found with her hooves melting so she needed to be destroyed without Sharon ever having ridden her. Bush kids learn to be resilient and to take the good with the bad.

On weekends, when we were home from boarding school and not too busy, there'd sometimes be tennis, cricket or skiing at a local waterhole, or a gymkhana or campdraft somewhere. We had also joined the drama group in Julia Creek and went in for rehearsals. If we ended up at a party afterwards there was no way to let Mum and Dad know we would be late, as there was no phone service. If we got home any time after 4 a.m. Dad would be up cooking breakfast, so we'd have a wash and get ready for the day's work. Mum told us years later this was payback, as they'd worry all night thinking we might've had an accident and Dad spent most of the night up the windmill looking for our lights. Once he knew we were close to home he'd start cooking.

In 1969–70 Lorena and I spent an exciting year travelling overseas. In between touring England, camping trips around Europe and hitching around Scotland and Ireland, we worked at bars, restaurants and as tea ladies. We found the winter in London depressing as we weren't used to not seeing the sun for months on end, and the cold was debilitating. We spent a month in America sightseeing and visiting magnates like Nelson Bunker Hunt, who'd had cattle on agistment at Etta, then we booked to come home via South Africa and that was wonderful. We drove around South Africa and arrived home in time to start the muster, so all thoughts of saving up to go back touring were forgotten.

It was a tough year for Mum and Dad while we were away as they didn't get rain until late February (our Wet usually starts in December), but they wouldn't hear of us coming home to help them move hungry cattle. Noel Daley, my future husband, kept a close eye on them, however, as he worked on Millungera, which was just over the river, and lent a hand when needed.

Campdrafting

BEFORE CAMPDRAFTING STARTED IN OUR AREA WE loved to compete in the local gymkhanas, the Cloncurry Show and one-day events. But drafting was a bit more of a challenge and chasing a cow was part of our everyday work, so we practised while we mustered. Campdrafting involves having a 'cut-out' yard with about nine head of cattle in it.

A person on a horse cuts out one beast, endeavours to take it outside into an arena, around a course of two pegs, then through a gate. But this doesn't always go to plan as there are certain rules to adhere to and a judge with a whip for cracking the competitor off when they deem the unlucky person to be out of bounds. There is also a time limit for completing the course.

Our mode of transport was an old Blitz truck. We'd load the horses on the back, pack mattresses on top of the cab for camping, then we girls climbed up on top of the mattresses, with food and water for the long trip to town. It amazes me how much effort Mum and Dad put in to taking us to social events, but we all loved the rare outings.

Dad always bred and raced thoroughbreds, so when my sister Lorena and I showed an interest in drafting, Dad bought a beautiful palomino Anglo–Arab sire, who looked like a solid stock horse, to cross with his thoroughbred mares to produce our cow horses. This was a huge success and in 1974, after Noel and I were married, I won a $1000 (that was a lot of money in those early years) open draft at Boulia on one of the progeny. Lorena and I broke in our own colts and loved to take them right through to competition. In those days, lots of the campdraft committees also put on rodeos and gymkhanas on the same weekend, so we'd compete the same horses in as many events as we could, including showjumping, barrel racing and steer undecorating.

Steer undecorating is a women's rodeo sport. A beast with a ribbon stuck high up on its neck is let out of a chute and a woman and her assistant 'hazer' ride their horses either side of the beast. The aim is to pluck the ribbon off the animal in the shortest time. It is a bit like the men's bulldogging and it gave the ladies another rodeo sport apart from barrel racing and roping.

The Saxby Roundup was our favourite weekend. We camped at a waterhole so we could swim the horses, bathe (there was a lot of soap lost while bathing) and have a roaring fire. At Saxby we all slept in a five-man tent and since Dad was the president, and Mum the secretary and treasurer for many years, the money was hidden somewhere in our tent. Dad always seemed to sleep with one eye open. In the old days, all the camps lit a fire so we girls had fun at night going from camp to camp socialising. One night at about 2 a.m. I made the mistake of returning to our camp to get a coat and was just sneaking out again when Dad quietly told me to get into bed. I never made that mistake again!

Once Noel and I started going out, I borrowed his horses for the ladies' draft. I was on a hat trick as he was pretty cool and had two good camphorses – his stallion, Rio, and a mare, Deestrap. These were the foundation of our stock-horse stud and all our family are still drafting those bloodlines today.

Campdrafting became our main social outing and we made lifelong friends among those also interested in the sport of horses. Before long, Dad bought us a new float to take to the drafts in place of the old Blitz truck. Lorena and I could now only take a single horse each, so we made sure it was a good one that would bring us some success. Lorena teamed up with her future husband, Rodger Jefferis, who also enjoyed the sport and had reliable horses, so a lot of courting was done at the campdraft venues as well as swapping horses.

Some of the horses we drafted we also trained for the Sedan Dip and Clonagh Stations races, and as Frank also had his own team of racehorses, borrowed from Dad, he walked them across to the venue riding another horse that wasn't going to race. This took him a few days but he'd always arrive in time with the horses eager to run. Nowadays at Sedan Dip there's a prize for the horse that wins a race, as well as an open-age draft, but back when we liked to train Dad's racehorses and ride in the ladies' race there was no such prize.

When Lorena and I married and children came along, campdrafting was even more fun as we'd all camp together at the drafts. The children were excited to see each other. They loved to compete and ride wild, and we'd all swap notes about our latest horses over a campfire dinner. Our children were all horse enthusiasts and daring riders, but one draft stands out when our daughter, Jaye, aged six, rode our stallion, Rio, to win the mini draft. Campdrafts start early in the mornings. Everyone must pull his or her weight to get the horses fed and watered before the day starts, so the kids learn responsibility at an early age. We support each other and try to be at the cut-out yard to watch each family member ride and help pick the beast best suited to take around the course. Then, of course, someone also must be on the camera to take a video so we can watch and learn from it when we return home.

My sisters and I were brought up to be independent women, maybe through boarding school or because we helped everywhere since Dad had no boys. When my husband, Noel, said he didn't want to campdraft anymore that was fine by me, so long as he didn't expect me to give it up as well. He retired from drafting for about fifteen years while I drove our Volvo bodytruck, carting my three or four horses to any draft in the vicinity of five hundred kilometres, usually meeting up with our daughter, Jaye, and her kids. I camped in a swag in the back of the truck with an esky full of food, so I was quite comfortable and often my grandkids shared my swag and torch. We both draft again now but have sold the bodytruck and travel in a bit more style with a small truck and five-horse gooseneck.

One of the great things about drafting is that no one can ever be sure of winning, as there are so many issues to deal with – venue, cattle, the horse, our nerves and the ground surface. Some surfaces are hard and slippery and not safe, others are very heavy, and some are nice. Each ground must be ridden accordingly, to keep safe and not give the horse or rider a bad experience. Consequently, each competitor is in with a chance if they do their homework. The whole family has had some success drafting, but the best part of it has been doing it on horses we've bred, broken in and started for competition. To name a few wins, Noel won the first Cloncurry Stockman's Challenge for horsemanship and cow-working skills; Jaye and I have won the Australian Campdrafting Association lady rider title twice; our sons, Kelly and Darcy, have won the under twenty-ones Cloncurry Stockman's Challenge, along with many other wins, so we've had plenty of proud moments. Every day is different and each venue holds different challenges, so a campdrafter can never rest on his or her laurels.

The legacy lives on now with our beautiful grandkids, aged between three and ten, still drafting our old line of 'Rio' stock horses. We all still love to get together at the odd draft to compete and play together.

Learning the Gulf

Sue Woodall

Sue Woodall, Almora Station, has lived in the Gulf for over thirty years. She was born in the Mallee country of Victoria, and when she was five years old the family moved to a farm near Barraport. Sport played a big part of her young life with the winters spent going to the footy and playing netball. In summer, there was tennis, basketball and swimming, either in the dam at home or in the pool in town. She loved the farm, riding her pony and helping with the sheep. Sue loves reading, collecting books and researching the history of her family and the Gulf.

FEATHERS IN THE JAM?

Sue Woodall

FOR THE NEW GOVERNESS ARRIVING FROM VICTORIA IN 1977, the language of north Queensland was confusing. The confusion started with the question, 'Where's your port?'

Sue was staggered to think that at the tender age of eighteen they thought she would be travelling with alcohol! She finally realised they meant her suitcase. On the long trip to the station, mention was made of road trains. Even though Sue grew up in the country she had no idea what they were. She was so grateful she never asked, 'Where are the tracks?'

Then there was rosella jam – surely they don't make jam out of parrots! Probably the most embarrassing misunderstanding came when Sue was informed that the men were going to fence the turkey's nest. Oh, how impressed she was with these environmentally conscious men who were going to protect that poor turkey sitting on its nest.

She learnt that 'flat stick' meant very fast and a 'donkey' heated water. The old Toyota was called 'Canardly' (can hardly go). She noticed 'ay' was quite often added to the end of a sentence. 'Nice day, ay?' She found it hard to understand the Boss and his mate George. The Boss mentioned that he thought she was deaf because she always said, 'Beg your pardon?'

A joke was told and she laughed at what seemed the appropriate moment, but she had no idea what they'd said.

Power was supplied by a generator that ran for only part of the day and turned off at night. Sue finally got used to its hum. Most days she wondered how she came to be a couple of thousand miles from home at a place where her parents couldn't even phone her.

She'd completed her HSC, not doing terribly well, and decided to move to Brisbane to live with a nursing friend of her mum's. She realised later that Maureen and her husband, Geoff, did not envision having this naïve young country girl in their house for nearly three months. She must have driven them crazy. She applied for many jobs along with the hundreds of other school leavers. She tried at a newsagency (where at least forty people were in the queue awaiting an interview), the Queensland Police Force (there was a three-year waiting list), a florist, a café (that looked so grotty she never even went in), a legal office, gift shop, the Queensland Sugar Board, Bullen's Lion Safari Park at Yatala (she needed a driver's licence), a snack bar in the city and a hairdresser's where she was informed the job was taken by 8.45 a.m. She was told at interviews for a couple of jobs that she was too old. She went to the Valley for a waitressing position after reading an ad that mentioned 'good conditions, good wages'. She found the right address, looked up and saw photos of scantily clad women and 'strip' on the sign. She turned tail and took off. She laughed with Maureen later … she wasn't sure if they wanted a topless waitress, which would have been hilarious as she was so flat chested she reckoned the management would have said, 'Oh love, I think you'd better wear a shirt.'

A Dutch bloke interviewed her for a job in a warehouse. A guard dog nearly ate her as she arrived, there was a nude calendar on the wall and he asked her if she was liberated and had muscles to carry stuff. She was grateful she never got that job.

She was introduced to some new experiences while in Brisbane. She thought the green tree frogs cute but cane toads disgusting. She became very adept at catching trains and knew every stop from Oxley to the city. She tried pawpaw for the first time and Orchy Passio-Nectar became her drink of choice. Her favourite revelation was frangipanis; Maureen placed the flowers in her room on her arrival, and the scent was delicious. As she walked to the many train stations she saw the trees with pink, orange, white or yellow flowers. They were so different from the English plants in her garden at home and became a favourite.

Eventually, she found in the *Courier-Mail* an advert for a governess job on a cattle property south of Burketown. She thought governesses were only characters in books set in the 1800s. She had never heard of Burketown – or the Gulf Country – for that matter. Surprisingly, even in Brisbane, many hadn't heard of this area in their own state. She phoned the Queensland Tourism Bureau but they were no help. Mr Ian McMillian from the Australian Mercantile Land and Finance Company in Eagle Street conducted her interview – a lovely man who pretty much gave her the job on the spot. Her wage would be sixty dollars per week with six dollars taken out in tax. Mr Daniels from Brodie and Co Stock and Station Agents, Cloncurry, in the great north-west of Queensland, would purchase her plane ticket. Mr McMillian told her they required her to commit for a year and then added, 'Maybe you'll fall in love with the boss's son.'

So here she was governessing on a cattle station in an area no one knew. For a girl who grew up in Victoria and had only just finished school, her job as a governess was at first daunting. There were the two younger boys and their older sister, SC, who was twelve. She was a happy girl who became a great mate – they laughed, yarned and had fun. They decided to dress a gas bottle in Mrs C's old dress and hat, named her Gladys the Gas Bottle, and she stood outside the kitchen window for many months. The two young boys were often asked to go mustering, which caused much angst as they fell further behind with their school work.

The school room was a large room upstairs in the middle of the house with no windows but six doors, four leading to bedrooms and two at each end opening onto the verandah. It was a cold room in winter (even though the governess didn't regard a Gulf winter as cold) and unbearably hot in summer. As the Wet approached – with no fans in the house and no power, for that matter – the children needed to be careful not to smudge their good work with sweat marks. She made them paper fans to try and alleviate the heat. The children all worked at a wooden table, with a shelf each in the old wardrobe to store their school work. Educational resources were few, excepting the wonderful *Reader's Digest World Atlas* from which she hand-drew a world map to put on the wall. They studied three subjects – English, Maths and Social Studies – and she was impressed by the children's handwriting and their knowledge of grammar. Their work was returned to the Primary Correspondence School in Brisbane. Even though School of the Air was available from Mount Isa the children didn't participate.

As she lived with the family, the children became like sister and brothers to her. After school and on weekends they played many games – pick-up-sticks, dominoes, Monopoly, snakes and ladders (a favourite of the youngest boy), chess, cheat, 500, switch, fish, and of course cricket on the front lawn.

Her bedroom was a small room upstairs at the back of the house. She loved her little room with its bed, dressing table (which they called a duchess), wardrobe and small table. The floor was covered in lino and the small window with a lace curtain. It was her sanctuary with all her bits from home. The children often came into her room to yarn, look at her photos and play a game or two. SC especially liked the female company.

The job description also included 'light household duties'. She washed the dishes, mopped the floors, made the boys' beds (but not SC's), folded washing and even cooked if Mrs C was away but was a nervous wreck because she couldn't cook. One of the most hated jobs was cleaning the green metal louvres that enclosed the verandah upstairs. Luckily it wasn't done frequently. Hands were often cut on them and the cloth dropped outside to the ground. Mrs C did the washing once a week in the Simpson wringer washing machine, a marathon job with the 'whites' going in first and the 'work' clothes last. A bonus was the generator being on for most of the day. As the Boss was on council there was always a pile of shirts that needed ironing. The governess did her own washing and became quite fond of the old wringer.

The governess who grew up watching *Countdown* on TV was introduced to country music, Slim Dusty, Charley Pride and even more obscure singers she'd never heard of. Every night the son played music on his cassette player that was heard by all in the house. One night howling started and the governess wondered what the heck it was. She learnt later it was Chad Morgan singing 'The Sheik of Scrubby Creek'. It still makes her laugh.

There was no TV or telephone. The ABC radio was the only means of latest news and music (and the music wasn't really 'the latest'). The family listened to the serial *Search for Elizabeth* at 1.00 p.m. (*Blue Hills* had finished the year before). The mail came once a week, her letters home were long and detailed, and luckily her family and friends wrote back. How she loved mail day. The RFDS base in Mount Isa not only handled 'medicals' but relayed telegrams to the stations. She heard via telegram of the death of her much-loved nineteen-year-old cousin Judy and couldn't have been lonelier and more heartbroken.

The food was different from meals she was used to. The meat and three veg was the same, except she ate beef instead of lamb. Barramundi was a new and delicious experience. Mrs C made bread with her eyes shut. It was wonderful. A whole high-top loaf could be eaten in one sitting, often with golden syrup or apricot jam, and the crust was fought over. If a batch of bread wasn't up to scratch it was because 'a germ was in the air', but this was a rare occurrence. The governess loved puftaloons, where the bread dough was fried in fat. She ate corned beef curry and rice for breakfast ... that was a big surprise. And if 'the tin' was in the curry it meant it was VERY hot. The Boss was the expert curry cook, as was his eldest son. The Boss also made the best corned beef fritters, which were eaten for breakfast. She'd never before had a rib bone, a treat on 'killer night', and wasn't impressed. Chicken was usually only eaten on birthdays. How she missed a good feed of chook. One of her favourites became oxtail stew. Who would have thought?

Despite being a country girl she thought this 'bush' was different. She grew up near irrigation channels and marvelled at the tropical rivers with the pandanus palms and cabbage and tea trees. The water was so clear, so different from the Murray about sixty miles from her home town. When the Wet arrived and the rivers flooded, she was amazed at the amount of brown water that flowed into the Gulf.

The dogs chased wallabies, not rabbits. She fed poddy calves instead of pet lambs. There were brumbies, dingoes but no foxes and, more importantly for her, no mice. She grew up in mouse-plague country and loathed the vermin with a vengeance. One reminder of home was the caw of a crow or screech of a galah.

She marvelled at the Morning Glory, the enormous white cloud that stretched across the horizon and floated over the house, and brought with it a cooling breeze. She told her friends down south about the Morning Glories and they laughed. She didn't realise 'morning glory' had a completely different meaning to many people. She was so embarrassed and always added 'cloud' when talking of this wonderful phenomenon.

She went mustering but wasn't very good. The Boss told her and SC to stop talking and get behind the cattle. She noted in her diary that night that the next day she was 'going to get those cattle, not talk and just ride like the wind!' Maybe a bit dramatic! She bought new jeans that happened to be light cream in colour. Why not blue denim? The first day in the cattle yards she ended up with a big splat of green cow poo on the front of them. It was warm and wet and she wore it like a badge all day. Again, why not blue denim?

Social events in the area were always eagerly anticipated. There was much excitement when in August, after a year of preparation, the three days of celebrations marking the Gregory Centenary started. The program included a fishing competition (twenty-five dollars for the largest bream), Old Timers luncheon, boat race, packhorse mail (where bushrangers held up the pack with orange water pistols), horse sports, race meeting and Centenary Ball. As requested, the son made a boat for the race out of cabbage tree logs for SC and the governess, but it wasn't terribly buoyant so they got into the cold water, pulling it and then pushing it. They ended up coming last but laughed a lot. She rode in her first ever horse sports, winning the Gretna Green on Dick from Brookdale and the Three-Furlong Flutter on Sally. She was just so excited but should have retired on a high. She never repeated that winning feeling. The family probably shut their eyes awaiting a buster. The old hall was decorated a treat, an enormous sunflower hanging from the ceiling. The women looked wonderful in their long frocks – Mrs C especially looked lovely. There was even a Belle and Matron of the Ball – a first for the governess. It was a wonderful weekend with the whole community and many visitors coming together.

She attended the Burketown Races, where jockeys were at a premium. There were only three. A ball was held on the tennis court as the hall was blown down in Cyclone Ted. She laughed when the song 'Tennessee Waltz' was played.

Another big event was the opening of the first ever church in Burketown. Despite not being Catholic, she was given the job of preparing the two boys for First Holy Communion and SC for Confirmation, teaching them The Lord's Prayer, Hail Mary and the prayer before confession. The day arrived and the children looked splendid, with the boys wearing their wedding clothes (from their older sister's wedding), ties and all, and SC looking great in a white frock and veil. The church was interdenominational with representation from the Catholics, Uniting Church and Church of England. There was no plate for the offertory, so an Akubra hat was passed around instead. It was a special day, with the children relieved they didn't have to go to confession.

The governess stayed two years. She left, travelling overseas and trying many jobs. Mr McMillian's word came true when seven years later she married the son who played Chad Morgan. She is often asked how she ended up in the Gulf. It sounds clichéd, but she replies, 'I fell in love with the best bloke I know.'

Polly Kim

The daughter of a surgeon in the Royal Navy, Polly Kim spent her childhood in various locations around the world. After travelling to Australia in the seventies, Polly settled in North West Queensland, where she fell in love with the laid-back lifestyle, the wild scenery and the solitude.

She now resides in a small mining town, where she has run the local hostel for the past twenty-five years. Over the years the hostel has welcomed thousands of travellers from all over Australia and the world.

Polly and her husband, Kim, have six adult children. Two are based in Europe, one in Brisbane, one in Melbourne and the other two are still in Mount Isa.

FROM ENGLAND
TO THE GULF

Polly Kim

I FIRST ARRIVED IN THE GULF ON THE BACK OF A TOYOTA tray-back ute along with the family from Wollogorang Station, and my school friend Sue. It was the end of the seventies and just after the Wet season. There was only a single car track to follow and guide us to the Territory border and beyond.

At that point I had no idea where I was, as I was fresh out of England and we were travelling on a working holiday visa. Little did I know then I would settle in the area and eventually run a helicopter mustering business, and then a backpacker hostel in Mount Isa.

I came from the edge of the Cotswolds so I couldn't have picked an area more different from my home. As we left civilisation we mused about the big drums of flour and vegetable seeds we loaded onto the Toyota before we left Townsville. We did load up with some fresh bread in Julia Creek as it was obvious we needed time to perfect the art of bread-making. I was told fresh veggies were flown in from Tennant Creek with the mail once a week, so the veggies at least had time to grow.

Arriving at Wollogorang was like stepping back in time as there wasn't even a telephone or town power, but it felt good to be so self-sufficient and having to improvise daily. Wollogorang is situated just over the border in the Northern Territory. It runs over 120 kilometres down the Northern Territory–Queensland border and has a forty-eight kilometre frontage on the Gulf. Trying to comprehend the sheer size of the property was hard considering a large farm back home was a mere two thousand acres. The station was very run down from years of neglect due to the previous owners deciding to concentrate their efforts on a marijuana plantation instead of nurturing their cattle herd! To help with the muster, the Lawn Hill helicopter was hired and this is when I met Kim, to whom I have now been married thirty-five years. Kim originally came from South Korea, where the Americans trained him as a pilot for Vietnam.

We set up a helicopter mustering business when there were very few other choppers in the Gulf area, as most people still mustered just on horseback and motorbike.

It was a great lifestyle that gave us about five months off a year during the wet season, when we usually headed south or overseas. We based the choppers out of various cattle stations: Lawn Hill, Calvert, Bauhinia Downs and Corinda. At one point we were the proud owners of the old Gregory Police Station, which came complete with its own jail, inmate outhouse and acre of land. The township of Gregory had just been subdivided so we looked forward to basing ourselves in a town and living in a house for a change, but the idea was short-lived as we were offered a ten-year sublease off Lawn Hill, which meant moving our camp to the Corinda Waterhole, west of Doomadgee.

We did spend one wet season at Gregory, which was most enjoyable – having the beautiful Gregory River at our doorstep. The road was blocked off in every direction as soon as it rained, due to the black soil surrounding the township. To amuse us while the roads were closed, the publican at the time used to hook up a piece of tin to the back of his car and we participated in mud skiing on the road. The skier was instantly turned into a mud monster, caked from head to toe. That year, such a wild storm came through that it blew down our jail outhouse and the old heritage-listed hotel rooms right off its stumps. Beyond repair, it was sad to see the old building unceremoniously dragged down to the dump.

I have some wonderful memories of the mini schools that were held at Gregory. They gave the children a chance to mix with their classmates and get to know their teachers better. It also gave the home tutors and governesses a chance to catch up and swap notes on how they were going. Until then, the only time the children met their school friends was at the sports day and Christmas barbecue in Mount Isa. The barbecue was held at Kalkadoon Park and the Rotary Club came out to run their train, Ferris wheel and enormous slippery slide, which kept the children amused all night as they went from one apparatus to another.

Not long after we took possession of the property at Gregory and before the previous owner left, Antony, my second son, who was about one year old, ended up with a nasty burn when he grabbed a hot cup of coffee off the kitchen table. The previous owner was flying into town, so we jumped on the plane with him as Antony needed to see a doctor. He ended up in the Mount Isa Hospital for a few days – they put him in isolation at first as they thought he had chicken pox due to the amount of mozzie bites on his body!

Poor little fella seemed rather accident prone. When he was two he broke a leg climbing onto his brother's motorbike only to have it fall on him. At first it was hard to tell whether the leg was broken, but my mother's instinct kicked in and I knew it was more than just a bruise. When I heard Kim flying in I drove over to tell him to not shut down the helicopter and to fly us to Doomadgee. Sure enough, Antony's leg was broken. A paediatrician in

Brisbane viewed the X-ray. I was very impressed, as that was advanced technology for the time. Antony was plastered up and I was given a spare roll of plaster to reinforce his leg if necessary.

A few weeks later, on a shopping trip to town, I realised he needed the plaster changed as his leg couldn't even fit in a shopping trolley child seat. Furthermore, the plaster was extremely dirty since it was impossible to stop Antony from dragging his foot on the ground. At the hospital he was given a fibreglass cast, which seemed like a good idea at the time. The only problem was when it was time to take the cast off, the Doomadgee Hospital didn't have the right equipment. One of the nurses and I struggled for what seemed like hours, but we did eventually remove it. Luckily for Antony, he had no more childhood mishaps and no lasting problems from his injuries.

During the mustering season Kim was away more than he was at home. Consequently, he missed the birth of our first two children by miles as he was in a different state each time. My first son was born at Bauhinia Downs in the Northern Territory. The birth was a classic do-it-yourself job. It happened to be the weekend of the Daly Waters Rodeo so everyone was away, except me and my two step-kids, Woojin and Andrew, who were ten and seven years at that time. I began to feel a bit uncomfortable while doing some gardening in the evening, but didn't think that anything was happening until my waters broke. I had only seen a doctor twice during the pregnancy and the last time was two weeks before when I drove the three-hour return trip to McArthur Station. All that bouncing around on the rough road had shaken things up for sure. We had a radiotelephone that I used for calling the doctor who told me to drive to Borroloola, but after agreeing to this I realised I wasn't going anywhere. It was about a two-hour drive to get there and I was in no state to drive. I did consider letting my ten-year-old drive as I had recently taught him while dragging the airstrip, but thought better of it.

I tried to get back to the doctor to say we would stay put. This was easier said than done as the radiotelephone reception was fading due to the night setting in. I had to lie down and leave the children to get through on the phone, which entailed waiting for the bright white button to go out and then pressing the black button. Once we got through I spoke to the telephonist who was based in Katherine and explained what was happening. They kindly kept a line open for us all night and they also looked at a map to find our nearest neighbours to try to get some help.

Eventually, six people turned up to give me a hand. From McArthur River Station, the mechanic arrived accompanied by his wife, and from Balbarini Station the manager with his wife and the horse shooter's wife and her son. Luckily, all the ladies had several children between them so had some idea what to do. At one point they looked like the three musketeers with tea towels around their mouths, but they did a great job of delivering my son with the help from the telephone exchange in Katherine and a doctor in Darwin.

The baby, who was eventually named Richard, arrived at about 5 a.m., at which point everyone was exhausted. I remember looking across our living room at everyone sprawled out on the squatters' chairs and suddenly getting into entertaining mode. With so many visitors in the house needing breakfast, I broke out the bacon kept just for special occasions. After all, they had driven miles to come to my aid, without any hesitation.

We wrapped my son in a sheet and placed him in the laundry basket as I didn't have a stitch for him – my original plan was to shop for the baby once I had gone to town to wait for him. One of my helpers from Balbarini had a six-month-old baby and drove home, returning with a bassinet and some clothes. Richard was fairly respectable by the time the RFDS picked us up to fly us to Katherine Hospital.

My second son, Antony, was born in Mount Isa, but again we only just made it in to Isa from Lawn Hill with the RFDS. It was the Scouts of the Air annual camp that weekend and we were supplying some meat for it, so I was wheeled into the hospital with a large Tupperware container of meat on my lap. I must have been keeping up with the family tradition, as it was sometime later that my mother mentioned all her babies arrived early!

Looking back, it's hard to imagine we managed to run our mustering business from camps on various stations when the only means of communication was a two-way radio. If we needed anything we sent a telegram via the RFDS, and after hours Kim and I could communicate, which was sometimes hard as everyone else wanted to talk too – this is called the galah session. Eventually we had radiotelephone channels, and finally the microwave system brought real telephones.

Life was always hectic, what with teaching the kids and minding the preschoolers, cooking for mustering camps, looking after animals and the garden, but there was never the stress you have in town when you have so many time restraints.

Some of the properties where we were based were foreign owned, which added another dimension to living out bush, as from time to time the owners visited and tried to apply their knowledge to running their business. This didn't always seem to make sense to the people who had grown up and lived all year round in the bush. The Japanese owned Calvert Hills. They left a Japanese manager and an Australian manager to run the property. The Japanese manager was a black belt judo instructor and was game for anything, including learning how to ride a horse and muster. To keep up his fitness for his judo he was often seen going through his daily exercise routine and if things seemed a bit quiet he carried an old bicycle tyre tube to do resistance exercises while riding a horse.

The elderly Australian manager decided to correspond with some Filipina ladies and went over to the Philippines to meet them. He ended up marrying one and she eventually flew into Calvert having no idea where she was. One of the first questions she asked was, 'Which way is the market?'

It only took two hours to fly to Mount Isa but the nearest shop was Borroloola, a two-hour drive away if you were lucky not to get stuck at one of the seven large river crossings. Mount Isa was a twelve-hour drive away on a road that was by no means an all-weather road. In one direction were the rivers and in the other, through Benmara, were vast black soil plains that turn to sticky slush with a drop of rain. After one wet season it took us days to get home from Borroloola, as we had to find the low crossings at each river as well as dig ourselves out after becoming bogged countless times. Furthermore, we hit a large wash just after the McArthur River when our wet brakes were not working. We stopped so abruptly that Woojin and I flew forwards and hit the windscreen and dashboard respectively. I jarred my back and broke the windscreen with my nose, but poor Woojin lost one of his beautiful new front teeth. We returned to the clinic at Borroloola with the hope that Woojin's tooth could be put back in his mouth, but sadly the nurse advised us that it wasn't possible and we needed a dentist. We had a nose mark in the windscreen for quite some time after that incident.

The Filipina bride became the main cook for the station, so the meals were quite out of the ordinary. One time we caught some black bream that she cooked up and decorated as if we were royalty having a banquet. Mealtimes at Calvert brought a league of nations together. Often we had up to eight different nationalities congregating around the table for meals – Aboriginal and white Australians, English, German, Filipino, Korean, Japanese, American, Brazilian and Dutch.

Benmara, being American owned, had an American manager who often visited. Kim's favourite saying at the time was 'Stars and Stripes meets the Rising Sun'.

A Brazilian multimillionaire owned Lawn Hill. He always visited with an exotic entourage and held some wonderful socials for the station folk. They left a Brazilian overseer to keep an eye on things, as well as various relatives and adopted sons who came from an orphanage he owned in Brazil. It was quite hard for them to handle the Australian workers, with far more rights and rules to adhere to compared with workers in Brazil.

I took on the housekeeper's job in the big house for a while, which was quite a juggle as my children were left with their schooling while I worked. I even ironed sheets and one time, when there was a change of overseer, nearly every piece of their clothing had to be washed and ironed as they reckoned it had become dusty on the flight up to the station!

When Kim first arrived at Lawn Hill he said he felt as if he had arrived at the end of the earth – he had to adjust to the hard water, the food and customs he wasn't used to. He also had to learn how to handle the cattle and try to understand what everyone said. That first year was quite a challenge for him, to put it mildly. The ping-pong table saved him, as this gave him a relaxing outlet and put him on the same level as everyone else. He was a talented player, after being the Fairfield RSL Sydney ping-pong champion the previous year.

The first time I arrived at Lawn Hill I was flown from Mount Isa in the Lawn Hill Cessna 206, as it was during the wet season. On the way in we took a detour to check the road to see if it had dried out. A whole line of vehicles was bogged in the black soil on the Lawn Hill to Gregory road. At first, the Toyota became bogged so the tractor was sent, and it got bogged, then the grader too, and last of all the dozer. At that point, with the four bogged, they realised they had to wait until things dried out.

During our helicopter mustering years we had the inevitable accident, from time to time. Luckily, nothing too serious happened to anyone or our choppers despite the work being extremely risky. Most of the day the choppers flew just above the tree line, at about ten to twenty feet above the ground, which meant there was no time to auto-rotate if something went wrong. If they had to be put down it would be a hard landing, at the very least.

One of the worst places Kim did an emergency landing was in the Forty Mile Scrub, west of Mount Surprise. Everyone was amazed he managed to land the chopper without damaging anything except the landing gear. The biggest problem was recovering the chopper as a road had to be bulldozed in to clear the thick trees away.

A few times we had incidents with shotguns. Twice the skids were hit by stray bullets from the passenger who was supposed to be just helping move the mob along, or shooting a beast for a clean muster. But on one occasion the rotor blades were shot at by a gung-ho manager who wanted to get his men's attention. Every blade was hit and the chopper gave a terrifying shudder. Luckily the bullets hit the tail edge of the blades so it was possible to patch them up and keep going. It would have been a different matter if the bullets had hit the leading edge, as that would have meant replacing three rotor blades at great expense.

Another time Kim was ferrying west from Lawn Hill and realised the chopper was on fire. He had just passed a mining camp and was climbing up to go over what was locally known as the China Wall. He landed quickly and smothered the fire with my down sleeping bag that he was lucky to have with him. It was the one I brought with me from England and was perfect for the job at hand, being stuffed with feathers. The fire was in the battery so there was no way of starting the chopper again, and he knew he had to start walking back towards the mining camp to get help. Luckily, he managed to reach there before dark.

Navigating over the vast area we covered was always a bit hit-and-miss as the only aid in the chopper was a compass, and a million-to-one detailed map Kim carried to help him find his way. He could easily be blown off course and be looking for a familiar landmark to get on the right track. It was always good when a station's name was on its roof, but some outstations and camps were hard to find.

While based at Lawn Hill we made our camp at the bottom of the hill, below the Aboriginal quarters, beside a bauhinia tree and on an overflow channel of Lawn Hill Creek. It was a great spot that gave us a little waterhole for some of the year and playmates for the children when the families visited the station. We set up our School of the Air (SOTA) television and video recorder in the annex of our caravan and showed movies to the stockmen at night. We were sent only two videos a week by mail from Mount Isa, but everyone was happy to alternate the movie each night. I owned quite a few turkeys that had the run of the camp too. We made a roost for them out of a piece of bamboo between a couple of gum trees that happened to be just outside the annex. They must have been watching the movies as well because one day someone put the TV on during the day and they began to roost, thinking it was night time.

One year we were involved in the Year Six and Seven SOTA canoeing camp at Lawn Hill Gorge, which was run by the itinerant teachers from Mount Isa. We were asked to man the base camp while the group canoed upstream for a night and then downstream for another night. Our eldest was eligible for the camp, which meant the two younger children and I minded all the equipment, including several four-wheel drives. One night when we were camped out on our own, I heard some rustling nearby. I looked out carefully from inside my swag and, to my horror, saw a lone buffalo inspecting our camp. I managed to wake Andrew up as I knew he would stay calm, but I prayed Richard stayed sleeping and didn't move. Luckily for us the buffalo spent a few minutes walking through the camp and calmly disappeared into the bush.

We were based at Lawn Hill when the Gorge was declared a national park. Until then we often had a day out there, taking the motorboat up to the natural spa and enjoying the fabulous water. The dogs enjoyed the trip too, but this became a bit of a problem once there was a ranger guarding the area. Quite a few times we only remembered the dogs weren't allowed anymore when it was too late and we were almost there, so they were tied up at Adels Grove until our return. The 'opening' of the Gorge was quite a memorable event. Queensland Premier Joh Bjelke-Petersen and a few from the Queensland cabinet came for the event and my mother happened to be visiting from England. The night before, we had a function in Burketown and then returned for the opening the next day. Kim decided to fly the chopper in and interrupted the ceremony when he came in to land but everyone, including the premier, appreciated him being there because he took anyone who asked for joy flights into the Gorge until his fuel got low and he had to return to the base. Joh and his entourage camped a night in brand new tents, which was quite a sight for this hidden paradise. It is now so well known that it is part of the grey nomad trail and a must-see if visiting North West Queensland.

When we moved to Corinda, which is located on the western boundary of Doomadgee and part of the Lawn Hill holding, we didn't have the luxury of an established station – just the ruins of the Turn Off Lagoons Police Station. In true pioneering style, we slowly built a homestead with power and running water. At first I scooped water out of the waterhole with buckets. A friend from Sydney welded together the frame for a building. He made four trusses, which were supported by three posts each, each post having a plate at the bottom with four boltholes in them. We had the help of a builder who worked at Doomadgee, but I'm still amazed we managed to position the forty-eight bolts in the right spots so the posts just slid over them. Once the roof was up we proceeded with the large concrete slab – twelve by fifteen metres – which required numerous trips to the creek with our trailer for sand. Everyone, including the very youngest, shovelled sand for weeks until the floor was done. We put in some partitions to divide the area, and made the outside walls so they opened to catch the breezes. Our bathroom was built under the tank stand, and Kim built a donkey for hot water from an old hot water tank that we found at the Doomadgee dump. He encased it in bricks, which insulated it very well, giving us scorching hot water not long after a fire was lit underneath.

We had about one hundred square miles of country to run a small herd of cattle, as well as a base from which to run the helicopter business. We only needed seven miles of fencing around the whole block, as the DPI had recently built a fence along the Doomadgee boundary to help with the TB eradication scheme. The Nicholson River ran through the block, which meant we had some fertile river country, but keeping the fences up all year proved to be quite a challenge, as every time the river flooded it took our fences with it. We became experts at building flood gates designed to float up when the river flowed through.

Our homestead had a wonderful view over the Corinda Waterhole, always teeming with numerous bird species, particularly towards the end of the year before the rains came. In the days of the drovers, this was the last water stop for the cattle for three days, when going west from Corinda and the Turn Off Lagoons.

Over the years I've had numerous visitors from the old country, all of whom loved their trips to the Gulf. While driving up to Corinda with my brother Pete, one of the children mentioned how busy the roads were that day. His reply to that comment was, 'What do you mean busy? We've only seen three cars all day. And anyway, where's the road?'

It's amazing now to see the number of sealed roads in the area and to realise thousands of people visit Lawn Hill National Park and Adels Grove every year.

Michelle Low Mow

Michelle Low Mow was born in 1964 and was raised in Brisbane before she headed to the outback in 1990 with her partner, now husband, Rod. They went into tourism in the 90s and gradually built a base camp with not a lot, into the resort they have today. In 2018 they won the Caravan & Holiday Parks Award in the Outback Queensland Tourism Awards, and Rod won the Peter Evert Award for Outstanding Contribution to Tourism.

Now, after thirty-four years together with Rod and two wonderful children raised in the outback, there is nowhere else they'd rather be.

GETTING TO ADELS GROVE

Michelle Low Mow

ONCE I HAD THE TASTE OF OUTBACK LIFE THERE WAS NO turning back. It all started when we arrived in Mount Isa after a year travelling overseas. In Mount Isa I found work with Toyota spare parts and my partner (now husband) Rod approached Campbell's Coaches, telling the owner, Lloyd Campbell, he was the man to conduct the tours to Lawn Hill National Park each weekend. For the next three years Rod ran all the tours into Lawn Hill from Mount Isa, travelling 280 kilometres north-west to camp on Riversleigh Station, and then on to camp in the National Park, fifty kilometres further north.

Riversleigh Station then offered Lloyd the opportunity to build a permanent safari camp on the Gregory River as a base for the tours to see how they developed. So Rod came home one day and asked if I would consider moving to Riversleigh and building the camp. The plan was that we would go up each March, clear the grounds, put up the camp to run the tours for the season, then pull it down each October for the wet season. I gave Rod one year to see if I liked it.

At the beginning we had the camper trailer, a few tents and a trailer outdoor kitchen. Millions of prickles surrounded us – we tried to poison them and then burn them, but nothing we tried worked so we borrowed the grader from Riversleigh, graded the ground clean and started afresh. We then went about planting lots of seeds, over and over again, as the birds thought this was a great feeding place and kept eating them all. We kept guard shooing them away. I have a photo of Rod trimming the grass for the first time with a pair of scissors.

The day before a tour, we drove to Mount Isa to collect all the food for the group and any building things we needed to keep improving the camp. Rod then toured the groups around Riversleigh and I toured the groups around Lawn Hill Gorge.

As we only had a shower with a bilge pump, in the first three months we argued about who would get to go into town to collect the guests and have a proper shower there. But then a friend of Lloyd's came up and built us one. Well, then it was a fight to stay at camp because, even to this day, they are the best showers in Australia. No reason to go to town anymore. There were solar panels and batteries for the little power we needed, we cooked everything on a wood barbecue and started a veggie garden, protected from the wallabies as they ate everything.

During our four years there we learnt lots about plants, birds and reptiles. We met some great people, and coaches and school camps started coming in. The school camps were great as the children used to track through Riversleigh, Lawn Hill and Adels Grove, and do night walks, canoe, abseil and swim. On my tours coming back from Lawn Hill we would drop into Adels Grove to visit Barry and Di Kubala, who owed the property from 1982 to 2001. (Barry was the founding member of Savannah Guides – a group of tour guides that operate across northern Australia – which we still proudly belong to today.)

We would have a look through the Grove as there was a walking track to the river where we could swim, then have a Zooper Dooper icy pole – a reward after the twelve-kilometre walk, canoe and swim. It was a long day but totally worth it. Rod would put traps in the river on Saturday night and catch yabbies to make yabby scrambled eggs for breakfast the next morning. With leftover damper toasted on the barbecue, breakfast was just yummy.

A retired guy by the name of Shorty worked with us. He was great, but you never knew what you might come home to when he stayed at camp. One day he said he would peel the potatoes for me while I did the tour to Lawn Hill. I came home to ten kilos of peeled potatoes for eight people – he wasn't sure how many to peel so he peeled the lot! Another time a small grass fire began and he used a rake to put out. It was a plastic rake, and luckily we had quite a few, but he kept on using them until all of them melted! We asked how the fire started and he told us that after breakfast he cleaned out the wood barbecue and moved the ash away from the camp so it didn't look untidy – he just forgot to let it cool down before moving it. I could go on forever about Shorty.

In February 2001 we were offered the chance to buy Adels Grove. Never in a million years did I think this was a possibility and we really couldn't afford it; however, we rounded up four partners and officially took over Adels Grove in March 2001. The day I'll never forget.

In our first week there we were introduced to the RFDS, which held a clinic at Adels every four weeks. I remember Doctor Don lining up Rod and myself at the first clinic. We had done so much cleaning up he thought it was a good idea for us to have our tetanus injections. Thanks, Doctor Don. To this day, we are so lucky to have him as part of the outback community. We have the best medical service in the world.

Our first year at Adels Grove was an eye-opener. We brought everything from our camp at Riversleigh and moved it to Adels Grove on 12 March after one of the biggest wet seasons in years. Lawn Hill Station moved their equipment from Riversleigh to Lawn Hill on the same day so we followed them halfway, then started falling through the road. We were in the eighth vehicle – the first seven had made it mushy. After digging out our vehicles, the bus fell through and ended up staying there for the next three weeks.

We started with a seven and nine kVa generator that needed cranking, and wasn't that fun at times! Then I upgraded the fax machine to find that we didn't have enough power to run it, so I had to send it back until we got a bigger generator. After fifteen years we have upgraded to a 150 kVa generator set, so it is fuel we worry about now. We're hoping to look at solar soon.

Having dealt with the RFDS on many occasions for broken bones through to saving a life, when a gentleman came to the counter and told me a guy had passed out in the Grove, I said, 'Okay', and started to follow him. I figured he didn't just pass out after he asked, 'Do you have a defibrillator?'

I grabbed the defib and ran, calling to a staff member to ring the RFDS and stay on the two-way for updates. It was a relief to find a nurse doing CPR and I connected the defib and oxygen. It was the most rewarding experience when, after working for twenty-three minutes, he came to. Forty-five minutes later, after assistance from all involved, the RFDS arrived. By this time the patient could talk with the doctor and complain of a sore chest. All this led to me receiving the Queensland-wide Spirit of John Flynn Award from the RFDS in 2016.

We had two wonderful children – Haydn in 2002 and Charlee in 2006 – with the assistance of the RFDS. I felt very safe when it was time to have children, but they both came early. Haydn was ten weeks early. I was only up to reading on the internet what happens at twenty-nine weeks, so when my waters broke I had no idea what was in front of me. After I arrived in Townsville later that day, all the specialists got together and said, 'Right, let's deliver this baby.' My reply was, 'Okay, but what do I do?' Not to be outdone, Charlee came six weeks early. I knew what to do that time.

Only a few years later we were signing up with the Mount Isa School of the Air to go through primary school and more adventures. Before long, it seemed, Haydn was heading to high school to board.

* * *

All of our wonderful visitors to Adels have played grandmothers to the children while they were growing up. We have, however, had some funny times with some guests. Once we retrieved a camper trailer that had come off its wheels and axle! You would have thought they'd have noticed before it got to that stage. Another time, two people got bogged and sat until we found them twenty-four hours later. They had read the manual from cover to cover and it said, 'lock in the hubs'. They had no idea what a hub was.

In the many years of living in the outback I have met some amazing people, from our worldwide visitors and friends on neighbouring properties, to all the women in the CWA and their husbands. I have been overwhelmed by the community and how they rally together in any situation and, believe me, there have been many.

Adels Grove has grown in leaps and bounds over the years, with staff coming in for each tourist season then heading off at the end of their contract to the next part of Australia for the next adventure, sometimes coming back to us the following year. Remote living is certainly not for everyone, although we are finding remote travelling certainly is, with over twenty-eight thousand people travelling through each year to enjoy this wonderful part of Australia.

From 2013 to 2015 Adels Grove was shortlisted as a finalist in the Queensland Tourism Awards and in 2016 was judged state winner and national finalist in the hosted accommodation category. We are very proud.

Sylvia Hammann

Sylvia Hammann has lived in the Gulf of Carpentaria,
Australia all her life. She became a fisherperson and
fished for many years in the same area with her husband,
sometimes living on a boat and at other times living off the
land. She is now retired and lives in Karumba, Queensland,
a small fishing and tourist town. She has three children and
sixteen grandchildren.

A COUNTRY BUMPKIN
WENT A'FISHING

Sylvia Hammann

I WAS JUST A COUNTRY BUMPKIN LIVING IN THE SMALL
Queensland–Northern Territory border town of Camooweal.
I had such dreams of travelling the world then. I even had my
journey marked in red on a map. Never did I dream when I
met my husband, Gunter, I would end up a fishing person.

When we went to Cairns to live, Gunter got hooked
on mackerel fishing. With three children to care for I was
unable to get involved in the fishing but did my bit, helping
to unload, clean and restock the boat for the next trip. At
the end of the season I took it on myself to clean and anti-
foul the hull, mainly because I was little and could slither
on my stomach in the mud to get at the underneath bits.

I soon learnt mishaps happen unexpectedly in the
fishing business. Once, my husband went reef fishing and

failed to return home at the expected time. After giving him an extra day to arrive I reported him missing and a plane was sent up to search for him. Luckily, after two days he was spotted being towed in by another vessel. His main motor had broken down and in those days there was no radio on the boat.

In 1971 we sold up in Cairns, bought a secondhand caravan and an old black Bedford truck into which we loaded all our goods and chattels and headed for the Gulf of Carpentaria. We went to Burketown first but decided it wasn't where we wanted to settle. The kids thought we were a circus coming to town. The way we were loaded up, we probably looked like one.

We drove north-east across the top road, 230 kilometres from Burketown to Normanton, then just a bush track the stations used. It was supposed to have been a short cut, a three-hour drive, but after crossing numerous gullies, opening and closing gate after gate, and with all the tyres on the truck deciding to take turns going flat, it took us all day. When we finally reached Karumba, a further seventy kilometres away, I refused to go any further, so we set up camp on the beach at Karumba Point. We had the beach to ourselves. There was an old toilet with a hole in the sand, which was handy as there weren't many trees close by, and a bore-water tap that was only turned on for two hours a day.

Gunter returned to Cairns to get our boat. Before he left we drove forty kilometres back along the Normanton

Road to Walkers Creek and filled every container with fresh water to last the kids and me until he got back. The older children had bikes and rode to school across the mud flats. I couldn't drive the truck as it was too cumbersome for me to handle, but, stocked with plenty of food, I didn't need to. When we ran out of bread I tried to make my own. After two weeks of duds, my children offered to ride to the store and buy a loaf of bread! After that, no more bread-making and the kids relished a decent sandwich for their lunches. When Gunter finally returned with the boat, I greeted him with the words, 'Did you bring any water?!'

The kids and I were sick of drinking boiled lagoon water. Later we learned there was a freshwater tap outside the fence of one of the fisheries houses.

Before we could start fishing Gunter needed to fly back to Cairns again to get another dinghy as he had lost the other on the way around. While there, it rained in the Gulf and the unsealed roads became impassable. He could only drive back as far as Croydon, 230 kilometres south-east from Karumba. He left the Toyota there and came the rest of the way on the railmotor to Normanton, and from there he came down the Norman River by dinghy. We got the Toyota later when the road opened.

The new dinghy was a punt and I believed him when he said it was unsinkable. We fished on the other side of the Norman River and worked two sets of cord nets. I went out with him in all kinds of weather, thinking I was safe. The unsinkable punt nearly ended our fishing career when it capsized in the middle of the river one rough night. I hadn't gone out to check the nets that night as there was a midnight tide and I couldn't leave the kids on their own. Early in the morning Gunter came in dripping wet and exhausted. He had waded in from the fairway buoy. The punt grounded on a sandbar, having drifted with the tide out of the channel with Gunter clinging to it. The nets sank somewhere in the river. He was adamant his fishing days were over.

At low tide we found the nets, were able to retrieve the punt and get the outboard working. That afternoon the tide came in and we couldn't resist ... we ran the nets out again.

Living conditions got a little easier when the council built an ablution block and installed a freshwater tank on the beach. The tank was kept locked and we were allowed to fill our containers once a day. The water for the showers and toilets was turned on in the afternoons. During the holidays, though, so many people would camp on the beach we had to line up for a shower.

When my sister Irene and her family came to Karumba to fish, the kids and I were happy to have some company at last. With Irene's husband, Ernie, to fish with, Gunter took the boat further away. We would get some violent storms during the wet season and one night when the men were away we got a really bad storm. The caravan started shaking and everything fell off the shelves. As soon as I got the windows closed the kids and I abandoned the caravan and jumped into the Bedford truck to wait it out. I looked across to see how my sister was faring and when I saw her and the kids huddled in the front seat of their Toyota I couldn't help laughing. I spent the next day sewing my annex back together.

There is always a threat of a cyclone during the wet season as well, and it was one of those times when one hovered in the Gulf. That night my sister woke me and said the police came and told her a cyclone was heading our way and we should get ready to move out. Neither of us knew where to go or what to do, so we went back to bed. Thankfully, the cyclone changed course during the night.

Fishing got better when a buyer started taking our fish into Karumba. Before that we took our catch to Cairns to sell. The buyer also started a prawn-processing factory where I worked during the season.

Eventually we sold our boat and went back to fishing in a dinghy. One day my youngest son, David, and I went with my husband to help him pull in a net he had set in a creek a few miles up the coast. As we drove in we struck something and broke the shaft on the outboard motor. The tide was still out, and the net lay in the mud. Gunter tried to walk out to untie the net from the anchor but he kept bogging down in the mud. As I was lighter he sent me out. The only way I could get there was to crawl on my hands and knees as quickly as possible to stop myself sinking, then lie on my stomach as I untied the knot. Covered in mud, I made it back to the dinghy and it took all my strength to pull the net in. We tied the dinghy to a tree on the bank and the three of us walked home.

* * *

In 1974, Karumba was inundated with floodwater; Karumba Point became an island. From the beach we watched as rooftops, cars, wharves and poor, helpless animals were washed out to sea. We waved to the Karumba residents as they were evacuated to Weipa on the vessel *Brewarrina*. We were relieved we weren't forced to go as well. When the flood receded, the stores in Karumba dumped everything. One store dumped hundreds of cans of food into a hole the floodwater had gouged out. We drove our dinghy in from the river and loaded up with as many cans as we could scrounge out of the mud. They had no labels and we guessed the contents, but food was food. There was a prawning company on the Point and they opened their store to the Point residents and we could buy meat and perishables – so we didn't fare too badly during that time.

We had a go at prawn trawling on an old navy boat converted to a trawler – I was cook and deckhand. It was a good sea boat but nothing worked on it. We missed out on a lot of prawns due to machinery failing just as we were ready to shoot away. I had David with me, and whenever it got rough he became seasick. One day we had to take shelter behind a sand island surrounded by reefs. Alas, we ended up on one. When the tide went out the trawler rolled on her side. Has anyone ever slept standing up? Well, that was how we spent the night. It was a relief when the tide came in and the boat stood upright. We steamed back to port immediately as all our fresh water had leaked out.

When we trawled for tiger prawns the deckie and I must have consumed gallons of Milo to keep us awake and warm while we worked throughout the night. Next morning, after we winched up, everyone caught up on some sleep, except for me, as David would be just waking up. I busied myself cleaning the nets and the decks until he had his afternoon nap and I could finally shut my eyes. Trawling was an experience, but I was glad when we gave it up and went back to barra fishing.

Disaster struck when Gunter stood on a stingray and the barb went through his ankle. He then spent ten months in the Cairns hospital with golden staph. While we waited in Cairns for him to get better, I went to work to keep us going.

When we returned to Karumba and started fishing again, we bought another boat. We parked it beside the caravan as we fixed it up, but when launching day came it took six four-wheel drives to drag it on a trailer over the sand down to the water's edge. David and I fished for a few years on the boat until he had to go to school. By that time, land had become available and we moved from the beach to live on our block. I stayed on land then and went to work in a prawn factory and later in the supermarket until the children finished school and I returned to fishing.

As the saying goes, there is never a dull moment, especially for fishing and me. One afternoon we went to check the nets we had set in one of the creeks off the Norman River. It was dark when we started back and on the way I experienced a kind of void. One minute I was sitting on the back seat of the dinghy, and the next I awoke to find myself lying headfirst in the dinghy's nose. I was mystified as to how I got there and then I heard Gunter moaning and complaining of a broken neck as he tried to sit up. Both of us had been thrown forwards off the back seat. Another fisherman had come into the creek and set a net without a light near the mouth. We hit it with some force. I don't know what he must have thought when he checked his net and saw a huge hole in it – we had to cut it off the propeller. I shudder to think what would have happened if we had been thrown into the water.

One wet season, the road to Normanton was out and the Norman River was in flood. Gunter developed a toothache and the only way to get to Normanton to see a dentist who was working there at the time was by dinghy. Most of the way we guessed the outline of the river, but in one spot the banks disappeared altogether and we had to decide which way to go. There was a difference of opinion, and we drifted in midstream and had a big argument. Finally I gave in and thank heavens I did. We got to Normanton, drove right up to the store and tied the dinghy to a street post. On the way back the outboard broke down. The wind was blowing the wrong way, so we couldn't drift home on the tide. We rowed to the bank and tied up to a tree, knowing a fisherman would be coming by to check his nets. He didn't until the next morning. That night it rained and mosquitoes were out in force. Gunter rubbed petrol over his arms and legs to deter them. We spent a miserable night and I was afraid to go to sleep in case I stuck my legs over the side, thinking a croc would be watching us for sure. When the fisherman saw us he kindly towed us home before continuing on to his nets.

We ran into trouble once when we went up the Bynoe River, which is about fifteen kilometres from the Norman River mouth. While we were anchored in shallow water a whirlwind swung the boat and somehow the anchor rope got tangled around the prop. We towed the boat further upstream until we found a sandy bank to beach it. When the tide went out and the boat was out of the water, we dug out the sand and tunnelled under the hull. It was I who had to wriggle under and unwind the rope. I made my husband stand guard as my legs stuck out of the hole, and after seeing the huge crocs that lived in this river, I wasn't taking any chances.

After all these years fishing among the crocodiles, it was inevitable to have an encounter with one. It must have been their mating season that month we fished up the Norman River, as huge crocs were around every bend of the river. I had never seen them so close together before. One must have fallen in love with our boat or maybe it had its eye on me. It swam past us every day and loitered around our anchorage in full view. It even had the cheek to lie against the stern one day.

We decided to go and fish elsewhere, but the day we came back from checking our nets we saw the croc lying up on the bank no more than twenty metres away from our boat. It was big! When it heard our voices it stood up and slid into the water. I thought it would go and find some more sunshine, but we didn't know it lay submerged behind the boat, where we filleted. When I leaned forward to pick up more fish, the croc flew up out of the water with his mouth wide open. I screamed with fright and jumped back away from the side of the boat. It frightened the life out of my husband. Undeterred, the croc swam lazily around the side of the boat, in no hurry to move away, until we started to make a lot of noise by banging fish trays together. Even then it seemed to look at me as if to say, 'You'll keep', and then slowly dived. As soon as we finished processing our fish we picked up our nets and left. I was a nervous wreck for the rest of that trip.

Our next trip was to another river where fish were plentiful, the weather was calm and there were no crocodiles that I could see. Ours was the only fishing boat there. A week later Gunter came down with the flu and took to his bed, leaving me to tend the nets. Well, I've never had to work on my own before – we always worked together. I knew I had no choice but to fire up the dinghy and go and check those nets. They were full of fish.

I stood knee deep in jewel fish on the back deck and had to fillet the little buggers. Gunter had never let me fillet before, so now I had to learn very fast. I guess I mutilated a few before I got the hang of it, but I got them done eventually and then went straight back and pulled some more nets out. I wanted to pull the lot out of the water but couldn't get the anchors up on two, so they had to stay there and I had to keep checking them every morning.

It seemed that Gunter wasn't getting any better and I was going to call for a helicopter to fly him back to Karumba. Even when he began to improve, I still wanted to go home. David turned up in his boat and helped to pull up the nets. The weather changed and got rough – it was dark as we steamed up the channel in the Norman River. Gunter put the boat in reverse to come up beside our tie-up buoy and the thrust of the motor broke the propeller shaft off the main motor. Water was pouring in so we had to rapidly tow the boat onto the bank before it sank. Thank heavens that didn't happen while we were steaming in.

Gunter became very sick another time while we were out, but luckily David was in the same river at the time and helped me pull in the nets so I could drive our boat back to Karumba. I decided then it was time to give up fishing and stay on the land, where it was safer.

Gunter and I still live in Karumba and now I write to keep myself busy in my leisurely retirement. I have had two books published so far and am currently writing about our life fishing in the Gulf of Carpentaria.

Ms Anon

Ms Anon resides in Running Creek.

SLIGHTLY LESS THAN PERFECT?

Ms Anon

I'VE DECIDED I MUST BE THE WORST 'STATION WIFE' IN the Gulf Country. I look on with awe at my friends who can whip up a sponge, castrate a steer, grow orchids, fix a barbed-wire fence. Not me. When I work in the cattle yards everyone knows Husband is desperate. I do not tag, brand, earmark, needle or, heaven forbid, castrate. I can work the crow's nest and am handy on the crush. I'm capable of letting the cattle out of the dip but hate it when I must count them. Some say to count in fives, others say twos. However, sometimes they come out so quickly it's hard to keep track. I figure one or two out won't hurt, you just need to look confident when you return and mark the numbers on the chalkboard.

The crow's nest can cause much angst. After a couple of days I have a syndrome called CNA (crow's nest arm). My arm aches and aches from unaccustomed use.

I have mentioned to the family that I'd like the gates in the pound all painted different colours. As Husband speaks quietly – and, some say rather unkindly, mumbles – I have trouble hearing what he says over the noise of a full cattle yard. Did he say 'weaners' or 'fats'? I figure if he only had to say 'green' or 'red' I'd have a better chance of understanding where to direct the beast. I worked with Son-in-law recently and he yelled out very loudly the direction of the cattle. I know he was 'taking the micky', but I quietly loved it as I could actually hear.

Last month I was in the crow's nest when husband yelled, 'Calf pen!'

To this I replied, 'Which one's the calf pen again?'

Despite the dust and sunglasses, I know he rolled his eyes at me as he said, 'It's been the calf pen for twenty-five years.'

Sorry I asked.

* * *

I quite enjoy 'the dip' as I find it fascinating watching the different ways the cattle enter the plunge dip. Older cows know where to go and execute a high and graceful jump, whereas a young beast will often fall in. I started judging their efforts, giving them a score out of ten for entry, height and splash. Some of those gorgeous old Brahman cows get a 9.5.

One of my least favourite jobs is holding the tail while the mickies are castrated in the crush. I was shown how to twist the hair at the end of the tail. I nearly broke three fingers. As said tails can be very slippery, I've told Husband someone should invent a glove or a velcro-type strip to aid with grip. The only gloves I have are gardening gloves (which I don't use) and I doubt they'd do the trick.

Last year I was promoted to the back yards pushing the cattle up. I was rather proud of my efforts managing to keep the yards full. I was even doing a bit of drafting. My pride was rather dampened when I heard Daughter telling her father that night, 'I don't know how Mum didn't get killed.'

One of my peeves is when I try my best to get a few old cows up to the next yard. I yaaahoo, I jump up and down, I take my hat off (like Husband) and wave it. No, they just won't budge. Begrudgingly I ask Husband for help. He goes 'Haaa' and waves his hat and they move on like quiet old milking cows. At these times, with a tear welling in my eye, I would like to pick up some dried cow poo and throw it at him.

I've also decided unloading trucks is not my forte. Son returned after dark with loads of cattle and, as any dutiful mother would, I went down to the yards, torch in hand to assist. I scaled the multi-level trailers, yelling and poking with my poly pipe. Finally, Son looked at me and said in a rather terse tone, 'Mum, I just want you to hold the torch.'

To be honest I was rather hurt, until I heard Son say to his father, 'I looked up and saw Mum hanging off the trailer and thought to myself, this isn't going to end well.' I realised he was just concerned for my safety. Or was he?

Husband says for someone who comes down to the yards so rarely, I'm full of ideas. He means I whinge. The slide gate comes to mind. To call it a 'slide' gate is a joke – it's a push-and-pull gate, with very little slide. You nearly have to be a body builder to use it. I don't regard this as whinging, but, rather, constructive criticism.

* * *

I do not shoot. I do not like guns. Someone suggested I should have a gun for safety, but I could just see myself taking a couple of toes off my foot. Husband's dear grandfather said every woman should have a .410 shotgun – a snake gun. Sorry, Pop, not me. I'm happy to wave the snakes on. Which reminds me of an olive python that decided to join me one evening while I watched TV. As is always the way, I was on my own. He (snakes are always male) was about two metres long and lounged on a ledge made of besser bricks. I rang Husband the next morning telling him about my visitor.

He asked, 'Well, where did he go?'

With just a touch of sarcasm I said, 'I didn't stay up all night to keep him company.'

The snake returned the next night and we enjoyed a bit of David Attenborough together. Or maybe he didn't enjoy it as he was not there the following night.

* * *

I don't like machines. I don't drive the forklift. When I'm on my own, round bales of hay are placed in strategic positions so I can roll them into the yards. Even this can be dangerous. I was dragging a bale around by the wrap when I lost my grip. I landed like a sack of potatoes on portable panels, resulting in a very bruised arm and leg. Family returned and asked me what the heck I'd done to myself. It was a bit embarrassing to say a bale of hay 'threw' me.

Starting the engine (the generator) has been one of my least favourite jobs. Something will always go wrong when Husband is away, as was the case this day. I started the engine, the most dreadful noise came out of it and what I gathered was oil sprayed everywhere. I quickly turned it off and on inspection found a very large snake wrapped around the fan. So it wasn't oil. Luckily Mrs W was here and with her engineering ability she managed to take off the appropriate pieces and remove the snake. It came out in one piece, very black and very dead. The engine started like a dream. Way to go, Mrs W!

A while later I went to start the engine, not too enthusiastically after the snake. I tried and tried but it was lifeless. I started the 'big' engine instead so all was well. On

Husband's return I proceeded knowledgeably to tell him about the engine not starting.

He replied, 'Of course it won't start, it hasn't got an alternator or starter motor. Remember we sent them to town?'

No, I did not remember.

I especially do not like to tow. I'm useless at it. I always pull at the wrong time, either too fast or too slow. The 'towee' (the one who does something stupid like getting bogged) is usually agitated before the towing starts. The poor 'tower' (me) then must put up with this bad temper. I mean, I wasn't the idiot who got bogged or let the battery run flat. I was once asked to go and help dislodge a tractor bogged in the creek. I nearly started hyperventilating at the mere thought. I was in the Toyota with the radio up loud, singing along as I revved and tried to pull the tractor out. I finally realised I'd stalled the car, so quickly restarted it. Seconds later Husband was at the window asking, 'Have you got the bloody thing going?'

To which I replied with a hurt look, 'Yes, of course I have.'

Not one of my better moments.

* * *

Pulling cattle out of bogs is fraught with danger. Husband pulls the beast out and I'm given the job of taking the rope off. Husband always says, 'You'd better watch this one.'

After the rope is removed I take off as fast as I can, watching behind me. The poor beast had no intention of getting up, while Husband sits in the Toyota laughing. My only concern with his little joke is the one time I take no notice, the beast will get up.

Which reminds me of a water run we did last year. We came to a dam with a dead cow floating about ten metres from the bank. Before there was time to think Husband said, 'Well, you haven't got any shoes on, you might as well go in.'

The worst part of these scenarios is the dead-animal smell. Luckily I am good with smells, which I guess means I don't gag. I took off my shorts and waded in, tying the rope around the cow's leg, waded back and waited while Husband dragged the cow to the bank. THEN THE ROPE CAME OFF. I got the blame for not putting it around the leg properly and he got blamed for not towing it in the right direction. Despite this disagreement, as I was already wet and, of course, had no shoes on, I went in again. Cow was removed, and I felt Husband owed me BIG TIME! I also learnt a good lesson – always wear shoes.

* * *

You might think I'd redeem myself in the garden. Nope! I love gardens, but not gardening. When I buy a new plant Husband whispers to it, 'Welcome to the graveyard.'

Sister-in-law and Good Friend bought me cacti for my birthday. Kinder presents I couldn't ask for, as they are still alive a few years later.

On arriving in the north, I didn't even know you inoculated pumpkins. Down south the bees do the job for you.

We had an enormous tamarind tree just in front of the house. It towered over the two-storey house, which gives you an idea of its size. The leaves were the bane of my existence and I would sweep out shovels full every day. Of course, on my watch this enormous tree died. Husband cut down the branches, but the huge stump remained. After much pleading, I took the task to hand and decided to burn it down. Oh my goodness, didn't it light up. I was so concerned I was going to burn the house down, I kept watch for an hour, hose in hand. The men were bringing cattle into the yards and thought the house actually *was* on fire. The only damage was blistered paint on the verandah. Again, not one of my better moments, but I did get rid of the stump and I hoped Husband would take me more seriously next time I asked him to do a job for me.

* * *

Vegetarian alert. I do not 'kill'. I've been known to help carry the meat to the butcher shop. I will cook the 'killer meat' of rib bones, liver, sweet bread and whatever else they bring in for dinner. I usually eat eggs.

Speaking of cooking: yes, I've had my failures. An old chap talked for many years about the biscuits I made that were so hard even the dogs wouldn't eat them. He used to take a pocketful just to get rid of them. I decided to make lamingtons one day, but didn't even get to the icing stage. I took the cake out too early and it sank quickly. I was having a bad day so I karate chopped it. You have no idea how far a cake can travel with a good whack. Husband happened to come in at this stage and commented I could have used the outside of the cake. He was very lucky I didn't give him one of Bruce Lee's best.

Husband said to me, 'Why are you writing about being useless?' Quickly adding, 'Not that I think you're useless.'

I told him that this is a community service. I figure there are young women new to the bush who are feeling a bit overwhelmed. They can read this and think, 'Gee, I feel useless, but not as bad as her.'

Good luck to them all.

Prawn fishing and ghost nets

Riki Gunn

Riki Gunn's background is in fisheries, natural resource management and Indigenous engagement. As founder and coordinator of GhostNets Australia from 2002–15 she worked with thirty-one Indigenous communities around the Gulf, enabling local people to receive a real wage for natural resource management. Riki is a member of the Global Marine Litter Network hosted by the United Nations Environment Programme; is on the Steering Committee for the Global Ghost Gear Initiative hosted by World Animal Protection (formerly WSPA); Director of FISHI International; and Treasurer of the Ravenshoe Community Centre.

GULF WATERS WARRIOR

Riki Gunn

At sea

'HAVE A JOB AS COOK ON A PRAWN TRAWLER IN THE Gulf of Carpentaria,' I wrote to my mother. 'Please send cookbook.'

Naturally she dined out on this tale for many a dinner party, for not only was I a lousy cook but, with a degree in performing arts, was probably the least likely of her five children to go fishing. This was in the mid 1970s and the start of an amazing journey that culminated in my sharing lunch with the Indonesian Minster for Fisheries, Ibu Susi, and her entourage in January 2015.

I took to life on a trawler instantly, although I wasn't immediately good at it. The first thing I had to get used to was that nothing stays still – ever. The stove in the galley was the first indicator of this – the oven door was equipped with a hook latch, while the top of the stove had a metal 'fence' on all sides to prevent pots from sliding off. In very rough weather I jammed the cooking pots in with other pots and pans. My worst disaster, before I got in the habit of securing things into place, happened after opening the oven door just as our vessel took a lurch to the port side. The roast shot out, flew across the galley, landed halfway up the bulkhead, slid down the wall and back to me as the boat did its return roll to starboard. What a mess!

We stayed at sea until the twenty-tonne freezer was full or, worst scenario, we broke down. Supporting us at sea were mother ships that we met up with every month to get fuel, oil and other necessary supplies. These were my favourite days for we received our mail, fresh vegetables and caught up on all the gossip about other crews and their antics back in port. I no longer take fresh vegetables for granted. These days I grow my own.

Cooking, as my mother well knew, was not my forte, so I soon graduated to the deck. Unfortunately, I wasn't a natural at this either but liked it much more. I loved being in the open and the physicality of the work. It was dangerous work and no place for a klutz, for there were moving bits and bobs everywhere, some with huge weights and pressures on them that could kill you in an instant if you did the wrong thing. But ignorance is bliss and in the beginning I was not that aware of this at all, so battled my way through without mishap. Thank God.

It didn't take me long to find my true place on the boat – the wheelhouse. Within the minimum allowable 'sea time' I obtained my skipper's ticket. I loved the challenge of hunting down a minute patch of prawns in an endless ocean, navigating with no landmarks or GPS and, most of all, finetuning the gear (a configuration of nets, boards, chains and ropes) so it worked at its optimum. This is an art. Little did I know in the future this knowledge would be relevant to a completely different field of work.

Remember, this was the seventies! So, although I had a skipper's ticket, it was difficult to get a job utilising the asset, even as a mate (second in charge). However, eventually I did.

Life as a skipper was extremely hard and I think I was too young and inexperienced for it, but I am glad I could test my limits. I was only twenty-five. The mental anxiety created by being responsible for five people's safety at sea was overwhelming. This is a job that is so dangerous no insurance company (not even Lloyd's of London) would provide basic WorkCover. Before I became a nervous wreck I chucked it in and was happy to settle for a mate's job, which was now easier to get with my reputation for catching prawns (we were the number two boat in the fleet). These experiences left me wiser to my strengths and weaknesses.

Things changed when I met my life partner, Neil. We made a good team and before too long we got together to run a twenty-metre trawler and did this happily for twelve years. Within that time we experienced a lot: a couple of cyclones we either had to ride out or were, luckily, in port for; a fire in the engine room; having to trawl for the dead body of a skipper from another vessel; and of course droughts, for it is true a drought on land is a drought in the water and at these times there were no prawns. This is especially relevant to banana prawns (one species that is mainly caught from March to May) that have a symbiotic relationship with floods and droughts.

One flood was so extensive Karumba was isolated by road for three months. Consequently, our banana prawn catch for that season was a record. Not just for us but for everyone. When we came into port to unload after fishing for only twenty-four hours, we were told we had to wait our turn. Three days, they told us. As these prawns were not frozen but in brine we knew they would not keep that long. We needed to off-load them ASAP. While we were still scratching our heads pondering the dilemma, a mate of ours who owned a fish and chipper asked if he could buy about two hundred kilograms.

'Great,' we thought to ourselves. 'Wonder how many more locals want some?'

We put the word out we would sell anyone prawns for five dollars per standard, garden-variety bucket. To put it mildly, we were swamped. It so happened it was the Easter weekend, so the town was bursting at the seams with friends, visitors and parties of recreational fishers camping on the beach. Before long people were queued up for a block with not one but multiple buckets and containers of all shapes and sizes, waiting to buy prawns

Everything went along swimmingly until two officers from the Boating and Fisheries Patrol turned up in uniform – with no bucket. Not a good sign. Neil quickly ushered them into the wheelhouse while whispering to me to ask the crew to stop work for the moment and keep people back until we knew what they wanted.

They didn't beat about the bush once on board. 'We've had a complaint,' the senior officer started, 'that you are selling to the public without a proper licence.'

'Shit, who made the complaint?' Neil asked.

'We are not at liberty to say.'

'If I pointed a gun in that direction would I get the person who made the complaint?'

With the slightest of smiles, the officer nodded while handing over the necessary paperwork. With the exchange of a cheque for two thousand dollars we too were now owners of a Buyers and Sellers licence.

Months later in the supermarket I ran into the person who had made the complaint.

'It wasn't me,' she started.

'Doesn't matter,' I replied. 'Whoever it was did us a huge favour, for now we have a licence to buy and sell direct to the public.'

The 1980s were a tumultuous time for the fishing industry, as governments around the world started to realise some limits needed to be applied to sustain fish stocks. With improvements to refrigeration and navigation, we could stay at sea longer and go further off the coast looking for new fishing grounds. Something had to change before the fishery collapsed. So, bit by bit, we dealt with more and more restrictions: parts of the fishing grounds were closed so juvenile prawns were protected; our time at sea was limited to maximise the effectiveness of spawning events; the allowable size of nets was reduced. Mostly we were happy to comply as we understood the need for these changes, for many of us wanted our children to be able to fish as well.

One piece of legislation incorporated a modification to our nets with the aim of reducing the unintentional catch of marine turtles. I later learnt that northern Australia, particularly the Gulf of Carpentaria, was home to six of the seven species of turtle in the world. These magnificent animals were under serious threat – and trawling was one of the many culprits. The modification, called a Turtle Excluder Device (TED), was an unwieldy contraption fitted within the net to enable turtles to escape. The first we knew about the TEDs was when the United States government embargoed our prawns.

Not wanting the Yanks telling us what to do, we collectively took on the government, fighting this further control on our freedom to fish. Surprisingly, we won. Unfortunately, the government then took the case to the Supreme Court. Unsurprisingly, we lost. TEDs were now law. Ironically, decades later the fishermen are thankful for the TEDs. No longer do the prawns get squished by the heavy weight of a turtle trapped in the net. A better product equals a better price, which is the exact reason why the TED was invented in the first place.

Then, in November 1992, disaster struck us. The Australian Government finally took away our right to fish altogether. With limited consultation and no compensation, they literally tore up over two hundred licences in the Gulf of Carpentaria, forcing trawl fishermen to sell their vessels. We were left stranded high and dry – without a livelihood – but fortunately still with a home, unlike many others.

Beached

AFTER SIXTEEN YEARS AT SEA, LIFE ON LAND AGAIN WAS to be a new adventure for me. This was just the beginning of a knock-on effect that rippled through the town of Karumba like dominoes. Christmas was a sad event that year, with many of us licking our wounds wondering what we could and should do.

In the 1990s, Karumba's reputation was bigger than the actual town. The real thing was often disappointing to first-time visitors as it was a flat, dusty, unattractive one-pub town on the banks of a river that is muddy all year, lined with mangroves that attract sandflies and home to the odd croc or two. It's the people of Karumba who give it its larger-than-life reputation. The town was built on characters who lived the motto 'work hard, play hard'. When I arrived in Karumba in the seventies I found a town full of men under forty. Woohoo, party time! It appeared everyone, if they were not running from something – the law, the wife, themselves – was after adventure and the big bucks. For in those heady days the prawn industry was like a gold rush – either a bonanza or a bust.

These were interesting times, as Karumba was fast becoming a tourist destination. The live cattle trade was growing and a proposal was in the air to build an unloading facility to export zinc mined inland. I loved learning about why these new people visited Karumba. The more I learnt, the more I was astounded by the complexity and diversity of this place I thought I knew.

I learnt that:

- A patch of seagrass in the Norman River estuary is incredibly important to dugongs. Without this 'McDonald's swim-through' they would not survive their migration around the Gulf, as the distance between the other patches is too far.
- Those flat, lifeless salt pans surrounding Karumba are not lifeless at all but are pit stops for shorebirds on their annual migration between Russia and New

Zealand. By the time they get to Australia these small birds are exhausted and use the floodplains to rest and beef up their energy levels.

- The Morning Glory phenomenon, where we experienced the sudden decrease in temperature and an increase in winds, was a cloud formation. A visiting team of German scientists who had invented a machine that measured the number and intensity of these rolling clouds explained the uniqueness of this phenomenon in the world. It is predictable in only two other places globally – the Gulf of Mexico and the Gulf of Aden. They are all shallow bodies of water rimmed by land on three sides in a tropical climate. All three factors create the perfect conditions.

- Cherry beer was introduced to Karumba by the Belgian crew of the first dredge that came to deepen the Karumba channel, enabling bigger ships in and out of the port. Cherry beer – different!

During that time I got intensely involved in community projects and had two major ones on the boil: a two-kilometre raised boardwalk between the beach and the town, and the Barramundi Hatchery and Discovery Centre (the Barra Farm). Both were to give me huge headaches, frustrations and failures. The process helped hone my skills in project management, negotiation, Indigenous politics (Native Title and Land Rights were big issues then, and still are), government bureaucracy, community engagement and consultation. The boardwalk and the Barra Farm were created to help raise the tourist potential of the town and to inform visitors about the special features of the landscape so they would, in turn, respect it as I did.

The major project was the Barra Farm, an aquaculture facility for breeding barramundi with which to restock the Norman River. Along with the exploding number of grey nomads visiting the region through the winter months came a growing animosity between commercial and recreational fishers. Each considered the other was raping and pillaging the limited resource. So when a small group of commercial fishermen dreamed up the crazy idea of creating the farm, I thought what a great idea – put back in what has been taken out. If I knew then what that simple idea took in terms of time, money, frustration and heartache I would never have embarked on it. So it's fortunate I didn't.

The plan was extremely modest. The Queensland Government's fisheries research department in Cairns, the Northern Fisheries Centre (NFC), would breed the fish in their excellent facility. We would rear the newly hatched larvae, which were flown to Karumba, in an earthen pond prepared with the right type of food. Three weeks later, when the fish could fend for themselves (although only thirty millimetres long), they would be relocated to the river. See? Simple. But regrettably this did not happen, for the fish (they had to be Gulf of Carpentaria stock) for some weirdly unknown reason would not spawn in Cairns. Our solution – easy peasy – we'll get our own brood stock and breed them in Karumba. After all, they are probably only homesick.

To cut a very long story short, there were continuous trials and tribulations inherent in this procedure. Sometimes we were astoundingly successful, but often desperately unsuccessful. As we battled our way through all these issues the organisation grew. First we needed the infrastructure to breed fish, then we upgraded so water was heated, or flowed better, or was filtered better – it just kept going on and on until one day we looked around and found we had created a state-of-the-art aquaculture facility, all from grants, volunteer labour and 'borrowed' equipment.

Looking after fish is also a time-consuming job, not something for volunteers, although that's how it was operated for the better part of two decades. To create income, we turned to tourism. In the beginning we charged people a modest sum to feed the fish – this is a spectacular experience. Although we gradually built up the tourism appeal with videos and informational displays, the guided tour and the fish feeding were always the real drawcard. Each guide developed their own spiel. An interesting fact they imparted is that all barramundi change from male to female. One of the female volunteers had a good line to describe this.

'And when the fish get to about five years old,' she would say, 'all barramundi grow a brain.' That invariably invoked a response from a male in the crowd.

'How do you know that?' he would challenge.

''Cos they don't change back,' she would shoot straight back at him.

At the end of the 1990s, I was confronted by a grazier who had come to Karumba expressly to drag me to a meeting in Georgetown, as my reputation for community work with a marine environmental focus had spread.

'I don't want to get involved,' I said. 'I have way too much on my plate and can't afford the time away.'

'Anyway, what's this meeting about?' I couldn't help asking.

'We are setting up a Natural Resource Management (NRM) Group and we need your input,' he said.

'What's that? Why me?' My curiosity was taking over.

The NRM balances the needs of primary industries (fishing, grazing, mining) with those of the environment. The organisation's Northern Gulf Resource Management Group looks after the southern half of Cape York and is based in Georgetown, halfway between Karumba and Cairns. What they lacked was local people with expertise in the marine environment and fishing industry – hence, me. Against my better judgement I went to Georgetown where I found the meeting very interesting. It really hit my core beliefs. By the end of the day I was seen bashing my forehead against the table, muttering *no, no, no* – for now I had a new hat to wear: Conservation Director of the Northern Gulf Resource Management Group. They had set me up nicely.

To gain an understanding of local environmental concerns we held industry workshops. The fishing workshop was held late in 2002, which I attended along with representatives from the gillnetting (barramundi), crabbing, NFC, and recreational fishing groups. Most of the discussion was straightforward as the fishing industry had things well in hand by then.

'What else?' we asked.

'Bloody ghost nets,' replied Claudine Ward, the Environmental Officer from the Gulf Commercial Fisherman's Organisation.

'What's a ghost net?' I asked, never having heard the term before.

'Derelict nets washing up on beaches,' she responded. 'We are sick and tired of getting the blame for the ones washing up on Cape York. They are not ours.'

'Why are they called ghost nets?' I asked.

'Because they still fish but don't belong to anyone, so it's as if they are operated by a ghost.'

'Really? I'll check it out,' I volunteered. So began a new phase of my life.

GhostNets Australia

THE PHONE INVESTIGATION TOOK NINE MONTHS. IT WAS a challenge as the region is eighty per cent owned or managed by Indigenous people, who can be difficult to contact by phone. I cold-called people, with one person leading to another or to a dead end. By the end of this period, though, I had a clear understanding that this problem covered the entire Gulf of Carpentaria; that nearly all the nets were foreign – from work already done by the World Wide Fund for Nature (WWF) in the Northern Territory – and who the interested players were likely to be in tackling the issue. So in 2004 we brought them together for a two-day workshop in Karumba with unprecedented attendance. They came from all four corners of the Gulf, as well as the Torres Strait, to strategise and plan a project, concluding with voting me in as the coordinator of the newly formed Carpentaria Ghost Nets Program. A huge honour, but a bit of an empty one as there was no actual funding to do anything. I felt like I was the captain of a ship run aground.

When funding did come through, I was invited to Canberra for the announcement and a photo opportunity with Ian Campbell, the Federal Minister for the Environment. I felt it should not be me but the newly elected Chair of GhostNets Australia, Djawa Yunupingu, for this was to be a project run by Indigenous people on their country and dealt with in their way.

The project design incorporated arming local people with the skills and infrastructure to manage the problem indefinitely, for it was inconceivable at that time that we could stop the flow of nets washing up on our shores, having no idea where they came from. It was a steep learning curve for all of us as it hadn't been done before.

So, after much negotiation I managed to convince Canberra that two of us should go – Djawa and me. I was so naïve in those days that I politely asked Djawa (by phone) if he was okay to fly by himself, as he was coming from Nhulunbuy (Gove) in the Northern Territory.

'Yes,' he responded. 'I'll be okay.' He added, 'We can meet in the Qantas Lounge in Cairns.'

'I can't get us in, I'm not a member,' I said, thinking it was my call.

'That's all right. I have Gold membership.'

Let the ground open up and swallow me whole. It was an important lesson in preconceived notions. Djawa was to help me navigate similar minefields over the years and I am forever indebted to him. One thing about Djawa was he never wasted words or bothered with unintentional slights or insults, especially when they were born of sheer ignorance. He is one of the smartest men I have ever met and well grounded to boot.

With the money finally in the bank, we held the first Steering Committee and started. The Steering Committee was essential for that whole engagement process. Although costly, time consuming and unwieldy – we had to have at least one person from each community – it was the sole reason we could succeed where similar projects failed. I am happy to say that we had no real splits within the group, ever. We had lots of meetings while we set things up, but after a while the trust was embedded and I got on with things without needing to consult every step of the way.

Being used to committees where people argue over the pettiest of details, it was incredibly enlightening to find we came to grand decisions in the simplest of ways. No wordsmithing, no over-analysing and no votes, for if there wasn't a consensus it wasn't going to happen.

Getting a Steering Committee plan and logo together turned out to be the easiest part of the project. The next stage was a lot more difficult. We had to find groups of people (who became rangers) to do the work, figure out ways to pay and communicate with them, equip them and, finally, train them in data collection. Finding rangers from each community willing to do this very hard and physical work was probably the easiest of these challenges, for all the communities had high unemployment. But finding a lead organisation to handle the money, pay and lead these people was extremely problematic. The main obstacle was that the work required teams of people sporadically – hard to pay them third hand.

This created two hurdles: first, creating the same trained crew that were available each time they were needed, and second, being able to pay them casual rates in cash.

Training and resourcing rangers became the central business for the next five years, until the Federal Government saw the value in establishing a national Indigenous ranger program – Working On Country. When these ranger organisations were fully functioning, they provided full employment to a growing group of people in each community. This in turn made our life much easier. In the beginning, however, we were stuck with trying to establish these ranger programs. This was not something that could be organised by phone or email – I needed to go to each community and talk directly with people. Each community was different and required a different model.

Until you visit these parts of Australia you are totally unaware there is another, almost third-world, country within. I had visited some of these places when on the trawlers, but being hosted by the Traditional Owners themselves was a different experience altogether. In Numbulwar (in the south-west Gulf) I experienced a smoking ceremony where evil spirits were exorcised from a house after a death. On Cape Arnhem I walked around a stone drawing of a Macassan (Indonesian) trading vessel. This was a large cutaway depiction made from small rocks of a three-tiered vessel showing all the cabins and holds inside the boat. The accuracy of the dimensions was uncanny as there was no way they would have seen it sliced in half like that. The stone drawing was made long before the British arrived on Australian shores. On Groote Eylandt we went spearfishing after getting bogged in a sand dune. In Bamaga I attended a wedding ceremony that had traditional dancing the whole night long. In Kowanyama I heard stories from the elders about 'the good old days' when the men worked in the cattle industry. In Pormpuraaw I learnt if you are travelling anywhere with cigarettes you should leave most of them in your swag, for if someone asks for one it is polite to give it. Leaving them behind means you can be polite and frugal at the same time. I don't smoke but it was useful information anyway.

In the Wessel Islands I experienced first hand the power of bush medicine. We were driving along in a gutted-out rust bucket of a four-wheel drive troopy, with me bouncing around in the back, when suddenly we stopped and one of the rangers ran into the bush. I had no idea what was going on as they spoke in their local language, but assumed he was going to the toilet. While we waited the chief ranger asked me in a mixture of broken English and mime what was wrong with my eyes.

'Don't know,' I said. 'Must be an allergy of some sort as they are very itchy.' (Miming rubbing.)

By this time the runner had returned with a handful of berries. He indicated I should squeeze them into my eyes. Not thinking of the dire consequences if this backfired, I did as instructed. Within a minute my eyes were fixed. Unbelievable! Better than Visine.

But my favourite story was from the backwoods of Arnhem Land. We flew into this small community airstrip in a light aircraft. As we were coming into land I saw four troopies and a mob of rangers waiting for us. As we disembarked the twelve rangers lined up so we could shake hands and say hello. I felt like The Queen inspecting the troops. On each troopy was a dead kangaroo, legs in the air.

'Is that lunch?' I joked.

'Yes,' the rangers proudly nodded. That wiped the smile off my face, because they had just hunted them with spears.

Not until I visited these communities did I realise the problems with language. In these communities reading, writing and numeracy were nonexistent because the main communication was oral. This was an important realisation for a core part of the project was data collection. We needed to know how many nets there were, where they were located (using a GPS fix), and a whole heap of measurements to help us identify the nets. To build this knowledge in the rangers, we employed field officers to provide onsite training as well as the tools they needed. One of these tools was a booklet developed by WWF that identified some of the nets. The rangers loved this book because it told a little about what the net was used for and who by.

One of the primary school teachers in the community of Numbulwar saw an opportunity to incorporate the rangers' work and the WWF booklet into the school curriculum. Together we arranged for the kids to go out in the field with the rangers. They helped with the measuring, data entry and sample collection. This, of course, gave the kids experience in the use of maths and English. But their favourite part was taking the samples back to the classroom, looking up the relevant match in the WWF booklet, then using the map of the world to see which country they came from. Suddenly geography became real.

On a cultural level the community saw this as a great way to get the kids to interact with the Elders (most of the rangers). During clean-ups, they often camped overnight. It was around these campfires that the younger generation heard stories that had been handed down for generations. A win-win for everyone.

In the beginning, only seven communities were prepared to do the work. We did not push any of them to join, wanting them to be both ready and willing, but we kept the communication channels open. Within five years, though, thirty-two communities from the Kimberley region to the east coast of Queensland just north of Cairns were happily engaged. Before long, we were making large inroads into managing this ghost net problem. Eventually we removed over thirteen thousand nets, rescued hundreds of turtles and recorded a huge amount of data. We were a success.

The first award we won was the Queensland Landcare Award in 2005. I thought this premature as we didn't have runs on the board, having spent most of the previous twelve months setting everything up. But, unbeknown to me, we were entered and won. I'm a cynic at heart so was not impressed. I knew the words 'Indigenous' and 'turtles' had got us over the line.

Having discovered winning awards was worth the pain of writing the submissions, since a lots of kudos accompanies the honours, the following year I applied for our first national award – the Banksia Sustainability Award. I had never heard of the Banksia Foundation, which seemed to be primarily aimed at improving corporate environmental footprints. That year they had a water category and waived the fee for us. It sounded like they wanted me to apply, probably because they had never had an application from the remote north.

When it was announced we were finalists I decided to attend the award ceremony alone, as I didn't want to have to put a ranger through the experience of endless boring speeches. After all, we had a snowflake's chance in hell of winning.

At the event, we sat through all the other awards as ours was last (the community sections are always last). My family, who attended the event to bolster me up, were liberally drinking the free wine and getting louder and louder, while I didn't eat or drink anything as I was full of nerves. Just before it was our turn, number-two brother whispered to me, 'Have you got a speech ready?'

'No, why do I need that? Not going to win.'

'Good idea to have three dot points ready in your head, just in case.'

When I was called to the stage my noisy family further embarrassed me as they cheered me along. Even when my name was called as the winner I still hadn't taken it in and needed a gentle prod from one of the other finalists to go up to the microphone.

Half prepared, I accepted the award on behalf of all the Indigenous communities in the Gulf of Carpentaria.

'Should I name them?' I whispered to the emcee.

'Why not?' he responded, having no idea what he had let himself in for.

So, visualising a map of the Gulf and starting with the top left-hand corner ... 'Gumurr, Marthakal, Dhimurru, Yirralka, Laynhapuy, Anindilyakwa, Numbulwar, Lianthawirriyarra, Gangalidda and Garawa, Mornington Island, Normanton, Pormpuraaw, Wik and Kugu, Napranum, Mapoon, Apudthama, Badalagal, Hammond Island and the Kaiwalagal mob ...'

I received a standing ovation. Only I knew I had missed out on Kowanyama and Yugul Mangi.

I've lost count of the number of awards we have won since, but for me that was the most significant. For the next Banksia, I let Djawa do the honours and after that other rangers got a turn in the limelight.

By 2009 our funding had run out. From a tragic beginning, the program was ending on a high. Things couldn't be better, or so I thought ...

Ghost net art

WHEN THE FUNDING DRIED UP IT WAS TIME TO TAKE stock yet again. Yes, we had done extremely well helping local communities manage this problem, providing them with the equipment, the skills and a livelihood. But there were still lots of things we hadn't done well, specifically: recycling the huge amount of waste generated, discerning the origin of the nets and, most importantly, stopping the problem at its source. We knew we couldn't do these things alone, so we concentrated on building effective partnerships. These were with visual artist Sue Ryan for the waste issue; Australia's eminent research organisation, the CSIRO, to help shed light on the origin of the nets, and an Indonesian non-profit organisation, the Arafura Timor Seas Ecosystem Action Program (ATSEA), to help with solutions.

We tackled the waste issue first. We had only two options available to us – burning the nets on the beach or taking them to landfill. Recycling was out since, apart from there being no such capability within Australia (for these nets were mixed plastic and full of sand and other grunge), the cost of transport to existing recycling facilities in the south was prohibitive. We decided we had only one alternative – reuse the net material for making bags, hammocks and other practical items. We trialled this idea in the Torres Strait at a workshop with the Hammond Island community. They made some really decorative bags, which they sold locally for twenty dollars each. Each bag took at least a day to make so it was obvious the income generated did not cover the work involved. Not a practical solution. Back to the drawing board.

One day a colleague suggested we create a one-off art exhibition utilising ghost net material. Interesting idea.

Who would exhibit it and who would pull it together? The colleague suggested a locally based person that he knew by reputation was experienced in working with Indigenous artists – Sue Ryan. So began our partnership with Sue and her partner, and the birth of the Ghost Net Art Project (GNAP).

GNAP took just as much involvement to set up as the ranger program, for once again we had to find people within the communities who wanted to have a go and skill them up in the use of this new medium (plastic is very different to work with than natural fibres), as well as get the art industry engaged with the concept so we could hold exhibitions. Our plan was to create workshops within the communities where the local artists interacted with well-known art mentors who were familiar with using this strange medium. Sue tried to match the mentors with the traditional skills of each community: for example, matching weavers with weavers. As skills developed, so did a portfolio of art pieces to be exhibited. The initial workshops focused on making baskets using simple coiling techniques.

Our first gig was at the inaugural Cairns Indigenous Art Fair (CIAF), with some artists from Aurukun in western Cape York. The Queensland government at the time was keen to showcase the state's excellent Indigenous artworks to the world. When we arrived to set it up the day before the opening, we were disappointed to find we were included in the kids section of the fair – we had expected to be up front with the main events. Additionally, we had three excellent baskets for exhibition that were not on display with the other Aurukun art pieces. And our pièce de résistance, a three-metre blue mermaid sculptural piece, was still in her box. She was very beautiful, with long black hair made of teased-out rope.

Incensed, Sue and the art coordinator for Aurukun, a fiery Frenchman named Guy, marched off to the event organisers. Eventually, and reluctantly (Guy was particularly persuasive), it was agreed that the mermaid would be hung in the auditorium. What a coup – prime position. Also, the gallery that was exhibiting the other Aurukun pieces agreed to showcase the three baskets. Then there was the haggle between Guy and the gallery owner over what price to set on them. It was clear he did not value the baskets the same as Sue and Guy. By the end of the first day the gallery owner had egg on his face as two of the baskets were sold for a total of four thousand dollars. Now, that's a living for the artists.

From that moment on, ghost net art was legitimate. Furthermore, it was not the flash in the pan many had predicted, for the first basket was sold to an eminent Indigenous art collector from England.

As she said to us later, 'Now I have bought this basket, watch everyone scramble to catch up.' So right she was, for a couple of weeks later I was contacted by the original gallery owner Guy had to haggle with so stridently.

'You don't know me,' he started, concluding with, 'I am keen to purchase any ghost net art piece you have,' without letting me get a word in edgeways.

'Actually,' I finally got in. 'I do know you. I was there. At the Cairns Indigenous Art Fair.'

'Oh!' was the last I heard from him.

Thanks to Sue's genius in bringing the right people together, recognising the potential of the medium and knowing what makes good art, ghost net art is now recognised as something of a phenomenon within the body of work that is Australian Indigenous art. Within only a few years of its emergence many of Australia's major institutions, including the National Gallery of Australia and the National Museum of Australia in Canberra (which also featured a ghost net basket on an Australian stamp) and the Museum of Contemporary Art, Sydney, have acquired pieces for their collections. International recognition started with the British Museum purchasing a piece. Since then, Australian ghost net art has been exhibited in Paris, Alaska, Singapore and Monaco.

Even though extremely successful, the fact remains that the art does not actually use much net, so our intention of finding a solution to the waste issue has not eventuated. One thing it does do exceptionally well, though, is create public awareness. Ghost net art attracts attention. It is colourful, textual, versatile and zany. It provides an opportunity for Indigenous artists, it transforms a negative into a positive and when it is presented at a public workshop, it is interactive. Perfect.

An end to ghost nets

THE MEDIA COVERAGE OF GHOST NET ART AND THE environmental awards we received brought the ghost net eradication project to the attention of a small group of researchers from the CSIRO. Up until that time we had been steadfastly collecting lots of information but did not have the wherewithal to crunch the data. We needed experts and here they were, knocking on our door.

Core to the issue was finding the geographic source of the nets – where the hell did they come from? By this time, we knew that less than ten per cent were Australian. We also knew from gear experts, various fishermen and the previous work of WWF that the nets belonged to countries as far away as China, Thailand and South Korea. What was not clear was whether the nets floated in from those areas, or were used by those countries closer to Australia. One solution involved determining the pathway the nets travelled to reach our shores. This is where CSIRO came in. Simplifying a complex mathematical story, CSIRO did some sexy modelling that gave us our answer. Most of the nets appeared to be coming from the Arafura and Timor seas, directly to the north of Australia. How could that be? Were all these countries fishing in these waters, or were Indonesians using nets made by these various countries?

There were lots of questions that only further research could answer – in Indonesia. I reluctantly took on the challenge but, as I don't speak Bahasa, we needed an Indonesian partner. Enter ATSEA. Learning they had already scheduled a meeting in Darwin, I wrangled myself an invitation.

The meeting went to plan and I met two wonderful Indonesians, Professor Subhat Nurhakim and Dr Tonny Wagey. They were keen to help even though they had never heard of the ghost net issue before.

'Come to Indonesia,' they said. 'We will organise a meeting with some fishing people,' meaning government as well as fishers. So I headed off to Indonesia to investigate.

I had many adventures in Indonesia, including some first-hand experiences with the corruption that is rife in the region and the slave trade still in existence. As this story is about the Gulf Country I will not elaborate further, but only add I found the fishermen rather shy but by no means hostile. They wanted to tell their stories and they welcomed the opportunity to do so.

The story that unfolded from all the local fishermen was the same. It was one of personal hardship brought about by depleting stocks, overwhelming competition from greedy foreigners and debilitating government corruption. Who cares about ghost nets in Australia when you have this to contend with?

Foreigners, with the support of corrupt officials, raped and pillaged the Arafura Sea. These fishermen did not care about the local guys, or even each other, for profit was the goal. The ghost net issue back in Australia was simply a by-product of this set of circumstances. The foreign trawlers from not only Thailand, but South Korea, China, Vietnam and Taiwan, deliberately drove through nets they found in their way, forced local trawler fishermen into dangerous fishing grounds close to reefs so their nets would get ripped up, and deliberately discarded their own damaged nets. The crew did not care – it was not their country, not their vessel and not their nets. When all the fish were gone, they would just pack up and find somewhere else.

Legacy

IN 2011 I LEFT THE GULF COUNTRY FOR GOOD. I HAD lived and worked there for thirty-four years. The Gulf shaped me and I am proud to say I left something behind. The Barra Farm is now owned and operated by the Shire Council and they plan to develop the tourist potential I envisioned years before. Rangers across the whole of northern Australia are now fully employed by the Federal Government, and those land and sea centres we struggled to get up and running are stewards of this vast land. The ghost net art phenomenon is still growing. Recently the Glasgow Museum purchased a four-metre sawfish created by Sue Ryan and Torres Strait Islander artist Ricardo Idagi (with a little help from me and other friends). But best of all, the nets have stopped coming.

In 2015 I had the honour of having lunch with Ibu Susi Pudjiastuti, the newly elected Minister of Fisheries and Marine Affairs, Indonesia. She told me then she had taken on board all the outcomes from our six workshops in Indonesia (which made me realise how well placed Tonny Wagey was in the Indonesian government) and put a moratorium on all trawling in Indonesian waters. Better still, she evicted all the foreign-owned vessels (not just trawlers). She meant business too, for later Tonny sent me a front-page article from an Indonesian newspaper. Although I couldn't read the Bahasa, the picture told the story. Behind a portrait of Ibu Susi was a vessel being bombed, blown up by the Indonesian navy. Message clear – Ibu Susi was serious.

Apparently it worked.

Graziers and managers

Kylie Tate

Kylie Tate was born in Atherton, Queensland. When she was a toddler she lived with her grandparents on Boomera Station, where her grandfather was the station mechanic. She is a keen fisherwoman, gardener and cook, and is known for her home-grown and made mango and tomato chutneys, jams and relishes. Her gourmet sausages have won the Sausage King of North Queensland award at the Cloncurry Show.

Kylie has lived in and around the Gulf her whole life. She has worked on Cowan Downs, Lorraine, Coolibah, Millungera, Neaumayer Valley and Canobie.

Kylie and her partner, Richard, have four children, two girls and two boys, and one grandchild.

GROWING UP ON REMOTE CATTLE STATIONS

Kylie Tate

I GREW UP ON COOLIBAH OUTSTATION, THE EASTERN half of Lorraine Station between Burke and Wills and Gregory Downs. Back then, Lorraine was split in half. My father was the head stockman of Coolibah and ran the eastern half when Ted Flamsteed was the manager of Lorraine, running the main station and the western half. My mother was the camp cook for Coolibah, as well as being a busy mum.

When we first moved to Coolibah I did my school lessons through correspondence. I got a pack of booklets in the mail from Brisbane and Mum and I would sit down and work our way through them. They came with cassettes and we muddled our way through for a couple of years this way.

However, after a few years my sister Anita started school as well and Mum found it very hard to teach us both, cook, garden and take care of the station complex all at once, so the decision was made that we go over to the main station during the week to board with the boreman and his wife. We could attend the little state school that was on the main station, where there were eight children as well as a teacher–headmaster and a teacher's aide, a lady named Thecla Lemson. Her dad was our grader driver for twenty-five years!

Thecla was my favourite person when I was little. She was a large Aboriginal woman who was a single mother to a little girl named Llewellyn. She was a lovely person who didn't have a mean bone in her body and was always happy and joking with us kids. In the afternoons she would take us down to the river and show us how to catch fish on hand lines, take us swimming and show us her little pet penny turtles that let us feed them. Her mum was Betty. She would always feed us fruitcake and cups of black tea. When I was little I didn't like fruitcake, but I ate it every time she offered it because she was one of those women who always fussed that you needed to eat, and you just didn't back-answer an adult when I was a kid, so I suffered the fruit cake because their home was such a nice place to hang out. I must have learned to like fruitcake because I actually really like it now.

A couple of years later we moved from boarding with the bore runners to living with a couple, Ailsa and Les, who were the gardeners. Les grew a massive vegetable patch that fed the whole station, Ailsa took care of Mrs Flamsteed's roses and the garden beds, and together they mowed the lawns and tended to the fruit trees. There were lots of fruit trees back then – oranges, lemons, mandarins, guavas and a banana plot.

Ailsa was a lovely lady. She was just how you pictured a grandmother to be – softly spoken, and she made us nice treats for smoko. Our favourite was pancakes that she sprinkled with sugar and squeezed bush lemons over. Les took some getting used to. He was one of those naturally grumpy old men who just tolerated us because Ailsa made him, but we must have grown on him because after a while he showed us little things, like how to sow the beans and peas, and how to know when to pick the bananas. Just little things you learn and it's not until years later you realise that you learnt something important. As an adult I have always planted a veggie garden, especially since having children. I think our kids should grow up knowing where their food comes from and have the basic skills and know-how to grow and produce their own food if they want to. So many kids grow up today with no idea where it all comes from before it arrives at the store.

After boarding away for secondary school, which I hated, I started a short course that taught me the skills to become a governess. After six weeks I would be qualified to be a home tutor, and with that I went home to Coolibah to help my mum teach my little brothers, then in grades one and two with Mount Isa School of the Air.

At first I spent a lot of time in the school room, but the boys wanted to play when I was in there so I ended up swapping with Mum. I looked after my little sister Stacey while helping to do the cleaning, the laundry, the cooking, the gardening and the animals. I didn't mind this at all, as I think at heart I have always been a homemaker.

A couple of months later, two lads pulled out of my dad's stock camp and I was put in to replace one. My dad was, and still is, a very hard taskmaster. He expects people to buck in and be useful at all times. I had of course been mustering and working down at the yards processing cattle as a kid, but not day in, day out, and as for everyone who starts out here, I learnt what hard work was about. In my first year I got so many roaring dressing-downs I seemed to be in trouble most of the time. I am sure I got fired five or six times that year, but Dad would go away, calm down, and we would just move forward without acknowledging I was fired. I just kept trying harder next time and hoping not to mess up.

I went over and did a short stint at the main station in the all-girls camp. Mike Munro from *60 Minutes* came out and interviewed us. It was funny – they had us fixing fences for the camera and galloping across the river crossing through the water on sunset. I got a short interview on my own, being the youngest girl in the camp at fifteen. It was all a little bit silly, I thought, but the other girls loved it and it was a talking point for some time.

I worked for my dad for a couple of years before moving over to the main station at Lorraine to work in the all-girls camp for the second round. It was a very different experience from home. At home we took great care to block our mobs of cattle up and walk them quietly to the yards to be processed. Here, the helicopter pushed all the cattle together while you got behind them and tried to keep them together as they ran all the way to the yards, where they were helicoptered in. It was crazy. It went against everything I had been taught about handling cattle. They were stirred up to the billy-o by the time you drafted them through the yards. All the galloping about was good fun, but I didn't want to stay where I didn't agree with how they did things, so I headed home again.

Ted Flamsteed retired after twenty-five years. The new manager decided it was not cost effective to have Coolibah operating on its own and our family was moved over to the main station. It was a huge change for us. My mum became the camp cook for Lorraine and my dad became the head stockman. Nowadays, the station is mustered with the station crew as well as the help of contract musterers, but back then the entire place was mustered with seven blokes and a girl. We worked practically every weekend and it was a tough year.

Management withdrew the school building from use and it was shut down. The families who had children at the school struggled to teach them through School of the Air and, over time, left the station. With a full-time job, my mum was forced to hire a governess to teach the three little ones still in school, meaning she worked just to pay for her.

My family left for Townsville and I decided to leave for Cowan Downs Station, out to the east on the Normanton road, and enjoyed my time there. Being a smaller block, things were a lot more laid-back and we did a bigger variety of work. I learned more about machinery and welding, as they didn't have a bore runner. We all took turns in the maintenance, and it was here I realised how much of an advantage my dad had given me over others. I was quite used to high expectations and getting told off if I didn't meet them. Because the property was smaller, we hardly ever worked a weekend, and because we were close to the Burke and Wills Roadhouse we spent most weekends in there socialising with the other local ringers. It was there I bumped into Richard Tate, my brother Paul's old head stockman, who had taken a job next door at Neumayer Valley, and we became close friends. If he had a weekend off he visited me, and if he didn't I went over to Neumayer Valley and worked with him.

One weekend at the dinner table, the Neumayer Valley manager, Bill, said to me, 'Girly, you spend so much time here working for nothing you might as well move over here and get paid for it.'

So, I gave my notice and a few weeks later moved over to Neumayer Valley. Back then it was owned by Sid Faithfull, who also owned Karumba Livestock Exports (Austra Live Ex) that operated out of Karumba selling cattle to the Asian market. It was a great experience learning about live export and on occasions we went up to Karumba to load cattle onto the massive boats that were then towed out of the channel and out to sea.

I'd thought about going and doing a stint on one of the cattle boats. I was fascinated with how it all worked, and when one of the blokes from our camp came back after a trip I questioned him about it. He'd had some terrific adventures and told us while they were out in the middle of the ocean, one night around 2 a.m. pirates with machine guns boarded the boat. They made everyone go above deck and lie facedown at gunpoint while they ransacked the boat, stole everything of value, then left as quickly as they came. After that I immediately gave up the idea of going for a trip on a cattle boat. I wasn't going to risk meeting pirates.

Richard and I spent the next year working together at Neumayer Valley and were camped out most of the time. Things were very dry and we had to supplement-feed a lot of the smaller, woody weaners in a little paddock we called the hospital paddock. They did it a bit tough and some got bogged in the mud while trying to get a drink down at the river. We went down each afternoon in the tinny and pulled out the ones that still had the strength to get up again or put down the ones who were not going to make it. The silty mud was like quicksand. In some spots I'd get out of the boat to tie a rope around the bogged weaner so Richard could tow it out, and would quite often sink and get stuck. Richard then had to tow me out as well!

One time, another of the blokes, Ian, came along to go fishing with us after we finished. We pulled all the bogged weaners out, were trawling down the river with a line out the back and came to a little narrow part of the river that was mostly mudflat, when up in front of our boat jumped this massive saltwater crocodile. He was about four metres long, not very happy to see us and started snapping at the boat. The water was barely two feet deep and Ian and I were screaming at Richard to put it in reverse. Ian started swinging the axe at the croc, which was getting angrier by the minute, and I screamed at him not to stir it up. Richard threw the boat into reverse and gunned it, forgetting about the fishing line out the back, which then proceeded to get tangled around the propeller and stall the motor. We had gone back only a couple of metres, but luckily it was enough to give the croc the space he needed to decide he would rather get out of there than eat us. When he stood up on the mudflat and took off running we realised just how big he was. He was about a metre tall, was almost as wide as the tinny, and a lot longer. If he had wanted, he could have had us for dinner as easy as pie. We were all very shaken up and pretty wary about hanging over the back of the boat to untangle the fishing line!

The six-mile yards at Neumayer Valley were right on the river. When we worked there we went down to the river to wash the blood off our hands from dehorning the weaners, then boil the billy and have lunch on the bank. Sometimes if we were walking cattle we would take our horses down there to swim them in the river. This time, we were on our second day processing weaners when we knocked off for lunch and had walked down to the river for a wash. We were halfway down the bank when we saw another monstrous four-to-five-metre salty sunning himself right in the middle of our camp. We never went swimming there again and boiled the billy back up the top!

* * *

At the end of my first year at Neumayer Valley I took Richard to Townsville to meet the rest of my family. While we were there I bought my dad's old Dodge horse truck and a lovely little blue quarter horse gelding, a mare and her foal, loaded them all up and began heading for home.

Halfway between Kynuna and Julia Creek our brakes went, but as there was no traffic it didn't matter too much. Coming into Julia Creek there is a railway crossing you are supposed to stop for, but we forgot about the brakes and left it a bit late. Instead, we bounced across the tracks and the next intersection before we could stop to turn around and head back out on the beef road. Luckily there was no train!

A little way down the beef road to Burke and Wills it started to rain. We came over a ridge to see right in front of us these two old blokes in a clapped-out ute full of firewood, going about forty kilometres an hour right down the middle of the single-lane road. Richard was madly beeping the horn and I hung out the window yelling to get their attention, as we had no way of stopping. Richard dropped back in gears, trying to slow down, when luckily one of the old blokes saw us. They swerved off the road and we went past, narrowly missing them, giving all of us quite a scare.

About halfway along we came over another rise to see an old bull walking down the centre of the road trying to avoid the muddy soil on the sides. Again, Richard was madly trying to go back down the gears and beeping the horn to get him to move off. The stubborn old thing refused and instead started running, still down the middle. We had slowed down quite a lot by the time we got to him, but not enough to avoid him all together. The sides of the road were quite steep and very wet from the rain, so there was no choice but to hit him up the backside. His rear end came up onto the bull bar and he ran along in front of us on his front feet with his testicles hanging over the bar. It was such a comical site we couldn't stop laughing. We slowed some more and he continued to run along in front of us, getting another couple of bumps up the backside before finally moving off to the side, allowing us to pass.

Two Mile Creek was running, so Bill met us at the creek crossing in the grader to tow us across. We bogged the truck right down to the tray and it took a heck of a lot to pull it out with the grader. The truck tipped right over on one side – at one stage we thought it might go over, horses and all. Finally, we got across and made it home, just before it rained for the next few weeks straight.

To this day, I think it was the most eventful road trip we have ever undertaken. We had so much fun and adventure in that old truck. We often reminisce about the old Dodge.

The following year, we decided to apply for a head stockman's position that came with married accommodation. We took the position on Coorabulka Station on the other side of Boulia and the edge of the desert. The closer we got the more anxious I became ... where were all the trees? This place looked terrible. As far as you could see there was just nothing. We finally arrived at a small station complex with a tiny little patch of lawn and a couple of ugly old Athel pines for shade. We were introduced to the manager and his wife, and to the two blokes who were to make up Richard's camp.

At breakfast the next day the manager informed me I would not be allowed to work in the stock camp, but I could 'share' the cooking with his wife. It was not what I expected, but, trying to make the most of it, I agreed to cook three days a week. I always enjoyed cooking and didn't mind it at first. I came in on a Monday, cleaned up everything from the weekend, then cooked and prepared enough food to last through to Wednesday. On Wednesday I'd start over, cleaning up from the day before and cooking enough to last through to Friday, then on Friday prepare enough to last over the weekend.

Over the next few weeks I got pretty bored, as there was very little gardening to be done with only a tiny patch of lawn to water and nothing else grew, so I took to tagging along with the blokes. I was quite happy to poke around doing any jobs Richard gave me. One day I was riding a motorcycle in the horse paddock, pushing out some heifers that had broken the fence and got in where they weren't supposed to be, when the manager came roaring up alongside me in his Toyota, got out and started screaming at me. 'What the effing hell do you think you are doing?' I was baffled as to why he was so upset and explained that the heifers had broken the fence, that I had fixed the fence and was now pushing them back out of the horse paddock. He proceeded to give me an earbashing about how I wasn't allowed to ride a company bike without first signing a release waiver that I had never heard of.

By the time we got back to the station and I met him at his office as asked, he had calmed down a fair bit. I, on the other hand, was bloody livid. I was not used to feeling like I was less than everyone else. I had always worked alongside everyone and been treated as an equal. I thought I was just as capable as the blokes who worked there and couldn't understand why this bloke kept treating me like I was not good for anything except cooking and cleaning. Anyway, I signed his release waiver and hoped that would be the end of it.

I was terribly homesick by this stage and really started to hate the place. It was just so desolate. There were creeks but they were all dry, so there was nowhere to go fishing. Back home I always headed down to the river to catch a fish or two in my spare time. Here, there was not even a good swimming hole. No birds or other wildlife came to visit, unless you count the nasty inland taipan snakes we got on regular occasions, but those were far from friendly and I have always hated snakes. I did find a cool spot where the bore head had rusted off below the ground, leaving a massive open hole going all the way down to the artesian basin. Because it was rusted off below the surface it couldn't be tapped, and it ran freely into its own big lagoon. The minerals in the bore water created a beautiful rich aqua colour and there were a few trees too, but they were very stunted little things. I took pots out there to catch some yabbies.

Soon after we arrived the managers went on annual leave for six weeks, we settled into work and made do with our new life. When they got home we were asked over to the office to have our three-month review. Neither of us was very happy but worked our butts off trying to make a go of it. The manager made sniping comments to Richard about his work, but anyone who knows Richard knows he is a workaholic who takes a great deal of pride in always doing things to the best of his ability. He has an extremely good reputation as a hard worker, so it rankled that this bloke, with his own reputation for being quite lazy, had been denigrating Richard. Anyway, we went into the office to have our review, at the end of which the manager said he was happy with us and would like to offer us a contract. Without having discussed it at all with me, Richard said a three-month trial worked both ways to ensure each party was happy, and he was not, and we wouldn't be signing any contract. Well, I was quite shocked but I could have whooped with joy! I was so happy I wouldn't have to stay. We gave two weeks' notice and went about packing up our belongings.

Richard moved back into the head stockman's position at Neumayer Valley. How lucky were we? We happily moved back to the Gulf and slotted straight back into our old routine, except we found out I was pregnant. This time I would be the camp cook, which, truth be told, I didn't mind one bit as I had horrific morning sickness that was not confined to the morning but lasted all day for most of the pregnancy. Later blood tests revealed I also had Ross River fever, so I was not the happy, glowing pregnant woman you hear about. I was sick and run-down for most of it.

We camped out for most of that year. I took a Toyota into the station once a week and picked up fresh stores, collected any mail that came and had smoko and a cuppa with the manager's wife, Ruby, and the mechanic's wife, Dot. I loved living out at camp and enjoyed cooking. I was used to my own company; it didn't bother me to be on my own all day. The Flying Doctor brought out an obstetrician once a month and I went into Normanton for a check-up. Apart from the Ross River, for which there is no treatment, I was fine and the baby was developing normally.

Caitlin-Jane was born a month before my twentieth birthday. I thought I would have plenty of time to settle in and get used to taking care of this little baby, but Ruby's car broke down while she was back in Isa and she was stuck waiting ten days there to get it fixed, leaving me as the only woman on the station to do the cooking and take care of the grounds. And a newborn infant.

I have always been a light sleeper and had Caitlin's little cot beside my bed, as she woke frequently during the night for a feed. One night I woke with a start and turned the lamp on.

Richard woke and said, 'What's wrong?'

'I can't hear her breathing,' I said.

I picked her up and she was bright red in the face. She had been sleeping on her back and vomited. Her mouth and nose were blocked – she was choking. Richard turned her upside down and started to whack her on the back. It wasn't working and she was turning blue. I panicked. I just grabbed her off him and we sprinted up to Ruby's house and pounded on the door. She came running out, took one look at her and placed her face under the cold water tap in her shower. It must have dislodged the vomit from her nose and mouth, she sucked in the biggest breath and screamed the house down. I have never been so thankful to hear a baby scream in my life and have not slept another baby on their back, despite what we have been told, since. We came so very close to losing her.

When Caitlin was six months old I took her into Normanton for her immunisations and booked myself into see the doctor as I had a bad bout of gastro that I didn't seem to be able to kick. Well, guess what. It wasn't gastro but another baby. I had just got used to this one and I was having another one! Bloody hell. What would I do if the next one came out a screamer like Caitlin? What was Richard going to say?

By the time I had driven home I was very happy about the whole thing. I mean, I wanted to have lots of kids. I grew up in a family of nine kids – I wanted about six, I thought. I arrived home and told Richard the news. He was a bit surprised but said, 'Oh well, we talked about having another one in a year or so, it will just be a bit sooner than we planned.'

Jasmine was born in February 2000. She was a big baby and from the moment she arrived she was happy and contented. It was a huge relief. Friends organised for us all to spend the weekend at Rainbow Beach, near Fraser Island.

I hadn't been on a proper holiday since I was a kid and we all enjoyed it immensely. We flew back to Townsville the following Monday to pick up our car and make the long, 1000 kilometre journey back home.

The beginning of the following year Richard started harvesting kangaroo skins in his spare time to earn some extra money. We were doing okay when we both worked, but with only one wage of $28 000 we were never going to get ahead. Richard did extremely well with the roos and we put a lot of money away. In just six months he made his entire year's salary; however, it eventually caused trouble. Richard agreed he would not work at night except on his weekends off but, soon after, he was told he could either be the head stockman or shoot for skins. Richard felt very betrayed and said if the management couldn't support him while he tried to put some money away for his family, it was time to go. So two weeks later we packed up for Cloncurry. Since we didn't have enough savings to live on, Richard went shooting for more skins.

The manager rang us a short while later. We heard they had already been through two head stockmen in the past month or so, so he was told to ring Richard and offer him a contract day rate to get him back and finish the mustering. Richard agreed at twice the rate he had been on and went back to the job, while the girls and I remained in town. He finished the mustering then went to work for Colin Fisher next door at Talawanta Station, digging out dams and shooting in his off time. When Mrs Fisher told me that she was looking for a caretaker for Balaclava Homestead, thirty kilometres out of Cloncurry, the girls and I moved there.

I enrolled Caitlin in School of the Air; we received our radio and all her school work in the mail, but we had a lot of trouble with the radio and missed more lessons than we attended. I would pack a lunch and the girls and I would set out in the car to either put out lick supplement for the cattle or to check the waters around the property. I got a part-time job at the local daycare centre to bring in a bit of extra money, which turned into full time.

Richard had moved across to Julia Creek and worked full time harvesting kangaroos. Every Friday the girls and I headed across the 126 kilometres to visit for the weekend, returning Sunday night ready to start the week over again. I had just completed a certificate in childcare, so when a position was advertised at the Julia Creek kindergarten – house included – I applied for and got the job. We moved straightaway – I was sick of driving back and forth every weekend and I just wanted us all to live under the same roof again.

I started a diploma in early childhood learning, set about teaching kindergarten, and a short time later fell pregnant. Matthew was born in March 2004. Jasmine was disappointed – she planned for him to be a girl that she was naming Pocahontas, but was quickly won over when he grabbed her finger and held onto it. Our second boy, Clayton, was born two years later in 2006.

By this stage we had taken over Game Meat Processing as well as Matilda Pet Foods in Julia Creek. Richard had several chiller boxes and several full-time shooters who harvested kangaroos and pigs for human consumption. In the beginning it was pet food, but things changed – the Russian market opened and there was a huge demand for the product. We were kept extremely busy with all the quality control testing and paperwork. Once a week a big fridge truck came in to load the product for meatworks processing. Then the Russian market crashed and prices for our product fell, as did the quota for the number of animals we could harvest.

I was unhappy living in town and just wanted to go back to our old life. I'd sent Caitlin away for boarding school, which broke my heart, as there was only a primary school in Julia Creek. I had been telling Richard for some time I was sick of this lifestyle, I never wanted to live in a town, which was only supposed to be short term and we had been here for seven years.

Richard's friend Nick came around one day to see if Richard would be interested in applying for a manager's job back home in the Gulf. Nick and his wife, Rachel, had a contract mustering team and did a lot of work for the company that owned Augustus Downs. I put our application in the next day and Richard received a phone call the following morning asking him to fly down to their head office for an interview. It all went well and two weeks later we packed up, yet again, and headed back to the Gulf. The closer we got the happier I felt. I was not one bit sad to say goodbye to that chapter.

* * *

It took us both a little while to adjust, but the longer we were there the happier we became. I could take the kids down to the river every afternoon if I wanted, they had acres of lawn to run around on, Richard got them their own two-wheeled motorbikes that had been his and his sister's when they were little, Matty stopped getting sick and put on weight, everyone was happy and healthy. Life was good again.

It was soon time to send Jasmine away to boarding school – I dreaded it, as Caitlin never settled in. She had problems where she was, so we decided she would move and the girls could start together at a new school. We ultimately chose Townsville Grammar because of its great attitude about keeping boarders very busy.

The second year back in the Gulf I invited all our family out for Easter. It was difficult for us to get away from the place, so we had a big family gathering here at Augustus. It was great. We took all the kids across to the Gregory River to go swimming – they floated around in tubes, made a rope swing, we had a cookout and took everyone to see the water running over Leichhardt Falls. Back at home the boys all went fishing while we girls and the kids set up a camp at the river and went swimming and kayaking in a waterhole. We had a terrific Easter and have made sure we've done it every year since.

In 2014 I was taking the girls in to Cloncurry to catch the plane back to school after the Easter holidays. We had to be there by 8.00 a.m. and it takes three and a half hours to drive into town, so we left at 4.30 in the morning. We made it past the dirt and onto the main road and after about six kilometres something went wrong with the front wheel of the car. The tyre bit in as I tried to correct our path and the vehicle rolled. As I felt it go I screamed, 'Hang!' We rolled over onto the roof and skidded along the road for about thirty metres. I am usually particular about seatbelts, but this morning I hadn't been. I didn't have a belt on, and neither did Caitlin. As we went over, my head hit the window, it smashed and I was thrown around the car like a test dummy. When we came to a stop I immediately asked if everyone was okay.

Caitlin responded straightaway, saying, 'I can't see anything ... where are we?' She had been asleep and was very disoriented.

'We just rolled the car,' I said. 'Stay there and I'll get you.'

It was still dark and I couldn't see a thing. I started calling to Jasmine as she hadn't made a sound, and after she didn't answer me I started to yell.

She then said in a tiny frightened voice, 'I'm up here, Mum.'

She was still strapped in, hanging upside down. It took me a bit to wiggle out of the floor space where I was jammed. My head ached and something was not right with my shoulder. I crawled across to her side and tried to hold her up with my good arm while I let the seatbelt go with the other one, but I couldn't support her and she came crashing down. I helped to pull her out of the window as I couldn't get the door open, then returned to pull Caitlin out as well. I sat them down and went back in to search for the medical kit. Caitlin had some glass in her knee, which I pulled out and dressed, but apart from that seemed fine. Jas had hurt her arm when I dropped her out of her belt but was clearly in shock.

Luckily, we were probably there for only forty-five minutes before a Toll truck came along. The driver stopped and wrapped the girls in towels and called Richard on the UHF radio. I knew I was hurt. I had the worst headache of my life and my shoulder felt like it was on fire. We didn't have to wait long. Richard and my brother turned up shortly afterwards, radioed Peter and Anne at Nardoo Station asking them to call the Flying Doctor, bundled us into the cars and we drove to Nardoo. Anne filled the girls with sweet, hot tea, redressed Caitlin's knee and wrapped a bedsheet around my neck to serve as a makeshift brace until the RFDS arrived with a real one.

Now the adrenaline was wearing off and I didn't have to worry so much about the girls, I started to feel a lot of pain in my head. I was glad when the doctor arrived and gave me a needle, as I struggled to cope. They put a neck brace on me, put me onto a splint, then into a vacuum bag to keep me still. It was awful; the pain in my head and neck was almost unbearable during the flight. I'd had as much pain medication as I was allowed but it didn't seem to be doing anything. When we touched down in Mount Isa, the girls were taken to the hospital in one ambulance and I was taken in another.

At the hospital, Jas was taken off to have her arm X-rayed and this poor nurse, Mum and Grandma were trying their best to deal with Caitlin, who was yelling at the top of her lungs, 'Don't come near me with that bloody needle!' She has always been terrified of needles.

My doctor cleaned up my head, gave me some local anaesthetic, stitched my head right there in the emergency room and took X-rays. I had a couple of broken ribs and a fracture in my scapula, which apparently wasn't too bad and would heal on its own with time. I was given some painkillers and we were all sent home. Back at Mum's, I wasn't feeling too crash hot. My face and head started to swell up, so back to the emergency department I went as I just couldn't handle the pain.

A CAT scan found a heap of foreign material still in my head wound so, again under local anaesthetic, they cut out my stitches, flushed out the cut, stitched it back up and sent me home. That night was awful. I was exhausted but couldn't sleep with the pain, and had a roaring fever, so back to the hospital I went. Another CAT scan found an infection under the skin, a fractured skull, and a bleed on my brain the size of a fifty-cent coin. The following morning my head was so swollen I could barely open my eyes and was unrecognisable when the surgeon came to see me. Off I went to surgery to be cleaned out again.

I came back in every day for weeks to have the wound cleaned and redressed, but then got permission to go home, as long as I went into the Burketown Hospital every day to get the nurse, Di Phillips, to look at it. Eventually Di told me that the wound had healed but it was going to leave one hell of a scar.

We have had more than our fair share of accidents. Matty had a little fall from his horse. The next day he couldn't lift his arm, his whole shoulder was swollen and he had a high temperature. We drove him into see a doctor in Cloncurry, and still his temperature rose. He was admitted to hospital and our doctor said she would be sending us to Townsville to see an orthopaedic surgeon. We spent the next three weeks in the children's ward. They eventually found Matty had osteomyelitis, an infection of the bone. He was very sick for the first couple of weeks, hardly moved from bed and was on a strong course of intravenous antibiotics from the time we arrived.

Weeks later, we were released to Ronald McDonald House at Townsville Hospital. After another five days, the infection was gone and we could go home. We'd been away a whole month so were keen to get back, and flew out that afternoon.

In July 2015, Jas was home for the school holidays. She was walking away a small herd of weaners on horseback with Richard. I was down at my veggie patch pulling weeds and watering when I saw Jas galloping up towards me with a look of sheer panic on her face. As she rounded the bend she started screaming 'MUM!' and I knew something was wrong.

Her dad's horse had been bucking, slipped its bridle off, taken off in a blind bolt and run Richard straight into a tree, headfirst. He was knocked unconscious after landing on his head. Jas tried to wake him but he wouldn't come to, so she rolled him into the recovery position and came for help. I grabbed the big medical kit and we took off in the buggy. About a kilometre up the road we came across Richard walking towards us. As we got closer I could see he was covered in blood and dirt. We pulled up alongside him, he looked very dazed and drowsy, and asked, 'What are you doing here?'

He was very stiff. I carefully helped him into the buggy and headed home. I drove him straight up to the shower in the outside bathroom as I couldn't see what was going on with him for all the blood and mud. As I took off his clothing I saw he already had a massive bruise over his shoulder and rib cage and thought it must be bad to come up so quickly. The large cut to his head was deep and bleeding freely, as heads tend to do. I was more worried about his neck as he held himself very stiffly. He asked me to ring the hospital in Burketown and check to see if Di Phillips was there, because he thought he might need a few stitches.

I thought, 'You have no idea, buddy. It's a bit worse than that.'

I called the RFDS and asked them to come and pick him up. They said to stay by the phone and would call back when they had a plane organised and an arrival time. I helped Richard out of the shower, carefully dressed him and sat him down and cleaned his head wound. I tried to put a sheet around his neck for support like Anne had done for me, but he refused. He got quite agitated and I thought he was in shock. He kept saying he was fine, but I could tell by the way he moved he wasn't fine at all.

The RFDS got to us two hours later. Some more staff members were now back at the homestead to help and a couple were sent down to the airstrip to pick up the Flying Doctor. They came in, took his vitals, administered some pain relief and set up their stretcher to cart him out to the back of the ute and down to the plane. He wasn't being very cooperative. His ribs and back were okay while he stayed still, but once he moved they began giving him terrible pain. The doctor told him he needed a neck brace put on before travelling. Richard said there was nothing wrong with his neck but his ribs hurt. I replied that I thought she should insist since he had fallen headfirst onto the ground. A neck brace was put on, they then put him into a vacuum bag, onto the stretcher, then onto the back of the ute, driven out to the airstrip and flown to Mount Isa.

I jumped in the car and drove the five and a half hours into town. He was still in the emergency department – they had done a scan and found an unstable fracture of the first vertebra in his neck. They couldn't tell me if he was going to be able to walk again, but he did have feeling in his feet so they were optimistic. He would be flown to Townsville the following morning.

Richard had several broken ribs as well as the major break in his neck. The neurosurgeon came in and explained it was rare to treat someone with this type of break. Usually if the person lived they were a quadriplegic; only one in a hundred walked away from this. He said the break in Richard's vertebra was quite extensive, but it was stable, and as long it remained supported rigidly for the next three months it would heal without too much lasting damage. That was a very sobering conversation. Over the next few days Richard went through a variety of scans and tests, which luckily showed no damage to his spinal cord, before finally being put into the new neck brace.

Richard's mum and sister went home and we were left on our own again. They had been a tremendous support during the worst time of our lives. We met with a physio, who ran a series of tests, physical and cognitive, and gave us the all-clear to leave the hospital once we worked out a long-term treatment plan with his neurosurgeon. The plan was that Richard could leave the hospital in a week, but would not be able to travel home for at least four weeks.

I tried to run things back home via the telephone. We had quite a few large contracts on the go at once and it was hectic. I flew back to Mount Isa, picked up the car and got home late that night, then spent the next day catching up in the office, ordering fuel, groceries, cattle supplements, et cetera, to keep things going while I was away with Richard. A friend offered us his small farm outside Townsville at Woodstock, so the kids and I packed the car with our swags, camping gear, all the dogs and enough clothes to last a while, and headed out before daylight the next morning to make the 1000 kilometre return journey. We drove straight through, only stopping to refuel, and reached the farm late afternoon, unpacked the dogs, got them sorted, threw our gear out and took off into town to see Richard.

He was eventually discharged. The farm was a forty-five minute drive out of town and I was extremely worried about how he would go in the car, even though they dosed him up with pain medication before leaving. The trip out was no fun, very stressful, with Richard in excruciating pain the whole way. The next few weeks went by with more of the same. Richard couldn't do too much for himself and was in agonising pain for a long time, but after six weeks we got clearance for him to be allowed to fly home. He caught a plane to Mount Isa, and another charter plane out to the station, while the kids and I packed up and made the big drive home, arriving later that night.

Richard was to wear the neck brace for four months. We flew to Townsville for his last review and he finally took it off. I was almost as relieved as he, not having to change the jolly thing every day. Six weeks later we had another review to see if Richard could go back to work full time and, although you could still clearly see where the break was, the doctor said he was fine to work if he was careful.

So, all in all, we are so very lucky to be here. We live in God's own country, we are well fed and considering all we have been through we strive to make sure we are grateful for every day we have.

I found a quote from the writer Alexandra Elle a while back that I absolutely love because it sums me up perfectly – 'I am grateful for my struggles because without them I would not have found my strengths.'

Hannah Crisp

Hannah Crisp (née Marsterson) was born in the late sixties in Mareeba and is the bookkeeper on Lorraine Station, whose homestead sits on the banks of the beautiful Leichhardt River. Like most managers' wives she has many roles at Lorraine, but this is the title on her payslip. Lorraine, a cattle station about 240 kilometres north-west of Cloncurry, is 605 000 acres (2450 square kilometres) and was first taken up in the later 1860s, with adjoining Talawanta as an outstation. Hannah was born into cattle and her family also grew tobacco. Her grandad had a butcher shop and slaughterhouse, so she thinks her genetics had a little bit to do with where she ended up.

YESTERDAY, TODAY, TOMORROW

Hannah Crisp

I DID MY SCHOOLING IN MAREEBA AND THEN WENT TO the Burdekin for two years of ag college. I spent a lot of time at Wyandotte Station with my aunty and uncle, and went nannying for a while in Brisbane where I was in charge of a little boy and twin girls who have since grown up and become The Veronicas. I went back to Wyandotte and met my husband, Michael. We spent our first year in Central Queensland on Michael's parents' property but we missed our friends and family and came back north with our cattle and horses, and took up a management position at Lochlea Station, which is north of Greenvale. We stayed for eight years and had our first two sons, Luke and Mark ... and so the story goes ...

We worked in the Gulf first at Beamesbrook Station, twenty-five kilometres south of Burketown, then spent four years at Cowan Downs 200 kilometres north of Cloncurry, followed by a year with Stanbroke Pastoral Company at Fort Constantine near Cloncurry, and then we were offered the job at Lorraine Station between Burke and Wills and Gregory Downs. We have been here for thirteen years.

Lorraine is like a small town; it never really stops. Something is always happening – mustering, fencing, poly pipe laying, farming, feedlotting, and a lot of other jobs.

Lorraine comes alive way before dawn each morning, with lights flicking on from all the buildings and, most importantly, the station kitchen light is one of the first on. Everyone makes a beeline for the kitchen to have breakfast, make their crib and head out to start their day. Vehicles are checked over and started, and headlights snapped on. Trucks, horse trucks, motorbikes and machines make their way out from the complex in small convoys.

Our house yards are very close, so we experience lots of calves bellowing for their mums. The dust stirred up by choppers yarding cattle is carried by the wind over to the houses. Whoever has worked at Lorraine I am quite sure will never forget the dust. The station complex is right on the Leichhardt River, which can be good and bad. We have experienced floods and droughts, and you learn never to underestimate the power of water.

At Lorraine, we have a large staff averaging about twenty to twenty-five, and up to about forty when we have contractors here as well. We have a farm and feedlot and some of the staff live out there during the year. I always tell the girls, 'Don't run out to the clothesline in your knickers because someone will see you.'

We have a fair mix of men and women, and I am very proud of all the young women who come out here to the Gulf and leave multi-skilled.

One of my favourite jobs is the butcher shop. I enjoy spending time up there doing the different cuts of meat and making sausages. We breed our own pigs here, so I break them down and turn them into ham and bacon, and everyone enjoys a big pork chop or a crackly roast – a welcome change in the kitchen.

Everyone enjoys the cool mornings because before long the Gulf humidity sets in for the day. I think the garden looks beautiful in the early morning light, with sprinklers going and the smell of wet earth ... it does something for your soul. We have lots of beautiful gardens and trees and lots of lawn – you feel as if it is a little oasis hidden in a little alcove of the property. Gardening is my passion, and over the thirty years we have been managing, there isn't one station that I haven't transformed in some way. At Lorraine there are a lot of old, established trees providing shade – frangipanis, jacarandas and poinsettias that you cannot fit your arms around. We have beautiful soil in which plants thrive and a never-ending supply of manure and mulch from the farm.

Lorraine sort of grips you with its history and country, and it is great to be part of a grand old station in the Gulf. We also have a resident ghost. It isn't a scary ghost but you can feel a presence. The old homestead was knocked down and we are in the process of rebuilding on the same site, so I wonder if it will take up residence in the new one.

Lorraine Station, like all Gulf properties in the later part of the 1800s, succumbed to drought. Owned by Fred Brodie at the time, it was foreclosed and taken over by the bank. They put on a manager, John Kirkaldy, to run the property. He never married but managed Lorraine for thirty-six years. I often think about his life – it must have been lonely, but he was well liked by everyone. His grave is situated in the head stockman's front garden.

In June 1915 Brodie put together a group that bought Lorraine back. Sir Sidney Kidman was on the board in the early years and his grandson John Ayers has not long resigned from being a director. Lorraine Station and Lorraine Pastoral Investments Pty Ltd have just had their one-hundredth anniversary in June 2015. The same families have passed it down for generations and we feel privileged to have been given the reins for the last thirteen years.

One of the shareholders, Anne Philp, has written a book called *Lorraine Station: An Early History*. All the station records are in storage at James Cook University in Townsville and the University of New England. This book gives you a great insight into the lives of people and how they lived back then. There weren't many conveniences, as we have now, and I am sure some of those women certainly did it tough. Anne mentions various women in her book from many walks of life, but they all come together on Lorraine. We have been trying to use historical names for new dams, tanks and bores, and I try to use as many women's names as I can find from the book. And yes, Anne has one named after her.

Eleven graves are recorded at Lorraine but we have found only three. One is John Kirkaldy's, and the other two on the high bank of the Leichhardt belong to two young fellows who died while working.

* * *

Everyone tells me I should have kept a diary. I didn't, but over the time we have been here I have seen some things people would never believe could happen. I have forgotten a lot of good stories but I will endeavour to remember some.

I have always wanted to write a book on station cooks because I have seen just about all of them over the years. Some were great, some were okay, and some were character-building. Throughout my life I have spent many days in the kitchen, so I feel I can say my little piece. I have had men, women and the odd backpacker cooking at times and they all had different ideas about what was edible, hygienic or how long you can leave something in the fridge. I am pleased to say no one ever had food poisoning, but that goes to show just how strong some people's constitutions are.

A couple of stories. I do all the beef cuts and make the sausages. Once I made different flavours for a change, including a batch with chilli that was hot, but not burning hot. Anyway, I marked them in separate bags but when the cook cooked them he mixed them all up, so no one really knew what they were getting. This cook had been stirring trouble for a while, asking people questions only a Harvard scholar would know the answers to, just to make out he might be a little bit brighter than everyone else. The crew put up with it for a while, until sausage night. One young fella, who could fight a bit, just happened to pick a chilli sausage and after one big mouthful promptly spat it out and said, 'Why didn't you tell me they were hot!'

With this the cook said, 'Well, I thought any dickhead would have worked that out!'

That's when the fight started. The ringer jumped through the servery and put the cook on the ground and gave him a proper choking. Among much hilarity, no one went to his aid – they all thought he had it coming. So, the young ringer comes up to my door at 7.30 and says, 'Hannah, I just choked the cook. He needed it so I gave it to him.'

My first response after finding out the cook was okay was to say, 'Thanks a lot, he'll pull out during the night and I'll be doing breakfast.'

The cook did the year out but wasn't quite so forthcoming with his smart comments.

Once, a lady was on her way to start work but the boreman found her broken down on the road. She was ceremoniously towed in the last twenty kilometres with a horse float complete with one very large horse, two dogs and four cats in the car. I should have gone with my gut instinct on that one.

Another lady rocked up, got out of the car half cut with a beer in her hand, and said, 'Thank God for f****** civilisation!' That one never went well either.

There was the relief cook who said she had cooked for a big family, so I thought that for three weeks it would be okay if I just helped her out a bit more. I should have started to worry when she said she was going to cook curry for smoko but was just cutting up the meat at nine o'clock for a nine-thirty smoko. I wasn't feeling too good about this, so I came up to check on the roast she was cooking for tea, just to make sure the veggies were on by six. I couldn't find her in the kitchen, so I opened the oven and the meat nearly galloped out over the top of me. She had just put it in there at six. I found her sitting on a stool in the pantry drinking a beer to calm her nerves, because she said she was worried dinner wouldn't be ready at seven. I quickly ran back to my house and grabbed my roast out of the oven, did some mashed veggies and we fed everyone.

Birthdays are special days and it is nice when the cook makes a cake for the birthday person when family is far away. So, here's to all the cooks who have been great over the years and have made that kitchen a great place to come home to, treating the crew like their own family.

* * *

During the early years on the farm Aussie labour was hard to find, so we have employed lots of foreign backpackers. We have enjoyed having them and I hope they have taken home a little piece of Lorraine in their hearts. One couple used to feed the cattle out at the feedlot. One day Daisy was in the feedout tractor and Jacko was in the loader, getting the weights right on the scales, and then went over to the molasses tanks.

He asked Daisy over the radio, 'Have you turned the pump and the auger on?'

She replied, 'Yes, I have, Jacko.'

Then he said to her, 'And that is why I love you, Daisy.'

All of us girls nearly choked because you would not hear an Aussie guy ever say those three little words, especially on the UHF. He was our hero for the rest of the day.

* * *

As the kids grew up we did a lot of campdrafting, rodeos, horse sports and athletics carnivals. We were able to be part of the Gulf community and made some great friends. During the day, even though we are working, a lot of fun things can happen. We have a social club here at Lorraine and in the afternoon everyone drifts over after work to have a drink and go over the day. Funny events are relived and often a little stretched at times in the retelling, especially stories from the stock camp.

Paddocks are large so we use horses, bikes and helicopters to muster. The choppers bring in the cattle that haven't come to water points, then the bikes and horses hold them until they have settled and can then be moved off quietly.

Things don't always go to plan, but most of our injuries do come from the stock camp. I am always a little apprehensive when someone gets hurt, until you can get out to them or someone brings them in to see exactly how bad they are. We are very thankful for the Flying Doctors; they help us out quite a bit, especially because we have such large staff numbers. Our grader driver had a stroke, we've had a few bad head injuries, convulsing babies, some very near finger amputations, a fair few broken bones and lots of cuts. But we have a very good medical kit and the Flying Doctor can talk you through a lot.

One young lady had an altercation with a horse and a bike. We had to put up a shade in a paddock as we couldn't move her. She was off with the fairies for a while and in a lot of pain, so the RFDS gave me instructions relayed through the UHF radio from a telephone in the office. I gave her a few needles for the pain and as it took three hours for the RFDS to get here; she wasn't in a good way. I was really glad when I heard that plane fly overhead. She made a full recovery, saying the thing that hurt most was where I gave her the needles, which made me laugh.

One of the things I love most about the Gulf is the wet season. We have experienced some great ones and a few fizzers as well. The build-up starts about October, with humidity that has sweat pouring off you. The horses are wet with sweat by seven in the morning just eating grass. The storm clouds build up and you get your hopes up thinking that it's so hot it surely must rain, but then it comes over cool and the clouds blow away and that is it for the day. Maybe tomorrow ... But that scenario can go on for weeks.

We get dry lightning, which I have seen at all times of the day, and with it that horrible feeling when you look up and see smoke twirling up into the hazy sky. Someone will take off in a chopper or plane to go and check on it, then anyone spare heads out with water tankers and machines to try to pull it up. Sometimes fires are let go as the country needs burning, but if it's too early in the season no one is game in case the Wet doesn't deliver. When the storms finally come, the thunder and lightning are magnificent. You hear the thunder rolling in early in the morning, about three or four, as it slowly makes its way closer, until the tin roof signals its arrival.

In April 2006, a massive flood came down the Leichhardt River. Over twenty inches (fifty centimetres) fell in one night. Up river in the harder country near Lake Julius, the Leichhardt broke its banks and continued to rise until it was forty kilometres wide. The water came up and over our banks and started to flow under buildings and through sheds. Vehicles were put up on grids and ramps, but still the water kept coming. It was higher than had ever been recorded at Lorraine, so we were all unsure just what was going to happen. The view from the air showed cattle bunched up on tiny little islands of dirt, clinging to the sides of turkey nests, and some dead caught up in fences and trees. Only the first round-up would tell how many baby calves perished, when the weaners were tallied. The farm was hit very badly with all the paddocks and channels gouged out, with water flowing through the machinery sheds up to the top step on the tractors, and lord only knows how many siphon pipes scattered all over the paddocks. It was heartbreaking to see everyone's hard work destroyed.

The water stayed up for about three weeks and then as it fell all was revealed. Some of our friends upstream and down had water going through their station homesteads and buildings. It flooded again in 2009, but very slowly and the damage was far less.

We have come through some dry years too and destocked, but thankfully the last couple of years have been manageable.

This is just a little insight into our way of life. It does get lonely out here even though I am surrounded by people. I miss my family and the friends I grew up with. I have lived in the Gulf for twenty years now and cannot see myself leaving just yet.

Tracy Johnson-Forshaw

Tracy Johnson-Forshaw is forty-eight and has been married to Ian for twenty-five years. They have three grown-up daughters, Courtney, Belinda and Nicole. Ian is a born-and-bred Gulf man. For over twenty years they have lived in the township of Gregory, approximately 400 kilometres north of Mount Isa and 120 kilometres south of Burketown. Gregory has a population of about twenty, ten houses and a pub, and sits on the Gregory River, a spring-fed, clear-running river all year around.

They ran a successful earthmoving and quarry business in the Gulf until 2017, when they decided to close and try something new.

STATION COOK

Tracy Johnson-Forshaw

WHEN I WAS TWENTY-ONE I TOOK ON THE JOB OF STATION cook at Gregory Downs Station (then Planet Station). This was my introduction to the Gulf, where I lived for a further twenty-five years. Cooking for ten hungry ringers, most of them in either their late teens or early twenties, was an eye-opener. I had never seen blokes eat so much. If they worked around the homestead they had breakfast at 6.00 a.m., morning smoko at 9.30 a.m., lunch at 12.30 p.m., afternoon smoko at 3.30 p.m., and dinner at 7.00 p.m. If they were away all day, breakfast was at 5.00 a.m., and they took sandwiches, cake and fruit with them. I got to have an afternoon nap on these days. Bliss! Besides cooking for the ringers, I made sure the kitchen was always clean and tidy, and I cooked for the manager, his little boy and the governess when they visited, and any truck drivers or contractors working for the station.

Breakfast consisted of cereal, toast, and a cooked breakfast, usually leftovers from the night before – rissoles and gravy, sausages, steak and gravy – and all with eggs. On special occasions we had bacon and eggs. I use to make up four two-litre jugs of powdered milk each night and put them in the fridge to get through breakfast. I was told to put a pinch of salt in each jug, as this made it taste better.

Smoko was cakes and slices. Once I had just pulled out a batch of patty cakes, nine dozen in total, and the ringers came home unexpectedly. They ate the lot in one sitting even before I had time to ice them. So, the Mixmaster was started again and more were made for the next feast. Lunch was always something cooked if they were home. It could be pizzas, spaghetti bolognaise, anything different ... as long as it contained beef.

Dinner too consisted of anything made from beef – Chinese, crumbed steak, corned beef, sausages, rissoles, or roast beef. Main meals were always served with veggies or salad. If I was making chips I washed, peeled and sliced a ten-litre bucket of potatoes to cook. Crumbed steak and chips nights were a big deal. Desserts and custard were always served, and if I ran out of time or was feeling lazy I opened cans of tinned fruit and made up jelly. The four litres of custard were always made with powdered milk and today I still make custard with powdered milk.

I was lucky, as the head stockman's wife, Katy, was a lovely lady who showed me the different cuts of beef. To test me, she arranged the cuts in the cold room and I had to tell her what was what. She also taught me how to make sausages, corned beef and ice cream.

The station had pigs, which sometimes added to the variety of meals I could prepare. When a pig was killed I made apricot pork spare ribs and fried rice, and Katy made her famous beef in black bean sauce. The couple who lived at the outstation, Ethel and Fred, grew a very impressive veggie garden and a lot of our fresh supplies came from there. Everything else came up on the freight truck once a week.

Once a couple of ringers helped me in the kitchen because they were on 'light duties'. I gave them the job of bashing the knuckle (round steak) and crumbing it for me. What a mess! But ninety pieces later they'd got the job done. Those ninety pieces only lasted for dinner that night and breakfast the next morning, with the boys making sandwiches with the leftovers for work.

One time the company managers were turning up for a brief visit. We spruced up the manager's house with new curtains, bedspread and fresh flowers – we thought it looked wonderful. That night I made rissoles and veggies for dinner and was promptly told they thought they would be served barramundi as we did live on the Gregory River! I was then asked if I had allowed for the diabetic lady travelling with them. I hadn't, of course, as it was the first I had heard of it; however, I was able to organise a lovely diabetic meal.

At 3.00 a.m. there was banging on my bedroom door and I flew out of bed thinking I had slept in. Standing there in all their glory were a couple of ringers with a forty-five pound barramundi between them!

Breakfast for the bosses.

Lives

Irene Moreland

Irene Moreland was born in 1950 at Lawn Hill Station near Mount Isa. This piece was transcribed from a recorded conversation.

MY YOUNG LIFE

Irene Moreland

I WAS BORN IRENE DOUGLAS AT LAWN HILL STATION ON
7 August 1950. We grew up there – me, my older brother,
David, and my two sisters – until I was five and my
parents brought us to the Dormitory at Doomadgee. The
missionaries ran the Dormitory. It was a big open shed; it is
burnt down now. It had a tin roof and board floor with tin
windows you pushed out with a stick to hold them open.

There were a lot of girls of all ages, from five to into
their twenties. It was very hard in those days. We had
only one blanket and we slept on the floor. There were no
mattresses. There were two rooms at the end of the shed
where the missionaries slept. There was no electricity, they
had big hanging lamps and no water. We carried the water
from the river.

There was another building where we ate. Breakfast was very early in the morning. We would go to the other building where the food was on long benches. We ate there, then I went to work at the hospital, and when the school bell rang, I went from the hospital to school, then from the school back to the hospital. Some of the older girls worked in the cottages in the community.

It was hard in the Dorm. We had no mother. The missionary, Mrs Roberts (Pearl was her first name), told me when my mother died in Townsville. I was only seven and my sister was five. My mother's sister, my auntie, was like my mother then.

At Christmas we'd have a sports carnival, and get a peg doll about as big as my finger. Other missionaries in other places sent them up. We thought they were great. Can you imagine the kids now if they got a peg doll for Christmas? Oh, and the hard-boiled lollies, I will never forget them. Such a treat at Christmas.

There were orchards in the mission with all sorts of fruits. All our veggies were grown here. There were ducks and turkeys, and the bread was made here too. The other mission rations came in on a boat and the missionaries, Mr Kaye and Mr Knott, went into Burketown in the old Chev to get them from the old wharf in Burketown. They crossed all those rivers, the Nicholson, Little Oakey, Big Oakey, the Gregory. The road was just a track and there were no supplies in the wet season. We couldn't go anywhere. No one could get out.

In 1967 I went to Brisbane. I got picked to go to Kedron Park College because I was the brainiest in our school, but I wasn't accepted into the college. They didn't accept me because of my darker skin, but my brother got in because he had brighter skin, so I went back to Doomadgee and lived with some of the missionaries for a little while until 1968, when I went to work at Talleyrand Station near Longreach. I was eighteen, but most of the girls were sent off to work on stations when they were sixteen. I went on the DC3 plane that flew into Doomadgee, Cloncurry, then Longreach. I worked in the house at Talleyrand, cleaning and washing. In the afternoon I'd collect the eggs and it was my job to get the cows for milking.

In 1969 I came back to Doomadgee again and stayed with my aunty. We lived in a tin house in the village with a kitchen and two rooms, concrete floor and no electricity or water.

In March that year I got married to Joseph Moreland. He was the one chosen for me by my parents. He was Waanyi and Gangalidda. He was twenty-one and I was nineteen. We got married in the school house, which was also the meeting house and church – now they call it the carpenters' shed.

We worked for the government for about two hundred dollars a month. I worked at the bakery and made breads, and at the health clinic with the Blue Nurses. The nurses drove into Doomadgee and in the Wet they came on the

DC3. After that I worked at the council office through the Community Development Employment Project.

I was twenty-two when I had my eldest son, Leon, twenty-four when I had Leanne and twenty-six when I had Ranaldo. I flew out to Mount Isa in the DC3 to have all the children. I have only the two boys now that Sister has passed away.

I was working when those kids were small and Joseph's mother looked after them. Even when they were grown up I was still working. I was still working on 17 September 2008 when Joseph passed.

Now I am sixty-nine. This is where I grew up, this is my home. All my children grew up here and I still go hunting and fishing. I have three grandsons, three granddaughters, one great-grandson and two great-granddaughters.

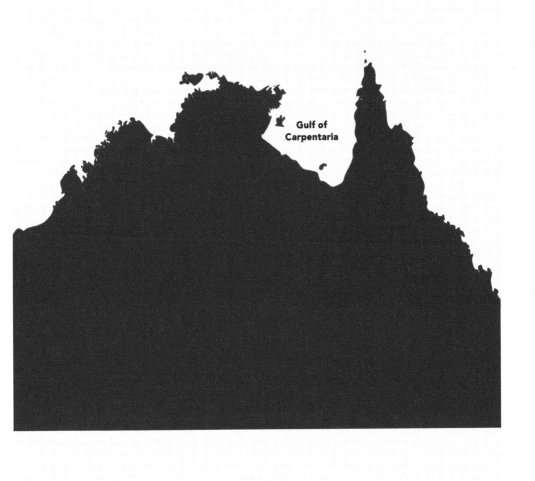
Gulf of
Carpentaria

Aunty April Peter

Aunty April Peter is a Garrawa woman. She was born at Westmoreland Station in 1937. This piece was transcribed from a recorded conversation.

MY LIFE

Aunty April Peter

MY NAME IS APRIL PETER (NÉE NORMAN). I AM A GARRAWA woman. I was born in 1937 at Westmoreland Station, near a swamp, on ti-tree bark. After I was born my mother took me up to the station and the station owners gave me the name 'April'. When I was three years old my parents walked with me to Burketown, 200 kilometres all along the coast until we got there. On the way walking to Burketown my mother died, thirty or forty miles out from there. Mum was buried in Burketown in the 1940s.

Dad cared for me after Mum died. He worked as a wardsman at the hospital. I felt lost without my mother but had Dad to care for me. I grew up in Burketown with Dad until Mr Black, the missionary, picked me up in the old truck and brought me and put me in the Dormitory here in Doomadgee. We older children had the job of carrying water from the river to fill up the missionaries' forty-four gallon drums.

That was where I stayed until I was eighteen years old and got married. After I married Eric Peter we went to Alcala Station near Cloncurry, worked there for two years and after that we came back to Doomadgee. Until another job came up, I worked as a dental assistant in the old hospital, and for Mr and Mrs Hockey doing housework and caring for their four children.

While waiting for another station job to come up, I had my first child, Warren, here in Doomadgee. After his birth we went out to Gleeson Station near Cloncurry, and then worked on various stations for five years. At Granada Station I was pregnant with my second child, Wendy, so came back to Doomadgee to wait for her birth. After she was born I went back to Granada Station to continue work, but left Warren here in the Dormitory. The last two stations we worked at before retiring from station work were Lawn Hill and Escott Station near Burketown.

My husband was a teacher, and I taught culture. I have loved living in the Gulf Country and working around the Gulf. While living here in Doomadgee we had our other children, Lurlyn, Erica and Esla. They were all born and raised in Doomadgee. All my children did their primary schooling here and then went off to boarding school.

In the old days, we shared with other families the bush food. Two or three families would go camping and fishing together on holiday camps. Nearing the wet season we'd get the Morning Glory cloud that brought the rain along. In the Wet, we couldn't get out of Doomadgee because of the monsoon rain. We got so isolated, we'd get our food in on the plane. All the women would get together too and go hunting for goannas, sugarbag, even dragging nets to catch fish ... just the women. We'd walk and get bush tucker for our children. In the wet season also we'd go and gather wallaby grass to make grass bags. That was our hobby while our husbands worked.

It is so harsh living out here in the Gulf Country, but I love it. I am so used to it.

Cass Carruthers

Cass Carruthers was born in Casino, New South Wales in 1949 as Carol Lorraine Mills, but lived all her young life, until seventeen, at Bottle Creek and Jackson Flat, sixteen kilometres out of Tabulam, New South Wales, on a beef cattle and dairy property. After her first marriage ended she moved from Mornington Island to Burketown, where she worked in a variety of jobs. She met her new life partner, Klaus Riffert, while working on a barramundi fishing boat. When Klaus passed away the barramundi fishing licence passed to Cass.

She now lives in Burketown but maintains strong family and friendship connections with Mornington Island.

A MOMENT IN TIME

Cass Carruthers

Mornington Island, Gulf of Carpentaria, 1980s

MY THEN HUSBAND, THREE CHILDREN, DOG, CAT, BIRDS and I arrived in Mornington Island in the early eighties. Before going to Mornington, my husband had been for an interview. While there he met Goobalathaldin (Dick) Roughsey OBE, his wife, Labumore (Elsie) Roughsey, Burrud Black Spider (Lindsey) Roughsey and his wife, Kardarr (Julie) Roughsey.

Labumore and Kardarr are true sisters, and Burrud Black Spider and Goobalathaldin are true brothers. Goobalathaldin sent back with my husband a small painting for me, telling my husband, 'She is our long-lost daughter.'

And so ... on arrival my love affair began with my adopted family, the Roughseys and the extended families.

I was welcomed with open arms by those beautiful elders of the community; their parents had long gone.

Being the deputy shire clerk's wife, I was given the voluntary job of overseeing Meals on Wheels. The staff – one female cook and me – delivered the meals and collected the washing. Through this work I met a lot of women in a very short time. From a very young age these women were shipped in on the sail boat *Morning Star* from the Gulf mainland. The *Morning Star* was owned by the government of the day that ran the church missions.

The island's mayor at the time was Annie Chong. She was also one of the stolen children, taken from the mainland at the age of three. Annie was born at Nudgjaburra, up off the back of Hells Gate on the border of Queensland and the Northern Territory. Hells Gate was notorious. It was the last policed area for settlers or would-be travellers from Queensland going to the Northern Territory. Those who survived to return described it as a journey from hell. 'Don't go through Hells Gate, you will be lost.' Most were apparently never heard of again.

The families referred to Annie Chong's mother as Queen Limerick. One of Annie's sisters was also sent earlier to Mornington Island, others to Palm Island and Aurukun missions. Lots of families were torn apart, broken up and sent every which way, with most of them never finding each other for decades, or ever.

I never pushed families to tell me stories. If they wanted

to, fine, but I think some stories were so damned gut-wrenching that parts would come and the rest just stuck in their throats like a piece of jagged granite so that if they continued, they would shatter.

Work on the island for women was very minimal. The council employed four, the hospital three, the school three, the store three, and the kindergarten one. Fourteen jobs for a population of about one hundred and twenty able, working-aged women. The population on the island at that time was approximately eight hundred and sixty.

The Community Development Employment Project (CDEP) was introduced to the island at that time and included a work-for-the-dole programme for Aboriginal councils. But only men were given the opportunity to work.

The project itself was, in most people's minds, wonderful. It gave workers a sense of worth, as jobs for men weren't plentiful either. Before the project started, gambling schools were huge. If you hunted or fished, you gambled. What else was there to do? There were a handful of amazing artists, authors, wood-carvers and artefact makers, but only a few. The men's projects were road construction, council garage work, a market garden, town clean-up, and a butcher's shop, as there were about three hundred head of cattle on the island. However, shortly after the butchery got going, the Department of Primary Industries came in and shot all the cattle. What a waste! From what I remember, about seventy head of cattle were yarded and tested for brucellosis, but none was found. Environmental damage? I don't think that was ever considered, since the prawn and fish trawlers came in sometimes as close as three hundred metres from shore, running diesel motors that destroyed seagrass and shell-food crustaceans all along the north-west side of the island.

The men were paid once a fortnight and most of them spent it on grog. The men thought it was Christmas, but it didn't put food in hungry bellies. The women and the families got nothing. At this time the women came into their own. They were up in arms and angry. Very angry! Before the CDEP began, when the dole cheques came in the women had more control over the money and bought food and other requirements for their families. One day, seven very pissed-off women approached me. I remember it was around late October and the dry wirlies were constant, picking up and spreading red dust everywhere, black cockies were flying in, the humidity was ranking up ... she was coming. Mango season. A crazy time in the tropics ahead of wet season.

The women asked for my help. 'We want to work for our own money,' they said. 'We don't know how to go about it.'

I suggested they gather more women who wanted to work and then we would ask the council to be heard at the next meeting. Twenty-five women came forward.

Wow! I thought. *Go, girls! Go!*

I wrote the letter, the women all signed it and were given a hearing at the next meeting. The council agreed these women should be given the chance to work also, and asked who they wanted to organise and run the work programme. They put forward my name. I was offered the job of Community Worker with another woman to assist me. We did community-based work, and coordinated the CDEP women's work.

And so, the women on Mornington Island began a wonderful and crazy journey.

By the end of the first week we had three teams. The first was the Cleaning Team, who cleaned old people's homes. The second was the Sewing Team, which set itself up with bolts of material and dyes. The third was the Cooking Team.

Most houses had gas stoves and there were outside cooking areas at every dwelling where most of the meals were prepared. Men played a big part, with around eighty per cent of them cooking on open fires and in walkamaries (firepits). A lot of the old-school women from the mission days cooked, but a lot of the younger women didn't.

Many Aboriginal people have laws about cooking land and sea foods. For instance, you cannot cook sea fish, turtle or dugong in the same fire as land meat, such as wallaby, goanna, wild duck or swamp turtle. If you do that, you or one of your family will become very ill (markirii). It is the same with washing your hands in the sea if you have butter or any land-based oil or fat on you. These laws are followed very strictly – small children are taught this law and many others at a very young age.

When hunters go out into waters or land that belongs to a different family, most of the catch goes to those owners.

For example, if the hunters harpoon a dugong, the hunters only get the head (although this is prized meat). But if the hunters go out and hunt in the sea or land that owns them, then the main harpoon-man gets the head, and the others in the party share the rest with their families.

Many Australian Aboriginal people believe that you cannot own the land and sea, that you are a caretaker only. The land and sea owns you and if you mistreat them, they will punish you, your family and your tribe by taking away your food, so you only take what you can eat for the day or carry with you.

The market garden grew a lot of surplus vegetables, so our aim was learning to cook vegetables and meat on gas and open fires, and to utilise and understand the value of vegetables in the diet. The aged-care hostel had just opened, and this proved to be a great place to learn gas stove cooking and how to blanch and freeze vegetables. On other days we did similar, but open fire cooking: fish, dugong, turtle and wallaby were plentiful.

Setting everything up for the teams took a few weeks, as the barge was on a six-week turnaround (if we were lucky).

And then the transport pain began – men and women on the same vehicle! This didn't go over very well with the community, to say the least. All hell broke loose. You would have to understand Aboriginal law to appreciate the conflict. Until the age of twelve, and before they go through law, boys can sit facing and talking to their mothers and sisters, but once they go through law they must face away, or vice versa. It is the same with conversation, which must be channelled through a cousin brother or a cousin sister. These moral laws are very ingrained within families. Husbands or wives cannot be travelling around on trucks with someone else's husband or wife, and brother and sister cannot sit face to face on the same transport. The laws on morals are very intricate and are not mine to tell. This is just an outline.

Back to the council meeting for us. Believe it or not, we got our own transport! (Well, I guess it helped we had a woman mayor.) The women all rallied together – they were so proud. More women joined us and, in the end, we had sixty-seven women working. Wow! We thought that was fantastic. Fifty-three more than before.

Once a month we met in work hours and all teams were required to attend. Everything was considered – conflicts were sorted and suggestions taken on ways to do things better. We finally ended up with seven teams: the Cooking Team; the Sewing Team, responsible for tie-dying, printing, making skirts, tops and shoulder bags; the Cleaning Team, servicing the elderly in the community, the aged-care hostel and the guest house; plus the four new teams – Hunting, Culture, Childminding and Catering. All team members were rotated every fortnight, except for the sewing supervisor and the three permanent childcare workers.

The Hunting Team: Their aim was to gather bush tucker and to teach younger women the art. Wallaby, rock python and goanna were hunted, dragnet fishing and crabbing taught, and mudshell oysters and a variety of shell crustaceans like mudbud snails were gathered. The food was distributed to the elderly in the community and to the aged-care hostel. The Hunting Team also took groups of the elderly from the community and the hostel for a day out each week. They would hunt, gather, cook and entertain under the huge she-oak trees along the beach. It was very, very popular. At that time very few vehicles were owned by families, so taking the old folk out didn't happen until the hostel got their own ten-seater bus. The old people cried tears of happiness and could hardly wait for their turn again.

The Culture Team: Aged, wise, women Elders and their groups – the Kaiadilt from Bentinck Island and the Lardil from Mornington Island – would go bush for women's business (song, dance, learning culture, reading footprints and reading the water). It took me two years to learn to read the water. Different ripples meant different fish, different shades and light reflections meant different fish again. The women recorded their own videos and had huge amounts of fun. Harvesting bush food – digging water lily and panuja bulbs – was important. These bulbs were wrapped in ti-tree bark and cooked in ashes or eaten raw. They have different but nutty tastes. Also collected were fruits – wild blackberry, wild grape, fig, peach, passionfruit and a soft, white wet-season fruit with lots of minute seeds that was very sweet. And the kids' favourite, the yum-yum fruit of the mistletoe that was like chewing gum. Then there was the honeybag of the native sugarbag bees. This is very precious and usually found in a live tree with a protruding, hollow dead branch that has only one or two tiny holes. Some native bees are as small as a fruit fly, others the size of a small bush fly. They have lovely, sweet, fat little round bottoms and they don't sting! There are signs about finding sugarbags but this little secret is not shared willy-nilly, so I'll leave that there. I was forever in love with my surroundings – so full of goodness.

The Childminding Team: The childminding centre opened. This was a huge achievement as it meant mothers could work and have their children looked after. This team had three permanent women plus the other carers who were either breastfeeding women, women with injuries, or those having social problems at the time. The Hunting Team also provided eighty per cent of their food.

The Catering Team: By this time my husband had been promoted to shire clerk. Every DC3 plane that landed had a different government department coming in, and those people needed accommodation and catering. We also catered for council meetings, sometimes at the drop of hat, and both the guest house and the government housing needed cleaning and linen washed. The Catering Team worked with me and Gloria, my workmate. This was a full-time job, made more difficult because of the six-weekly barge and shortages of meat. We became masters of disguise with our menus.

If a big party of government officials was coming, staying overnight and holding meetings the next day, hunters would be pulled off whatever job they were doing for at least three days before and sent out for meat. Of course, what they got depended on what was available and the breeding seasons. For example, dugongs run in herds. If calves were present (dugongs suckle their young), only one of the bulls was harpooned. Green-back turtles were not harpooned. One or two of the hunters would dive overboard with a rope and wrestle the turtle, rope him, tie him to the boat and head to the nearest suitable landing. The turtle would be hauled into the boat and left upside down until they got home. The live turtle wasn't slaughtered until the walkamarie was ready.

No one other than a handful of people saw the meat before it was cooked. Once the hunters arrived with their catch, refrigeration was of utmost importance if the food wasn't being cooked immediately, so my interactions with the hunters were crucial.

On the first night a welcome corroboree was held, with the traditional food cooked in the walkamarie pits. I was given meat for cooking lunches the next day, which were cooked at my house and taken to the council meeting for a serve-yourself meal.

We served barramundi, whole baked red emperor and coral trout. For mornays, we used rock cod or trevally and queen fish for nammis – raw fish pickled in vinegar, garlic and chillies. Being an avid cook, I brought a lot of herbs, spices and dried fruits with me to the island.

The menu read: roast lamb and vegetables (wallaby); curry or stewed lamb and vegetables (wallaby); roast pork and vegetables (dugong); stir-fried lamb and vegetables with rice (wallaby); stir-fried pork and vegetables (dugong); sweet and sour pork (dugong); sweet and sour lamb (wallaby); a variety of chicken dishes (if chicken was available); fried or grilled fish mornay (plenty of that); crabs laid on; and prawns and bugs dropped off by trawlers.

We were quite often asked for our recipes ... and that was fun. The first reactions were of shock and guests turning a little green, but most took it on as 'Wow! I've actually eaten wild meat!' and couldn't wait to tell their families of this great experience.

And finally, the women also built their own women's shelter with the help of one man who was a bricklayer and builder. They had a great time doing this for themselves. Those women were magnificent.

* * *

My dad Burrud Black Spider and I would sit from time to time and yarn. Dad was a big songman. We sat cross-legged near an outside open fire with wood smoke drifting around us in the slight breeze. Dad would clap his clapsticks and sing to the spirits.

A serene calmness settled around us as if we were floating on the waves of the breeze, lost in time. When Dad stopped singing, I never realised – you'd just sort of be aware of the silence of the moment. I waited until Dad spoke first. He would then tell me a story.

He told me about when he and his siblings were taken from his tribal parents and put into dormitories at the mission on Mornington. His parents came from Sydney Island, a small island adjacent to Mornington on the windward side. They were only allowed to visit the children a couple of times a year. He wasn't allowed to go back to his parents until he was twelve years old – or when the missionaries said he was twelve. He didn't know how old he was, but he said it was 'a long time before the soldiers came'. World War II, I guessed. During these stories, he would clap his clapsticks and sing with the spirits, a cry of guttural sadness, the stolen essence of his Dreamtime.

During one of my sittings with Dad Burrud, he clapped and sang with long, flowing notes. In the silence he placed his thin, frail black hand on my chest and said, 'Spirit say, daughter, your name, Yulma yul.'

Yulma yul means when the Wet is finished and in comes the gentle southern breezes and a time of plenty.

As I absorbed my dad's passing on of the Dreaming spirits through my body, I felt an overwhelming sense of peace, of coming home. This sense I feel many times living with my families.

The dulnul run

EVERY YEAR THE DULNUL RUN BETWEEN SEPTEMBER AND November. This is a fish that to me looks like a leatherjacket, though it is not. They come in the thousands and thousands. All along the northern shore of the channel between Mornington Island and Denham Island, from Dugong River to Cemetery Point, families all had their own places and camped and waited with their dragnets.

There is a lot of law around this fish. All fish guts must be wrapped in ti-tree bark (no other) and buried. You must not break any bones of the fish. Pregnant women were not allowed in the camps, because any fish bones broken meant the baby of the woman closest would die or be deformed in some way. A lot of the dulnul were dried whole in the sun and kept up to six months.

Dragnets – square casting nets about fifteen metres long – caught them. The head, or lead dragger, would put his or her big toe into the toehold at the base of the net, face out to the incoming catch, and drag the net, which was fed by those on the beach, out to its full depth. Once the net is set, a feeder goes to the centre of the net and, like the lead dragger, stays absolutely still until the catch, the dulnul, travelling down the shoreline begin to enter the curve of the net. The lead dragger then curbs the net around, carefully surrounding the fish, while the feeder supports the top of the net, especially if the catch is a big one. The feeder on shore then begins to slowly drag the net to the lead person, and then up the shore with the catch safely enclosed.

* * *

Every now and then, Mum Elsie sent word she wanted to go visiting, meaning she wanted to visit family in the cemetery. The cemetery was situated west of the Gununa township on a flat ridge, back off the point at the end of the channel between Mornington Island and Denham Island. After visiting the families we went and sat under the big tree, just down over the bank. This tree was big and shady, and we brought wood to make a fire, boil a billy for tea and cook ash damper. Mum would sing to her families.

Just off that same point was a dubalan. A dubalan is a road, or track, or path of an ancestral hero. This was the track that Thuwathu, the Rainbow Serpent, travelled on. At dead low tide on a high road of sand that reached out to the sea, a group of men would spread out, most only wearing jocks, a rope around their waist and carrying spears. They had the appearance of moving black sticks. These sticks then hunched down with spears resting between sand and shoulder and waited for the tide to come in. As the tide came and surrounded them, they rose, spears at the ready. So still were they that the only thing moving was the tide. Every little while a spear flew.

I was mesmerised. Was this reality or fantasy? A scene before me of life gone by. Suspended. Beautiful. A surreal moment in time that wasn't meant to last.

Camping

EVERY YEAR, WITH THE WET SEASON FINISHED IN APRIL, the groundwater settled and the so-called winter coming, the month of May was a serene time for camping and hunting. Crabs were full, fish were fat and full of eggs, wallabies were fat, and the wet season wild fruit was still plentiful. Humidity was gone, there were light dews in the morning with fresh sea breezes following during the day. Paradise!

At this time of year, Mummy Elise, Mummy May and I went on camp in Mother's Day week. Mummy May was born on Bentinck Island and was trilingual. Well, I guess most of the families were, speaking the Kayardild language from Bentinck Island, the Lardil languagefrom Mornington Island, and English. Mummy May told me she was brought over to Mornington Island in 1947 in chains. All the Kaiadilt people were herded up and chained together. Mummy May was a teenager at the time. She said there were a lot of very fierce battles between the Lardil and the Kaiadilt people, and the missionaries and the police tried several times, with spears and guns, to capture the Kaiadilt. A lot of people, mainly men, died.

Wurdu Creek, about fifty kilometres from Gununa, was our camp destination and this year it was my second trip to Wurdu in as many weeks. The first trip always involved a challenge between the Wilson brothers, Brother Bruce Chong (Annie Chong's eldest son), and me to see who would make the first track of the season to the top end of the island. The dry season track was still too wet, as most of it was across salt flats and creeks, so we made our own track along the ridge that ran almost down the centre of the island. Brother Bruce and his younger brother, Darren, driving his battered Toyota ute, always had a head start and tried to fox us all the time. With me would be my second son, David … his given tribal name is Bawu, meaning lone pelican. We would try to follow Bruce's tracks in our short-wheelbase Nissan.

The ridge was rugged, graduating from ant bed flats, kerosene and swamp grass, through to cabbage bushes and bujarri trees. Leaving behind the gelbels (plovers), we would make our way through harder ground-cover brush, which climbed up the side of the ridge, to pockets of taller brush, their roots wrapped and strangling jutting sandstone rocks. Finally, on top of the ridge, were taller trees, gunnanu (corktree) – used to make canoes (kinnu) – with ground cover of whistle grass with rice-like edible seeds. Following tracks here was impossible. We would have to stop, get out and search for them. One minute you'd be up on the ridge, the next down in a swamp. There are a lot of swamps on Mornington Island but they have hard bottoms, so no vehicle becomes stuck and they are hard to track. Thank heaven it's not quicksand! However, you do walk it first. So off we would go, but soon Bawu would start laughing and say, 'Mum! This is the second time we have been to this very same spot in the last half-hour.'

'Far out! Bugger Brother Bruce! He's foxed us again!' I'd reply, smiling.

After all, this was the fun of the challenge. So off we'd go again, studying the area around us for hundreds of metres to find where Brother Bruce had snuck off to ... usually across a rocky patch to disguise his tyre track.

While we searched we'd pick native blackberries (kirrirr) and jirdal tree fruit, very like a small peach and purple when ripe. These grow along the sand ridges and were in full fruit at this time of year. With us would be the honeysuckers, with their soft, smooth song, other tiny fruit-eating birds fluttering around, and the little grey shrikethrush that darts among the grass seed heads as you walk. Quails marched in lines across our paths like little soldiers going into battle and the cheeky willy wagtail flitted from bush to bush beside us as we searched for that tyre track. It was on these journeys too, we would randomly sight tiny, mysterious, startlingly sky-blue birds, finches maybe. Mum Elsie said they were called malmal and lived in hollow logs.

We would surprise the sand goanna on his daily stroll and scare the frill-necked lizard into a warning, statuesque stance, spreading out the spectacular frill that surrounded his gaping jaw as if to say, 'Come any closer and you're mine.'

On our approach grazing wallabies would stand up like royalty, glare with indignation at the invasion of their kingdom, then lope off majestically, saying, 'Leave it to the aliens.'

This is why it takes three to four hours to get to Wurdu Creek. But what a challenge! How great was that?

We made camp, lit two fires, then Bawu and I would go to the creek fishing and within half an hour would have two fat silver bream, a nice big grunter and two very big, heavy mud crabs. If the tide was out we'd go for oysters. With the sun low, I'd have damper in the ashes on one fire and whole crab and fish, neither gutted or scaled, cooking in the ashes in the other fire ... enough in case Brother Bruce and Darren arrived, or breakfast if they didn't. They had gone to Balaliya at the north end of Mornington Island, judging by their tyre tracks.

This night, they did return bringing cooked whistle duck and wallaby. We all shared our feast and yarned well into the night, counting the satellites (not a lot in those days), making out the star patterns (Bawu's favourite subject) and watching the trawlers sneaking into the outer reef of the bay for the night ... must be a wind coming up.

Next morning, we headed back to Gununa and home, but the weekend after was when Mummy Elsie and Mummy May and I went back to Wuru Creek for our yearly trek.

For our week away we carried a twenty-litre canteen of water (for emergency only), a tomahawk, axe, shovel and two three-pronged spears. We had plain flour and baking powder for damper, salt, leaf tea, vinegar, lemons, limes, potatoes and sweet potatoes, but no cooking pots or utensils, not even a mixing bowl. All our food was cooked in ashes, except for shucked oysters or mudbud snails off the mangrove roots, which were cooked in milk powder tins with wire handles. For mixing damper I used a garbage bag and sat cross-legged with the bag open across my lap. There were no plates – our plates were branches of leaves and brush arranged so the food lay nicely on them. The half twelve-gallon drum for tea always sat on the side of the fire (called 'ever-ready blackfella tea'), so there was always a cuppa for the hunters and gatherers as they came into camp.

Mangrove root oysters are to die for and were cooked in ashes while they were still clinging on the green mangrove root. Oysters off the rock at Wurdu Creek Bay are black-lips. Just up from Wurdu is White Cliffs – the oysters there are milky oysters and there are acres of them. We carried a flat boulder to camp, placed it in the ashes with the oysters on top, and then slowly turned them as they opened. We used a stick to pull them out and ate them with hot ash damper. Heaven! Absolute heaven!

Mornington Island just ruins you for life – if you move anywhere else the seafood never compares. There is such an abundance of it here.

We would set up night camp on the sand ridges overlooking the mouth of Wurdu Creek and the oyster beds that stretch out into the small bay. Among the oyster beds is an ancient fish and dugong trap, weathered and beaten up by the timeless rushing of tides. Two fires would be going and a brush windbreak cut. It would be quite warm, with a sweet, briny smell in the sea breezes.

Day camp was under a stand of she-oaks at the bottom of the ridge. These only grow around the shore and nowhere else on the island. Mum Elsie sat in the shade of day camp, or lay down for a snooze, as she had leg problems and couldn't walk far. Mummy May would go back up the creek about one hundred metres to the pandanus stand on the side of the ridge to dig out our freshwater spring. Wherever you find pandanus growing on land away from creeks, rivers or waterholes and dig close by them, it is almost guaranteed you will find water. Hundreds of freshwater springs are around the island if you know where to look.

I would go and look for crabs while I waited for Mum May to come and help me dragnet at the mouth of the creek. This net was only small, about seven metres long, and we dragged for baitfish, yulaa (garfish), sandfish (whiting) or river mullet. If you were lucky, on a good tide there would be lovely big prawns. I would then go fishing and Mum May would go for oysters, so within an hour we had enough food for our night's dinner and breakfast as well. We'd dig a hole in the wet sand and bury our fish, and tie up the crab to keep cool for the evening cooking.

Early each morning Mummy May would take her handmade bujarri tree dilly bag and go fruit gathering or panja digging at a swamp about one kilometre back over the ridge, inland from our camp. The bujarri tree (soap wattle)

276

has broad green leaves and thin curly seed pods used to make soap. Birds eat the seed pods, the branches are dragged through the water for poisoning fish, and the bark is used to make string bags. I would go and collect water from our well and enough firewood to use in the day camp and for the night fires, then move Mummy Elsie to the day camp where she would write her stories, published later as the book *An Aboriginal Mother Tells of the Old and the New.*

For lunch we usually ate bush fruit food, damper and tea, then went looking for shells, until by mid-afternoon it was time to catch dinner, cook potatoes in their jackets and damper in the ash beds. We would yarn and tell stories for a couple of hours by the campfire, watching to see if the trawlers would come in close. Mummy May was terrified of them, fearing they would come ashore and murder us. Mummy Elsie would laugh and growl and make fun with her of her fear.

It was on one of these trips Mummy May told me a story of the Kaiadilt people of Bentinck Island, passed down from grandmothers to mothers to daughters, how long, long ago strange beings arrived on Bentinck. Mummy May's English was not very strong, and together with her hand and arm actions it was quite a puzzle – until Mum Elsie made the story clearer by flattening the sand in front of us and asking Mum May to draw her story with a stick in the sand. She explained, 'This is the floating thing with sticks out of its belly and three sticks rising up from its belly. The strange beings had shiny hats, shiny shoulders, a round shiny belly, and a shiny spear.'

The first explorers recorded as going into the Gulf of Carpentaria were on the Dutch ship captained by Willem Janszoon, the *Duyfken*, which sailed part-way down the eastern side in 1606. Janszoon made the first recorded European landing in Australia here, but several of his men were killed and they sailed for home, calling the place Cape Keer-Weer or Turnagain.

The Spaniards, Torres and De Quiros, sailed in separate ships from Peru in 1606. After a murderous and plundering raid on the New Hebrides, the ships were separated by fever, bad weather and a mutiny. De Quiros sailed for Mexico and Torres attempted to reach the Philippine island where Spain had a colony in Manila. Torres sailed through the strait named for him, but made no mention of sailing into the Gulf.

In 1628 another Dutchman, Pieter Carpenter, visited the area, sailing completely around the Gulf. So maybe these aliens who landed from the sea, with the weird hats and the shiny armour, were from Pieter Carpenter's ship.

In the middle of the 1980s, Mornington Island was 'rocking' and the council was prosperous. They ran the 'wet' canteen, with all profits going back into the island's infrastructure. They received grants for helping to build the aged persons units and to buy their own barge, the *Gunagul*, that ran from Mornington to Karumba weekly, so now food and supplies were much fresher and more plentiful.

The wet canteen was strictly run and only open for two hours, Monday to Saturday. Every person over eighteen was allowed a six-pack of unopened beer per day unless they were barred by the police or council for whatever misdemeanour they were charged with. Families sat around on the lawns yarning and laughing and playing cards. Friday afternoons were the best and sometimes the worst when all groups on the island – teachers, nurses, police and visitors – came together. In my experience with Aboriginal people, if they had a grudge or wanted to fight someone they had to have an audience, a big show was needed, so these were carried out at the canteen or the general store. Some of these were very funny, others not so. One learned not to take sides.

There was only one phone, run by the exchange at the council office during office hours, and only one channel on the TV, the ABC, and even that was very hard to see as reception was so bad. When the store manager started bringing in videos, this was welcomed with open arms. With people working, they could now afford video players. But, sadly, with this came porn videos, then soon after the first filtering in of drugs, the first rapes, murder and then the first suicide. We knew this happened on the mainland, but when it happens in a small community it becomes monstrous and that monster had our community reeling.

Stricter laws were put in place by council and police, but it was like shutting the gate after the horse bolted.

Eventually I moved to Burketown, to another group of amazing women. Another life and, of course, another story.

Margaret Henry Chatfield

Margaret Henry Chatfield, artist, belongs to the
Kurtjar People of Cape York and is the eldest of three
children. She has two brothers, Leslie John and Trevor
William. She has lived in Normanton for most of her life,
where she completed her schooling and married. She has
four beautiful children who were educated in Normanton
until the family moved to Cairns to better their education.
Her now grown-up family continue to inspire her to keep
painting, to ensure her mother's and aunt's stories of
their homelands are kept alive and to help others on their
journeys.

THE LIFE OF MY MOTHER AND FATHER

Margaret Henry Chatfield

MY CLAN GROUP IS THAT OF THE KURTJAR PEOPLE WHO are the Traditional Owners of Delta Downs on the west coast of Cape York. My grandmother's name is Jessie Edwards and my grandfather is Bill Buckland, who is of the Kukatja clan. His birthplace was Vena Park. My grandmother's birthplace was Delta Downs Station (now named Morr Morr Station), where she lived all her young life until she was taken away with the family in the early 1900s by the property owners of Lotus Vale Station, to work as a kitchen hand there. My aunt Lilly was born in approximately 1915 at Delta Downs in the homestead that I believe is still there today. My mother, Alma Henry, was born in 1919 near the banks of the Smithburne River, and even though most

Aboriginal women in those days traditionally used hollow logs to give birth, both women were born in comfort.

I want to talk about my mother's and father's lives and will start with my mother, Alma Henry. My mother was two and my aunt was four (just small girls at the time) when they witnessed the drowning of their mother on the banks of the Smithburne River, just below the homestead. My grandmother walked out onto a tree limb, which lay in the river, to pull her line out of the water. She tripped and fell and, unable to swim, became tangled in the weeds that were very thick. She drowned while struggling to get free.

The property owners took care of those two little girls and their lives changed dramatically due to a very strict upbringing. It was a new world for them. They now had a foster brother and two sisters the same age and, unfortunately, apparently they did not go to school. They worked from a very young age, scalping dingoes, killing pigs for their snouts and eagles for their talons. They could fix fences, and kill and cut up a beast when needed.

As time went on they became women in their thirties and remained very dedicated to their foster mother, who still worked the property as an old woman, loving her for caring for them all these years. Her own children moved away much earlier to marry, but those two grown women just stayed by her side no matter what.

Both women knew all there was to know about property life. Those wonderful women could do anything they were asked. Eventually they did marry in their late thirties and then moved to Normanton. They felt very guilty for leaving their foster mother behind, but also felt they needed a life, as it was now or never.

Neither of these wonderful women ever once held any animosity towards their foster parents for the disciplined lifestyle, and only loved them dearly. To the end of their lives, they were the ones at their foster parents' side if they needed help. They did secretly have their Dreaming stories of hunting and gathering with their parents, but didn't dare utter a word to anyone, except to each other and then to us children as we grew older. When we went to school my mother worked at the post office as a cleaner, staying until her retirement.

My father, Leslie Wilson Henry, was a humble, generous and talented man, the youngest of a very large Irish family, having nine sisters and two brothers. He was born in Brookfield, Brisbane. His father was a minister and the family moved to Mount Garnet.

At a very young age my father worked across a variety of fields, commencing work in a tin mine at Mount Garnet – Mount Garnet Tin – then on to Mount Mulligan mine near Chillagoe in north Queensland.

On 19 September 1921, disaster struck at the mine. That day, my father was unable to go to work because of a stomach problem. My dad lost all his friends and workmates who died in the disaster and he lived with that horror for the rest of his life.

Between the ages of seventeen and forty years, it is unknown what was happening in his life. In his forties he declared he was younger than he was to enlist in the army in World War II and served his country in the infantry in Papua New Guinea as a lieutenant. After the war, he stayed with his sister Ollie Weiland to recover from the trauma of the war years. He also developed malaria and throughout his life suffered from the effects of this and from having to take quinine as treatment.

He moved to the Gulf to live and work as a fencing contractor on various properties in the area. He met my mum on Lotus Vale Station. They married in 1952 and started their family of three children, Margaret, Leslie John and Trevor William Henry. Our family then moved to Normanton, where my dad worked for the council on the sanitary truck for the rest of his working life. As a family man, my father was a warm and gentle-natured man, and our life with our parents was full of love.

Life on a family-owned station: Almora

Ann Jones

Ann Jones is May Colless's second daughter. Her lasting affinity with the Gulf grew from her childhood years living on Almora Station near Burketown, with her parents. Ann has a Bachelor of Education with further study in Special Education and Speech Remediation. She has taught from primary to university levels in Queensland and Papua New Guinea, where she and her husband lived with their five daughters for many years. Ann's experiences growing up in the Gulf inspired her to document that way of life during the war years in her book *Put the Billy On* (Glasshouse 2008), which won the IP Picks for the Best Creative Non-Fiction Award in that year. Ann now lives on Bribie Island.

MY MOTHER, MAY COLLESS, ALMORA, 1936–45

Ann Jones

IT WAS HOT AND STEAMY. IT HAD BEEN HOT AND STEAMY
every day throughout the long week since the family left
Sydney. Now the coolness of the night gave some relief as
the T-model Ford edged its way along the ruts in the black
soil towards their destination. May Colless reflected on
the circumstances that brought the family to the Gulf and
sadness overwhelmed her as she remembered their thirteen-
month-old son, Peter, left in the cemetery at Goodooga.
He had drowned in the shallow bore drain that passed the
cottage at Mulga Downs, the sheep property where her
husband, Geoff, was overseer. Coming to the Gulf was a
new beginning for the family, an adventure to help ease
the pain of separation and personal loss. With Geoff and

her two little girls, Marie and Ann, May felt confident of coping with the isolation that this adventure might bring. She hoped so.

As the day faded a large, square building loomed in front. The car came to a halt and a cloud of dust enveloped them. Through the gloom, a light flickered before an approaching figure.

'G'day, Geoff.' This was Fred Muller's greeting as he opened the gate to let the newcomers into the yard. Fred left next morning to go south and Geoff took up his position as manager of Almora, a sheep station on the banks of Running Creek, one hundred kilometres south of Burketown and owned by Synott, Murray and Scholes.

May was the eldest daughter of a family of ten. She was born in Longreach and grew up on her parents' property, Wahroongah, a sheep station on the Barcoo River near Isisford. At twenty-one, May Watt married Geoffrey Colless, a young jackaroo from Ruthven Station, a property adjacent to Wahroongah. She was familiar with the sheep industry and living in the bush, but this environment was very different from the flat, treeless plains of western Queensland.

It was 1936, May was twenty-seven, and her new experiences seemed endless – educating the children, coping with the climatic extremes, finding ways of communicating with the outside world, seeking medical help for her family and others in emergencies, and learning the cultural ways of the Aboriginal people in her employment. Despite these challenges, her new surroundings excited May. The homestead, a Queenslander, overlooked the savannah that grew in the heavy black soil. A natural garden of parkinsonia and mimosa grew on the grasslands and enclosed a cluster of basic corrugated iron and timber structures.

Wide verandahs framed with white posts and decorative balustrades circled the two-storey house. Four bedrooms surrounded a large lounge/dining room, each room separated by VJ walls, with doors leading into the living room where May's piano stood. It had been shipped up with the family's possessions on the *Leisha*. May's oil paintings and the wall vases, typical of the day, decorated the walls. The vases were filled with fire plant, a weed with fiery red bracts growing prolifically around the yard, and colourful cuttings from the spectacular display of bougainvillea covering the archway leading from the front gate.

In the main bedroom, the only furniture was a double bed standing in the centre of the room and a dressing table against one wall. A tester, which supported the mosquito net, was attached to the bedhead. Lace curtains dropped to the floor from windows and hung on doors leading out to the verandah. The furnishing of the other rooms was just as spartan. With double doors opening onto the verandah from each room, the whole house was designed to catch breezes during the long, hot summer.

As was the practice, one of the single bedrooms was designated as the 'guest room' and kept immaculate for guests, such as the wool classer at shearing time, or the visiting minister from whatever religion, passing by on his annual visit to the outstations. The inspector of schools visited once a year to assess the quality of the children's correspondence lessons. He used the guest room, as did the Flying Doctor when the homemade windsock guided the pilot of the little Tiger Moth onto the all-weather airstrip on the ridge in the horse paddock. Serious cases of illness or injury were often brought to Almora to be attended to by the Flying Doctor, as Almora was one of the first stations to be equipped with a pedal transceiver – Alf Traeger's invention that set up aviation medicine in the outback.

On one end of the back verandah a door opened into an area used as a bathroom. At the other end was the office that housed the pedal-generated wireless and the stock and stationery of the property's business. Along the side verandahs, wire stretcher beds, covered with horsehair mattresses and grey flannel blankets, rested against the walls. Above them, mosquito nets hung in folds from nails hammered into the VJs. These beds were favoured in the hot nights of the summer months.

Large hardwood tree trunks formed cylindrical posts and supported the upper level of the building. An enclosure of wire gauze surrounded four of the inner posts and formed the dining room. The dining room floor was concrete, but the surrounding floor was packed hard with ant bed that May covered with discarded hessian bags and hosed to keep solid. Within the room was the long, solid timber dining table with two benches on either side serving as seats. The combination, given tongues, could tell many tales that unfortunately remain within the walls.

A small, square structure, the meat house, stood to the right of the back door. Slabs of dry-salted corned beef hung from large hooks along the beams inside the gauzed upper half of the building and a massive chopping block, created from one of the ancient bloodwood trees in the paddocks, stood independently in the middle. Hordes of ever-hopeful blowflies clung to the gauze on the outside of the walls.

When a killer was brought in to be butchered, most of the meat became corned beef and was hung to dry here because of the lack of refrigeration. The only cool place inside the main house was the Coolgardie safe, a large wooden-framed, box-like construction made of wire mesh, hessian bags, and charcoal with a galvanised iron tray on top. This was filled with water and the bags hung over the side with one of the ends in the tray to soak up the water. The degree of coolness inside the safe depended on the amount of breeze that passed through the hessian.

To the left, in line with the meat house, was the washhouse with two cement tubs, a washboard and an old wind-up gramophone, which wound down frequently as 'Comin' round the mountain' screeched out on wash days. Further away and under the shade of some gum trees, the chooks scratched around in the chookyard. A room inside the enclosure acted as a storeroom for the grain as well as providing protection from snakes for the laying hens' nests.

Out the back a small corrugated-iron room stood alone and aloof from the general activities of the day. This was the lav, with a one-hole wooden seat and a nail hammered into an upright beam that held squares of discarded newspaper.

The stables to the left of the main building were used before the annual race meetings for the station's grass-fed racehorses. Trunks of ironbark supported the roof-only corrugated iron structure. Simone, a beautiful bay filly, was the favourite in the stables and nurtured for her many winnings at the local races.

Sometimes the clean smell of phenol wafted across from the sheep dip in the stockyards, built away from the house and near the shearing shed and the shearers' quarters – both important buildings in the homestead complex. Again, corrugated iron was the predominant material, with ironbark saplings forming the uprights.

Crystal-clear water from Running Creek, pumped up to the water tank by the windmill in the middle of the vegetable garden, was gravity fed for use in the house as well as in the yard. Tropical fruit, citrus, colourful shrubs and the rare beauty of this harsh countryside added to the attractiveness of the old Queenslander. The back garden produced fresh vegetables for most of the year, except in summer when cyclones ravaged the countryside and the monsoon rains turned the black soil into a quagmire, leaving travellers bogged, rivers overflowing, the plains flooding and animals drowning.

In January 1940, a cyclonic disturbance came across from Willis Island and the whole of the Gulf became one big sea of water. When the storm passed, the Flying Doctor Gordon Alberry, in consultation with his pilot, Ken Berry, took a chance against the odds to do his medical rounds and to attend two ill patients in Burketown. Flying in the little Moth was a precarious risk at the best of times, as the only navigational aids they used then were a compass and landmarks – fences, rivers, dirt roads and telegraph lines. They had no radios. The risks in this weather were enormous and, as the floodwaters obliterated the landmarks, the pilot relied on the compass to guide them over the sea of water to Burketown. They never arrived.

When it was realised the plane was missing, a widespread search by air and on foot began. Pilots from all over Queensland took to the air. The twin-engine Dragonfly from the Daly Waters–Cloncurry run, the Qantas Moth from Cloncurry, the Royal Netherlands Indies Airways airliner, passing through Longreach at the time, the twin-engine Dragon Rapide belonging to the Airlines of Australia's service from Cairns to Georgetown, and a flying boat from the Flying Operations for Qantas Empire Airways in Darwin joined in. Land parties, stockmen, managers and black trackers from Burketown, Gregory Downs, Punjab, Almora, Kunkulla and Planet Downs, some on horseback, some on foot, squelched through thick, black mud. They crossed swollen rivers, pulling their saddles on makeshift rafts, swimming with their horses. Snakes slithered past on the surface on the water. Bloated bodies of drowned animals brushed their legs. Submerged logs rammed their raft. They climbed out onto muddy banks to be welcomed by the myriad mosquitoes the monsoons brought to the north each wet season.

These men and horses were heroes, but the real catalyst in the successful outcome of this drama was the pedal wireless. Through a broadcast on the pedal wireless from Camooweal, to May at Almora, the missing men were located on a piece of grassy land in the middle of a swamp on Punjab Station. Geoff, his brother Don (overseer at the time) and the two stockmen rescued the bedraggled pair.

It was usually at this time of the year that May was kept busy as the nurse-of-small-ills. For major illnesses she called the Flying Doctor, but she had a collection of favourite cure-alls for common complaints. Castor oil was number one in the medicine stakes and renowned for curing everything – people seemed to suddenly revive their good health when the castor oil bottle came out. She handed out chlorodyne for dysentery, laudanum for pain and quinine for malaria, all very distasteful concoctions and to be avoided at all costs. She had a homemade mixture of sulphur and syrup for Barcoo rot, plastered antiphlogistine poultices on adults' boils and carbuncles, and hot bread poultices for the infections on the children's legs. Condy's crystals ran a good second to iodine for infections. Sometimes dabbed, other times poured over open wounds, these gave the best response in terms of reaction if not cure, with the victim's hair standing on end and blood-curdling screams emitting from the small fry's mouth, followed by prolonged bawling sessions.

Apart from having to suffer frequent treatments with iodine, the station offered an idyllic lifestyle for the children. They learnt to ride, though not without a few hard tumbles, especially from one of the ponies, a half-Shetland – a small fur-ball whose character belied his appearance. He was a cunning fox that took them unawares and pig-rooted without warning. But his behaviour taught the girls to be good riders, and at an early age they helped with the mustering.

For Marie and Ann, going walkabout with Winnie, Delma, Jacob and their children was always an exciting adventure. They played with nulla nullas, swung bull roarers, threw spears with woomeras and spoke with the children in the tribal language. They ate bush tucker, climbed fig trees for the colourful wild figs that clung to the branches and trunks, searched for conkerberries in the bush, hunted out sugarbag in the hollow trees and ate goanna tail cooked in the coals around the campfire. They shared the Aboriginal people's connection with their land, their oneness and interconnectedness with living things that was so much part of their spirituality and culture. They listened to stories of the Dreaming and their education was enriched.

When it was time for the girls to begin their formal education, their lessons arrived in the dark blue canvas mailbag from the Correspondence School in Brisbane, delivered on time by the mailman each week, except during the wet season when no mailman arrived, no mail came, and no callers visited the station. The roads became impassable and remained that way for up to three months, until the black soil plains ceased to be a quagmire. May found this time of the year very lonely as she had no contact with other white women for months.

The wet season brought other difficulties too, as the heat and humidity attracted swarms of insects. Flies were perennial pests. Fly veils were worn over the hats, but the pests managed to infiltrate even the finest and crawled into the corners of eyes. Infection from this resulted in red, swollen eyes, which often closed completely and caused the victim to be teased about their bung eyes. Mosquitoes and sandflies were the worst worry. At mealtime, cow manure smouldered under the dining table as a deterrent to the hordes of mosquitoes ... and the diners' appetites. On the table the carbide light flickered away, attracting moths, flying ants and beetles. Having the carbide light on the table was always a risk. If too much water entered the inner chamber, it gave out a few impolite belches as a gentle warning that something more serious was about to happen, then detonated, by which time some astute diner had grabbed the tin handle of the container and pitched the exploding light over the verandah rails.

Stores for the station came up from Brisbane to Thursday Island twice a year, in April and November, on the *Wandana*. From there they were transferred to the *Leisha*, then brought out from Burketown to Almora on the lorry. Most of the commodities were sealed in tins but sugar and flour came in bags. Weevils were particularly attracted to the flour, and as soon as the bags were unloaded May dipped them in the creek. The flour crusted on the outside and by the time the weevils bored their way through the crust, most of the flour had been used up for baking the daily loaves of bread and brownies for smoko. Prevention against weevil invasion was a continuing problem and often the ratio became unbalanced when the weevils in the flour became flour in the weevils.

Geoff and May enjoyed having Geoff's father, Henry, up to holiday each year away from the Sydney winter. He too arrived on the *Leisha* and became chief saddler and carpenter, and helped with the odd jobs around the homestead. He built the girls' dolls' prams and the chairs and tables for their mud-pie tea parties from packing and kerosene cases. He was the children's storyteller and teacher, and told many stories about his family, of how in 1874 his father had been in the thick of founding Australia's cultural history, driving a mob from his cattle property in Penrith to South Australia to establish Innamincka Station.

During one of Henry's visits, a pending new addition to the family became the focus of excitement at the station and Henry became 'mother' as May had to travel with the mailman to the hospital in Mount Isa a couple of weeks before she was due to give birth to Michele, to be sure of being at the hospital in plenty of time. It was a difficult journey as the roads were tracks formed by use only, rutted from wheels ploughing through mud in the Wet. They drove through the spectacular gorge country of Lawn Hill, beneath the shadow of the magnificent mesa, between sandstone ranges, past the ancient fossil beds of Riversleigh, delivering familiar blue canvas mailbags to the remote stations. Then it was the return journey for May two weeks later in the same manner, nursing her newborn daughter.

Henry was not the only visitor to the Gulf: the remoteness attracted a rich diversity of individuals ... people who needed to, wanted to, or just happened to live there in the seclusion of isolation – Afghan, Malaysian, Chinese and

Japanese, among others. The effects of the Depression were still being felt in the cities and men of all ages and from all circumstances took to the road looking for work just to survive, carrying only their swag, a billycan and a waterbag. If they called at the station they were offered a day's work in return for a feed and shelter for the night. These swagmen had many interesting yarns to tell and brought the world closer to the people who lived in these isolated areas.

Jenkins, the teamster, worked around the area creating firebreaks along the fence lines, goading his magnificent team of draught horses with his colourful language and his accuracy with the whip. Alice Ah Cup, a descendant of the Chinese migrants who came to North West Queensland for the gold rush in the early 1900s, was the station cook for a while. Alan Cashen – Cashen, as everyone knew him – was the kangaroo shooter. His home was a tent on the bank of a creek wherever the kangaroos were plentiful. Mr Bird in his bowler hat and his black suit stayed for a while and made decorative pot-plant holders from discarded kerosene tins for May. Often an old Afghan peddler clanged past in his horsedrawn van offering trinkets and treasures from the East, enticing the women with silks and luring the kids with chubby little cupid dolls and acrobatic monkeys on sticks. Willie Suki was another station cook and changed the menu from very conservative meals of meat-and-three-vegetables to gourmet Asian delights. Not only was he the cook, but during his time on Almora he provided the kitchen with an ample supply of fresh vegetables, especially Asian greens, from his vegetable garden.

May was also a fine cook. When fresh meat was unavailable, which was most of the time, she created a variety of dishes made from the dry-salted beef: boiled corned beef and cabbage, corned beef fritters, corned beef curries, corned beef shepherd's pie, corned beef rissoles. If sheep were killed, and after fresh chops and a roast leg of mutton were devoured as a welcome change, the menu became corned leg of mutton, curried breast of mutton, or corned breast of mutton served with white sauce.

Fish was seldom served. In the late afternoon when the work day was over, the Aboriginal women often took all the children down to the creek to fish – their tackle, a string tied onto a stick; the hook, a bent pin. Small catfish lured onto the hook were not popular as eating fish, so the catch was of no consequence when it came to changing the meat menu. But every year on Good Friday, to follow the Catholic tradition of not eating meat, the families from the stations gathered at a waterhole on the Gregory for a picnic lunch. Fish was to be on the menu. It was the men's job to light the fire ready for their big catch and amuse the children, while the mothers had time to chat. If the fish weren't biting, the children too noisy, or the stockmen lacked the skills to catch fish, they resorted to throwing a stick of dynamite into the waterhole and the whole surface became a sheet of fish floating belly up. Those who swam retrieved the catch, and there was much banter around the fire about the abilities of stockmen and their fishing skills. For a brief interlude, the struggles for survival in the bush were forgotten.

The Aboriginal people were a happy group and fitted well into life on the station, the women going about their jobs with a shy, quiet acceptance. The men, well respected as stockmen, had an affinity with animals, were excellent horsemen and loved working with them. When the stores for the month came up on the *Leisha*, they received their issue of tea, sugar and flour thankfully, but the night a killer was brought in they sat around the campfire feasting on the fresh beef and rib bones, and singing tribal songs to the beat of the nulla nullas and clapsticks.

To help the women cope with white man's ways, the station ran on routine. Monday was washday, when Winnie and Delma boiled the clothes up in the copper, scrubbed them on the washboard, rinsed them in the tubs in the washhouse, then slung them over the wire line between two trees, propped up with a forked sapling. On Tuesday, the clothes were damped down and rolled up in readiness for ironing with the old Mrs Potts iron heating on the stove. It took the whole day of sweltering effort by Winnie to complete the ironing. At the end of the day, too, the yard was immaculate with zigzag patterns from

Delma's broom, not a leaf visible. Each day of the week was allocated to certain tasks, except Sunday. Sunday was a day off. However, after a butchering there was an occasional change. When the final piece of beef was brined, the fat was rendered down to make kerosene soap in the copper that also boiled the dirt out of the clothes, loosened the feathers to pluck the chooks, and cooked the hams at Christmas time.

There was little change of routine in the kitchen. Every day the bread was baked and every day the meals were cooked, so the only change for the cook was at shearing time. The shearers had their own cook and the success of the shed depended largely on the cook. If the meals were good, the shearers responded by shearing well and quickly. If the cook failed to present plenty of well-cooked meals, the station paid the price with shoddy shearing and lazy performances.

Shearing time was a busy time for everyone. It was also mustering time, so lessons stopped and the children helped with the mustering, drafting, relaying messages to the house and working in the shed, provided they didn't get in the way of anyone, especially the roustabout. That meant they could not go near the shearers or the shearing stands, but were allowed to help the wool classer skirt the wool, stamp down the loose wool in the bins or pull the handle of the wool press. When the entertainment in the shed waned, they played on the bales waiting to be carted by lorry to the Burketown wharf for loading onto the *Leisha.*

One year, one of the stockmen hitched a ride with Cashen on his way to Burketown, with the lorry overloaded with wool bales and with a definite tilt to one side. Cashen arrived in Burketown but the stockman didn't. Cashen decided that only thing to do was to retrace his route and found the stunned stockman sitting in a clump of tussock grass on the side of the track, staring into space. Apparently, he had been thrown from his perch on top of the load when the lorry lurched dangerously when it ran into a creek bed and accelerated to climb the bank.

During the shearing May took on the role of radio operator at the pedal wireless each morning, to hear the early morning medical sessions with the Flying Doctor in Cloncurry. At other times she joined in the galah session, when people who were physically isolated talked to each other over the radio, helping to reduce the isolation and ease the loneliness.

Other changes to the routine occurred when the Burketown and Gregory races were on. Weeks before the events, May searched the mail order catalogues and ordered new clothes and shoes from emporiums in the southern cities. McWhirter's and T. C. Beirne's in Brisbane for new dresses and patent leather shoes for the girls, and Anthony Hordern's in Sydney for the stockmen's outfits – shirts, dungarees, elastic-sided boots, Akubras – and a bolt of material for May to make the Aboriginal women new dresses. These she sewed on the old Singer pedal machine while she taught the children their tables.

On race day there was a general exodus from the station. In Burketown the family stayed in the luxury of Harry Clarke's Hotel, but up at Gregory there was little accommodation so, under the shade of the paperbarks on the sandy creek bed of the Gregory River, tents were pitched among bush-style stables and campfires. Forty-four gallon drums enclosed the makeshift circle track, and away from the main affair hessian walls surrounded four posts and served as the lavs. These structures were used for two purposes – the comfort of the patrons and a shelter for the two-up players. If gusts of wind blew too fiercely and haste dominated care in the construction, those inside could be caught in very uncomfortable circumstances.

Over at the track the ladies stood around chatting, sheltering from the heat in the bower sheds, enjoying the companionship in their best outfits and matching hats, with their high-heeled shoes digging deeply into the bulldust. The men worried about their horses and race colours, and hoped the beer was cool. The bar had its own bower shed and the bookies stood in its shade for the convenience of the punters and drinkers. For three days and three nights nobody got much sleep, with the races by day and dancing at night. There was no dance hall, just a floor laid down in the open, but the protocol of a formal ball was adhered to. The men wore evening wear and the women wore long ball gowns and their glitter, a paradox of fashion and place. The battered piano was dragged out from the storeroom and dumped in the corner, and the adults danced until the early hours.

One year May indulged herself and ordered, through the McWhirter's catalogue, a beautiful pair of satin pyjamas. While everyone was up at the track during the day enjoying themselves, a mob of cattle came through the camps in the river bed, trampling down the tents and devouring anything edible and available, even the ball gowns hanging in the trees. May's new satin pyjamas were among them, and for many years after she laughed through her story about the cattle being responsible for the arrival of Michele nine months later.

In December 1941, disquiet, watchfulness and anxiety replaced the optimism of the Gulf people as Japanese planes suddenly bombed Pearl Harbor. Two days later Australia was at war with Japan; the country faced an enemy on its doorstep and was on high alert; more so the people in the Gulf with knowledge of the enemy activity in Pacific Islands, the bombings of Darwin, Broome and Townsville, and the Navy reports of lights in the Gulf waters. In March 1942, Japan invaded New Guinea and by August the same year the enemy army took control of Kokoda, very near Port Moresby.

With the resurgence of enlistments after Pearl Harbor, few stockmen were left on the stations and military authorities issued orders to the primary producers that it was imperative that managers of rural properties remain in their positions. As compensation for not being able to enlist for overseas service, the men were invited to play a dual role by joining the Voluntary Defence Corp (VOC) to be trained in guerrilla warfare, the use of machine guns (the Bren and Lewis light machine guns and the Thompson submachine gun), and in the demolition of explosives, grenade throwing and rifle drill. They were ordered to be always on stand-by as coastwatchers, to be available to infiltrate the deep mangrove swamps that lined the edge of the Gulf waters.

Geoff enlisted in the 23rd Queensland Regiment in April 1942 and was immediately given the leadership of men from Armraynald, Wernadinga, Inverleigh, Magowra, Maggieville and Delta Downs, stations east of Burketown. Aboriginal stockmen were included in the enlistments to be used as scouts and coastwatchers.

When notice came through that women and children were to be evacuated to safer areas south, May elected to stay with Geoff and offered her service to replace him as a Volunteer Observer in the Air Observers Corps when he was away with the VDC. She used Morse code during broadcasts for long-range radio communications, to cut through any interference. Unidentified planes, presumed to be enemy planes on reconnaissance, often flew overhead and May reported the incidents to the RAAF base in Cloncurry. She would send the Aboriginal women and the children to hide in the undergrowth down in the creek as the homestead, vital as a communication station, was an easy target for destruction.

Not all families left for the south. Two Burketown families, the postmaster's and the shire clerk's, were evacuated out to Almora and remained until the crisis was over. May enjoyed the company of the two young mothers and their children, but the routine for the two Aboriginal women was in tatters. Wash day was no longer on Monday but was an all-day, every-day affair with the old copper. The Mrs Potts iron stood on the stove permanently, the black kettle was continually being refilled and the oven remained always ready for the next batch of bread. Despite the disorder created with so many in the house and the tensions brought on by the threat of war, it was a happy time and there was always much laughter.

Just as May's guests had merged into an extended family, Geoff arrived home from Burketown with two girls, Kath and Violet. They, with ten others, were evacuated from Mornington Island mission on the *Morning Star* in darkness the night before and were to remain on the mainland for the duration. Kath and Violet joined the families at Almora and were given employment – Violet as a cook and Kath as a house girl. In the midst of this turmoil, May went off to the tiny Camooweal hospital with Billy Miller, the mailman, for the birth of Susan. She was then thirty-three years old.

By now the war was very close. Fierce fighting continued on land, sea and air in the Pacific Islands, and word came through from the RAAF that Japanese barges were found hidden in the mangroves around the entrance to the Nassau River. The people in the Gulf felt even more vulnerable to attack as unobserved Japanese infiltration was more than possible in such remote areas. Thousands of American soldiers arrived in the Gulf and were now camouflaged in their tents among the low scrub and bushland. They came with their Colgate toothpaste, PKs, Coca-Cola, coffee, hamburgers and Brylcreem, and brought a new culture to the people's very Australian lives of corned beef, kerosene soap and sweat.

When Geoff and May heard that Almora was to be sold, they decided to leave the station. The girls needed a more prescribed education than the random and informal home-schooling mixed in with the mustering and shearing and whatever else took May's time away from the lessons. Geoff studied for his qualification as a clerk of local government, became an Associate of Accountancy and in April 1943 was appointed to the Burke Shire Council. The whole family moved into the town. The authorities believed it was safe for the mission people evacuated from Mornington to return home, but neither Kath nor Violet wished to return to the mission, so the girls applied for release from the

Aboriginal Protection Act 1869. Violet joined the Irwin family at Riversleigh as a nanny to their two little boys, and Kath moved to Burketown with the Colless family.

May found town life very different from life on the station – she missed the open spaces and deep blue of Running Creek. In their place was a landscape of treeless saltpans, a pub, a cluster of service buildings and water flowing freely from an artesian bore, not through taps to the houses but escaping onto a lake of reeds and bulrushes. Herds of goats, scavengers by nature and necessity, roamed freely in the town and beyond, eating everything within reach and destroying anything that dared to produce a green shoot. But the goats had an important role to play in the Colless household. Cow's milk was no longer available, so the goats were milked – Marie's and Ann's job. Milking them was not a problem once you learnt the art of getting them to let their milk down and preventing them from putting their foot in the bucket, but getting them to come in to be milked was especially difficult if the stinker was around, strutting through the town playing Pied Piper, smelling the place out and leading the nannies out to the saltpans, kilometres away. Often it was dark before the goats were found and the creepiness of the night down beside the river, with crocodiles barking, flying foxes screeching in the mangroves and the wind whistling through the casuarinas trees, frequently resulted in the girls arriving home before the goats.

The second important role for the girls and the goats was to act as a team to get water from the artesian bore. The goats were hitched to a cart loaded with two four-gallon drums which was then hauled down to the bore drain, the drums filled with the hot water from the bore and pulled back up to the house to the family bath, a large, round galvanised tub set in the middle of the bathroom-with-no-water. The bore water was brackish and undrinkable, so the household drinking water came from a steel rainwater tank near the back steps of the house. This water was nearly as unpleasant, tasting strongly of the kerosene that floated on the surface to stop mosquitoes breeding.

During his year as shire clerk, Geoff initiated the harnessing of the bore water and built a public bath close by – a concrete tub sunk in the ground and enclosed by sheets of corrugated iron to form a bathroom. A stream of hot water ran from the borehead to the bathhouse and was harnessed with stones so the temperature of the water as it trickled into the bath was cool enough to be bearable. Neville Shute, in his book *A Town Like Alice*, mentioned this bath and had his heroine, Jean Piaget, lying in a Roman-style public bath. He used Burketown and its bathhouse as a prototype of the place he called Willstown.

Rationing of food and clothing was gazetted the year before the family's arrival in town, but various sources of supplies were still available. The chooks still found something to peck at in the sterile soil, and goats and fish provided a source of protein for the table. It seemed impossible to grow vegetables in the salty soil and sultry climate, but a couple of elderly Chinese men, descendants from the gold rush days, managed to supply the few local people with freshly picked vegetables at most times of the year. They lived down near the bore drain near their joss house and very close to Mr Suter's sanitary depot.

Dry-salted corned meat in a variety of dishes remained on the menu but was alternated with fish. The Shire Office and house stood within thirty metres of the Albert River and barramundi and salmon were there for the catching. While May attended to the household and the babies, and took the role of Matron at the hospital when no one else could fill the gap, the girls were occupied with either school or fishing. On weekends Geoff took them fishing in a little wooden dinghy. Catching bait was a two-girl job, one person on the bank with one end of the net and the other up to her neck in the briny water. Little notice was ever taken of crocodiles in the area, but one night, just as Geoff was about to tie up the boat, he heard a loud splash. He came back to the house looking shocked and announced that dragging the net for bait was to be abandoned from that minute. Very soon after, one of the locals in the pub complained about his best milker going missing and a second added that his dog had gone walkabout. A bar-room meeting was called immediately and a decision made unanimously that the culprit be caught and dealt with. Next day a trap was set, and an eight-metre-long crocodile took the bait. Word soon got around. School was cancelled for the morning, the pub emptied of its inveterates, the store and post office closed temporarily as the whole town gathered to see the giant of the river in a noose, hanging from a Casuarina tree up river with a half-eaten goat in its jaws.

In 1944 Geoff was appointed shire clerk of the Aramac Shire Council and the family drove down to Dobbyn, near Cloncurry, to the railhead with May, Geoff and the two little ones in the cabin and Kath, Marie and Ann sitting high on top of the load in the back of the lorry. It was a sombre farewell to the Gulf, their home for the past nine years, but a farewell not without fanfare. As the lorry ground along the sandy bush tracks of spinifex country, night descended and suddenly a strange glow appeared in the distance. At first, they thought it was an oncoming car but the light began to dance and sway like leaves in a breeze. Then suddenly it rose above the trees and stopped, poised in mid-air as if gazing down on them from the distance. Geoff stopped the engine and turned off the lights. May sat mute, one arm clutching the baby, the other grasping the toddler's leg. Kath's usual brown colour changed to cream, and Marie and Ann dived under the tarp that protected their belongings from dust. The light swooped down towards them again and stopped, hovering a short distance away. An abrupt wind whipped up, dust and grit swirled around the lorry and, with a sudden burst of speed, the light rose high above their heads again and vanished into the darkness.

The whole family sat in silence for a minute, alert to the hoots and screams of the night, waiting for the min min to return. Perhaps ten minutes passed before they moved. Then Geoff started the engine and, still in silence, they continued, thankful to be away from the eerie secrets of the spinifex and from those ghostly manifestations that had given such a flourishing send-off to their life in the Gulf.

Sue Woodall

Sue Woodall, Almora Station, has lived in the Gulf for over thirty years. She was born in the Mallee country of Victoria, and when she was five years old the family moved to a farm near Barraport. Sport played a big part of her young life, with the winters spent going to the footy and playing netball. In summer there was tennis, basketball and swimming, either in the dam at home or in the pool in town. She loved the farm, riding her pony and helping with the sheep. Sue loves reading, collecting books and researching history of her family and the Gulf.

ALWAYS CARRY A TORCH AND A BIG STICK!

Sue Woodall

ANIMALS HAVE ALWAYS PLAYED A BIG PART IN MY LIFE. I grew up with a dad who loved his sheep dogs and was so good with them working them with a whistle. We also had cats, cockatoos, ducks, tortoises, chooks and of course the pet lamb that was fed with a teat on the end of a tomato sauce bottle. My life in the Gulf has been enriched by animals – well, most of the time ...

Dogs can cause pleasure and pain. Tears have been shed when an unexpected death occurs, pride when they've performed well, anger when they have behaved appallingly. Two of my not-so-pleasant dog memories also include pigs.

I was walking early one morning with a couple of dogs. Why is it that dogs love to go walking? These dogs spotted a pig between me and the fence. I wasn't concerned until they decided to chase the pig in my direction. I wasn't quick enough and the pig and I collided, with the dogs in pursuit. As I lay on the ground with blood flowing from my knee the dogs returned, licking my face. What hurt even more was that when I returned home my obvious injury was not even noticed!

A month or so later I walked with more dogs than usual, about five. They spotted a pig, took after it and latched onto its ears. I went over yelling, throwing sticks at the dogs, trying to get them off the squealing pig. They finally did as they were told and what did the pig do? It then chased *me*, its so-called saviour. I ended up behind a sapling, stick in hand, hitting the pig in the snout while we played 'Ring a Ring a Rosie' around the tree. An angry pig clicks its tusks and these tusks were in overdrive. The stick got shorter and I thought I was a goner. The cavalry returned, grabbing hold of the pig again. I executed an escape, running as fast as I could, which wouldn't have looked pretty. I got home in 'a state', but of course all I received from my beloved family was gales of laughter. The dogs were all locked up for the day. I know they saved me in the end, but they got me into the predicament in the first place. I must say, over the years this pig has got bigger with every storytelling and is now a massive boar – the biggest I've ever seen.

There is a hierarchy to our pigs. There is the 'pet' pig, quiet pig and wild pig. We've had our fair share of pet pigs.

Tiny piglets were brought home with 'poor little fellow won't survive, Mum'. There was Blaire. I feel a bit bad about Blaire's name. She was named after a friend who lived next door and I have since apologised to her. Blaire (the pig) was awful. She was a piglet with attitude who wouldn't suck the teat on the bottle, but rather chew it. As a bigger piglet she chased chooks, grabbed them from behind and ate them. I lost three chooks this way. She loved husband John's cherry tomatoes, putting the whole tomato in her mouth with the juice dribbling down her chin. As she got older her attitude became worse. I was feeding the dogs one night and she jumped up and bit me on the arm, looking for her share of dog biscuits. I then chased her, falling over a piece of pipe, which made me even angrier. John reckons he's never seen a more destructive pig. She would go into the shed, find a box and shake it until everything was scattered over the cement floor. Blaire then got a taste for newborn kiddy goats that I'm sure she could smell. Now I don't know what really happened to Blaire, but I did comment that if she killed one more kiddy she'd have to be taken out to the back paddock. Blaire disappeared.

Babe, a big white boar, was probably the most famous, being featured in the Mount Isa newspaper. It was mentioned how Babe wandered up to a contractor pulled over on the side of the road who was answering the call of nature. On seeing Babe, the traveller jumped back into his car. Babe then jumped up, like a dog, with his front trotters on the window. The poor bloke didn't know what to do. Babe had a religious streak. He wandered through the house during Mass one night and never got the blessing he was after. At Easter visitors arrived, bringing hot cross buns, placing the box on the floor. Suddenly, one of the visitors had a look of shock on her face, mouth open and pointing. Babe was heading out the back door carrying a pack of six buns.

Paulie-pig, a big black barrow, is my favourite, but no-one else's ... they all hate him. If Paulie were a person he'd need therapy with all the negativity around him. He will lie down when I scratch his belly and is known to lie at my feet. It probably doesn't help that he gets into daughter Holly and Neil's yard, eating poddy calf food and whatever else he can find. He snuck into Holly's hairdressing van and stole conditioner. Neil chased him but Paulie was too fast, not even dropping the conditioner as he ran. Neil was not happy, and a couple of days later I wanted to comment that Paulie's hair had a lovely shine to it, but figured it was better to keep in the good books with my son-in-law. Paulie has been found with his front trotters in a helicopter and inside many vehicles. He finds a door open and looks for treats. He's stolen fruit and biscuits. He got into daughter Hannah's car and ate all her lollies. The only reason she found him was that his bum was beeping the horn. He did have a fall from grace after Gregory Melbourne Cup day. I brought all the tablecloths home to be washed and Paulie happened to find his way into the house. He managed to shred one cloth to pieces trying to find leftover chicken and champagne. Luckily, I could buy a replacement cloth. One morning daughter Bridget took the dogs for a run and realised Paulie had joined them. She took footage of him running flat out while a big pup looked back wondering why this pig was chasing it. It really is hilarious. Paulie is special.

We had so many dogs over the years I now keep a book, so there are no arguments about their ages and dates of arrival and departure.

There was Fight. Fight had to be seen to be believed. She had a blue eye where a beast kicked her and a deformed ear after a run-in with a wild pig. She used to jump up and her tail wagged so hard it hurt your leg. She went missing over at our outstation, Pandanus, late in the year after jumping off the back of the Toyota. We heard she'd been spotted at our neighbour's cattle yards and we went searching, but to no avail. After a month or so we thought we'd seen the last of dear Fight. On Christmas Day we had a call from the folk at Pandanus saying Fight just walked in, thin and foot sore. To me this was a terrific Christmas story, not about donkeys or shepherds, but an ugly, one-eyed dog who came home on Christmas Day.

Sooky was a dog that didn't live to an old age but caused a fair bit of mirth and anger. Bridget's School of the Air teacher asked her how he got his name and she summed it up with, 'The other dogs only have to look at him and he cries.' One day he pulled a piece of meat off the bench and got such a fright he ran out of the house yelping. But Sooky's call to fame was toilet paper. He'd sneak into the toilet, take the toilet paper out to the lawn and shred it to bits. We noticed after a few episodes he took only the better brands of toilet paper. Sooky had class!

Tango was everyone's favourite. He was a big boof-headed dog whose main mission in life was to greet Warwick, our mailman, when he arrived twice a week. Warwick couldn't understand how Tango knew it was mail day as he often waited at the creek crossing for Warwick's arrival. Tango then ran along the side of the car barking all the way. Warwick would get out and greet Tango with a pat, and I reckon if Tango could talk the conversation would have gone like this.

'G'day, Tango, nice barking today.'

'Thanks, Warwick, you're a bit late.'

'Yeah, the road was a bit wet.'

'I know, mate, I got a couple of mouthfuls of mud.'

As Warwick departed, Tango would chase the vehicle bidding goodbye.

Sally was our tree-jumper. As a big pup Sally started jumping at the African mahogany, trying to grab some leaves. Son Aaron would say, 'Jump tree, Sal', and off she'd go. As the tree got taller it became a difficult task for Sally. In her later years we held a branch down so she could get the high of a mouthful of leaves again.

When Hannah was hitting a ball in a sock under the rain tree Sally would try to grab the ball, making cricket practice difficult. Sally was a very good fielder when front-yard cricket was on the go. She fielded at silly leg but one day was knocked out with a hook shot. Much to Sal's despair, she was tied up during future games.

We got Toby, a dachshund cross, from the pound in Mount Isa and he just loved working in the cattle yards. His moment of notoriety came from a run-in with the law. At 1.00 a.m. John and I were awoken by the phone, never a good omen. I heard half the conversation.

'It's the police, is it ... oh ... okay ... you picked them up on the road ... Oh, okay.'

My thoughts ran riot. It turned out the police had picked up Toby and his mate Benjie (who had gone wallaby chasing) on the road and felt they should be returned home. The police van pulled up in the dark, with the culprits alighting from back. John greeted the criminals and thanked the police for their civic duty.

Nita, our kelpie–dachshund cross, was devoted to John. One day he went on a water run, pulled up at a trough and found Nita with him. He couldn't understand how she got there. He finally worked out she had ridden on the chassis under the tray. From then on, he made sure she was on the back of the Toyota.

There was Nitwit. Holly was about four and came into the house with a yellow substance all over her face. She wouldn't tell us what it was, so we got her to take us to its source. It turned out to be raw egg that Nitwit and Holly were enjoying in the chookyard. Holly later explained Nitwit broke the egg and she helped with the eating.

And Thorpy, who loved water, as does his son Hackett. They were named well. Thorpy was quite an aloof dog, until you gave him a squeaky toy. He was hilarious throwing it in the air, rolling over and running around like a pup. On a trip to town we would all buy a toy just to watch Thorpy have fun.

We had brothers Dumb and Dumber, who I couldn't tell apart. Hannah named Annie, who wasn't fussed on visitors. She wrote a story about Annie for school and it went something like this, 'My dog is Annie. I named her after my Auntie Annie. Annie is vicious.' Auntie Annie was very proud – I think!

Snakes aren't pets, but they certainly make their presence felt. Bridget stood on a three-metre water snake upstairs. Her big brother said, 'You should have seen her move, Dad.'

I sucked up a little children's python in the vacuum cleaner but managed to disconnect the pipes before he joined the fluff and dirt.

Every night a children's python we named Pete curled up on the louvres in the bathroom. He'd be lounging there while we all had a shower, probably looking for a frog for dinner. The two younger daughters were talking. 'I wonder where Pete the python goes every night?'

To which the other replied, 'Well, Mum is always last in the shower and Pete probably gets a shock seeing her naked and takes off.'

Trevor, the tree snake, lived in the besser bricks in the toilet and would pop his head out to say howdy. My mother was visiting and reckoned John was playing a mother-in-law joke on her.

We'd say to her, 'It's only Trevor.'

George finally caught and relocated him.

Snakes don't only make appearances at home. I was at the Gregory racetrack cleaning the toilets when I found one was hard to flush. I took the lid off the cistern and a children's python popped its head out. Not what I expected. A few years later Kerry and I were cleaning the jockeys' toilets when we came across a very big water python. We decided to relocate it and started flicking it out with our brooms. I flicked him out of the toilet, Kerry out the door and so on until we had him in the middle of the saddling enclosure. You have no idea how much effort it takes to flick a seven-foot snake with a broom. A car came into the enclosure, with Kerry and I thinking the driver was going to give us a hand. He then proceeded to run over the poor snake, leaning out the window, saying, 'The only good snake's a dead one.'

We looked at each other and didn't know to say.

I know snakes belong in the environment, but sometimes I wished they behaved themselves.

One night when I was on my own I heard a kiddie goat that I thought might be stuck in the fence crying out. I'd just showered, so headed off in my pyjamas and slippers carrying the trusty yellow Dolphin torch. I found the nanny and little goat down by the creek with a big water python wrapped around the kiddie's front legs. I must have had an adrenaline rush as I stood over the kiddie and bashed the snake with the torch until he let go. I grabbed the sopping wet kiddie and ran up the bank. When I phoned John to tell him, he asked me how big the snake was and I replied, a little sarcastically, 'Oh, I didn't take a tape measure.'

This was not the end of this saga, as a few days later I heard the same kiddie crying out. As it was early afternoon I thought it had lost its mother. I went over to the stables and found an even bigger snake wrapped around its back legs. I used a piece of poly pipe this time and saved the kiddie again. I'd like to report a happy ending where said kiddie gambolled up to me with gratitude in its eyes. NO! Blaire the pig ate the kiddie a week later.

Snakes aren't the only animals to behave badly. Dogs go wallaby chasing when they shouldn't. Tango, who was very tall, was known to pull freshly baked bread off the counter and eat the lot. One of my most distressing dog moments was when I'd purchased twenty new hens. Greg, from the Burketown nursery, brought them over from Cairns and I duly collected them. One of my twenty died in transit with another dying a few days later, but I was still proud of the eighteen left. Not long after delivery I went to give them a feed and found them all dead in the yard. Yes, all eighteen! John's young working dog was in there looking very pleased with himself. I was heartbroken and furious. I decided no dog was going to enjoy the dead chooks and made a big fire and burnt the lot. The chookyard smelt like a barbecued chicken shop. Despite my trauma, a nice surprise followed when Tracy and Annie both bought me replacement chooks for my birthday.

Another case of bad behaviour was when a boof-headed dog visited. I heard a commotion and ran towards the creek (not easy after eighty millimetres of rain), yelling at the same time. I found the dog and a goat in the creek, with the dog attached to the goat's ear. Before I knew it, I was in the water swimming after the goat/dog, yelling. I finally got close enough to grab the goat and hold onto it while abusing the dog, who had a very puzzled look on his face. I got the goat back closer to the bank with a couple of pandanus prickles sticking into me and found John, Neil and Luke looking down, trying very hard not to laugh. Goat saved, John helped me out of the creek and said dog was returned to its owner.

Not long after this episode I heard, 'MUUUUM ...' to which I replied, 'What do you want?'

John came through the door laughing, as I'd answered the goat!

Poddy calves play a big part of our day-to-day lives. Little calves are brought in after losing their mum or being attacked by dingoes or eagles. It was always the children's job, with reward being ownership of the poddy. When the children all left home it became my job, and I loathed it. I have many friends who I know have never uttered a swear word. I challenge them to come here and feed poddy calves for a week – I'm sure a profanity will sneak from their lips. Poddy calves have no manners. They take great delight in standing on your foot with their sharp little hooves. They aren't happy to just stand: they then twist said hoof. They brush past you with their poopy bums and tails. And for me the worst behaviour is that while you aren't looking they sneak up behind you and suck/lick your leg. It's disgusting. Some poddy calves just won't drink. You sweet-talk them, you get angry with them, you force milk down their throats but, no, they never drink. These calves often survive, and the one that has drunk from day one dies after three months for no apparent reason. Don't they know the price of calf milk?

Horses are an ever-present part of our lives, but one animal I have little to do with. The last time I went riding I was thrown and ended up with concussion. That was nearly thirty years ago. I do seem to get the job of bathing wounds when the horses are injured, though. And on one occasion, I became the undertaker. Of course, this was when everyone was away.

I went out to start a pump and noticed an old horse, Mule, standing in the cattle yards. I went to investigate and found his mate of many years, a mare, Tara, dead.

I removed poor Tara and as I did so Mule trotted along with the vehicle, whinnying. So there were Mule and me, tears in our eyes, taking Tara to her resting place.

Not all animals are pets. Green frogs are the bane of my life. Why, when there's a tropical creek at the back of the house, do they live in my toilet? I have three gripes with this: 1. They get under the rim of the toilet, which won't allow the water to flush. 2. Sometimes they decide to jump on one's bottom while one is sitting on the toilet. Not something you really want to happen to visitors. 3. Why do they poo everywhere when there's a perfectly good toilet? I will not kill a green frog so I therefore must relocate them.

One day I asked Neil to do a 'frog run'. He headed off in the Toyota and was going to drop them off at the creek as far away as possible. He returned not terribly impressed. The bag I had them in came undone and in the tray of the Toyota there were many frogs of different sizes hitching a ride.

Yes, I don't like wrestling goats from snakes or doing a few rounds with a wild pig, but on the whole who'd miss all the fun?

Three stories from Bowthorn Station

Kerry McGinnis

Kerry McGinnis was born in Adelaide in 1945, the eldest daughter in a family of five. Her mother died when she was six and when she was twelve her father, who had been a drover and stockworker before his army service, took them back to the bush. They spent a few years in the Northern Territory travelling the stock routes and running brumbies while their father took jobs breaking in horses or pumping on different stations. When she was fifteen they began work as contract musterers, and then drovers, along the border country and in the Gulf.

They purchased the unimproved Yeldham Station, put down the first bores and introduced fencing and stock to the country. Four years later they bought Bowthorn, where Kerry spent the next thirty-six years until heart surgery made it impossible for her to live so far from regular medical assistance. Kerry wrote two autobiographies while at Bowthorn and six novels, all set in the bush, from her current hometown of Bundaberg.

WRITER

Kerry McGinnis

Water

WATER IS THE LIFEBLOOD OF THE LAND AND BOWTHORN
Station, between Lawn Hill Nat Park and the NT border,
in the late sixties had an amplitude of the stuff, with any
god's quantity of it in its many creeks, and the huge gorge-
holes in the Nicholson River. There were old boreholes
sunk by mining companies in the previous decades and
left to trickle like artificial springs, as well as real springs
dotted throughout the ranges and natural dams in the large
swamp areas that held water for the better part of the year.
But the worst waterhole on the place, with the least depth
and the shortest lifespan, was the one in Accident Creek,
where the previous owner had chosen to erect the shed that
was our base camp.

The reason was simple enough. It was where the road into the property ended, just three miles inside the eastern boundary. Jim Boyd was a townsman, an ex-publican, and I daresay the water looked permanent enough at the start of the season, sparkling in the sunlight and brimming with lilies, but it's the opposite end of the year that counts, and that's when you should be checking before you build. The shed was no grand design, because the builders left halfway through the job. It stood on the bank of the creek, a large windowless, ceiling-less, unlined structure with a rough-cast concrete floor, partitioned at one end and with a verandah down either side. No generator, of course, and plumbing was do-it-yourself, using a couple of four-gallon buckets with which to haul water direct from the creek.

It was laborious, but life in a camp is, and at least the water was good. We'd bucketed worse from bores where soda created a white scum in the tea-billy, or the chemical content made the water too hard for soap to lather up. Eventually we rigged a little petrol motor on the creek bank and pumped water into four interconnected forty-four gallon drums mounted on a stand at roof height, with a pipe leading down into what served as the kitchen. The pipe didn't quite reach the sink, but it was still better than carrying water. A bathroom, thrown together from timber left lying around when the builders quit, was also hooked up to the supply, and we counted ourselves almost civilised.

So much so, I decided – as the one who spent most time at the shed – to start a garden.

This proved to be a mistake. The initial idea was to grow a few veggies – we lived on tinned and dried ones, so the fresh variety would be healthier and more economical. After all, a couple of pumpkin vines and a few beans wouldn't take much water. Only it didn't stop there, of course. A bit of lawn would lay the dust and if I was watering that much we may as well have a shade tree or two. I picked up a couple of poinciana pods at Doomadgee, and was offered cuttings from the gardens. My sister hauled home ferns gathered from the springs in the hills, and the boys hooked up a standpipe that worked straight off the pump. We already had a K-wire fence around the place and a bit of judicious patching kept the chooks out.

Then summer arrived and daily the water level sank back until the foot valve lay exposed. We dug a soak and kept deepening it, until the lift was beyond the capacity of the pump. The veggies were finished by then, and without its daily wetting the lawn gradually dwindled. When we started carting water there were only the potted ferns and a few young trees still in their tins left to worry about. It was just a poor year, we told ourselves. After all, we'd dry-bogged the trailer getting here, back in March. We were wrong. Year by year the hole silted up and, short of using a bulldozer to dig a deeper hole, there was little we could do about it.

From then on water problems dogged our summers. Early storms that filled the hole, even if they didn't run the creek, were a blessing. We rigged a cable across the hole and suspended a couple of sturdy posts from the cable to act as stirrers to keep the sand moving. We built a Chinaman's dam upstream, hoping the resultant surge and dump of the inflow in a big run would scour the hole, but the seasons turned against us. Storms were light and infrequent. Nineteen inches fell one summer, sixteen the next. We tried drilling a bore, but our rig was of the percussion, not the rotary, type with the diamond drill head that was needed to get through what the geologists termed the 'Constance capstone layer'. This was a band of stone, up to thirty feet in depth, they told us, spread out like an apron across the country from the roots of the Constance Range on Lawn Hill.

The maddening part was that by then we knew of a dozen different sites on the property where water was in endless supply. Only there was no road to them, they lacked a horse paddock, and we had already started replacing the tumbledown stockyards at Accident Creek. So we soldiered on, fighting nature (never a good idea). By now, ours was the toughest couch grass in Queensland. You could have sown it in the Negev Desert and it would have flourished. The trunks of the poincianas grew ridges to mark the driest summers, interspersed with smooth sections that denoted plentiful storms, and I discovered (there's an upside to everything) that bougainvillea like being dry.

And then there were the petrol engines – small, colicky, stinking things, forever choking on their own carbon. Noisy, hard to start, and with fuel tanks far too small for the job. We wore out several of them. They were balanced on a rising bank, judiciously staked about with steel pegs to prevent them shaking themselves loose or dislodging the belt or rupturing the seal on the intake or outlet pipes ... Nothing good could be said about them. I grew adept at fuelling, bleeding and priming them, and periodically whipping off their heads to decarbonise their innards. Starting the pump was the first task each morning, and the endless bother of keeping the tank full (we had progressed by this time from the linked forty-fours to a proper overhead job with a large capacity) was like a weight oppressing one's day.

In the middle of one season when the stock camp happened to be home, I trod the familiar path to the pump at midday with my usual flagon of fuel and was brought up short by the sight of a large Blucher boot, new looking, complete with insole and laces, lying on its side next to the engine. It had not been there that morning. I mean, I couldn't have missed it. Had it been there, I couldn't have avoided stepping on it.

Where it came from and how it got there was a complete mystery. We dubbed it 'The Boot' and conjectured endlessly about its origin. There hadn't been a visitor for months. There were no tracks to explain it. We kept cattle dogs – nobody could've snuck along the creek without an unholy racket ensuing, and if they had, why would they leave a single boot behind? It was no country for barefoot rambles. It wasn't a rider's boot – more the sort of thing a fencer might wear. The only possible explanation we could find was that it must have been dropped from a plane – jets regularly passed above us, en route to Singapore somebody told us, but you couldn't open a window on a jet and toss something out. Our own travels were very firmly of the *terra* sort, but even we knew that! Which left the alternative of a small plane, but that just brought us back to the question – why? Why would anybody chuck away a perfectly good boot?

What can't be explained must be accepted. The season fled by until summer was once more sucking life and energy from the land. The bauhinias shed their leaves, the spear grass whitened, the bulldust on the roads deepened, and day by day the water in the creek receded. When what had been one long expanse was broken into a chain of pools I went down into the creek bed with a shovel to see which of them I could link by a channel to the shrinking water supply about the foot valve. And there, half sunk in the silt but with laces and insole intact, I found the mate to 'The Boot'.

Pioneering life demands immense practicality, there's not much room in it for mysteries, so the 'Boot II' went into a drawer marked *Peculiar* and life continued, all the way to the mid eighties when the mining companies were once again investigating the western Gulf Country. They came in waves, seeking diamonds, oil and the ubiquitous *base metals*. These were more sophisticated outfits than those that smashed their way into the ranges back in the fifties. They dashed around in their four-wheel drives, with their satellite phones and rotary drill rigs, punching holes down everywhere. And as they were practically on-site, and willing to give us an afternoon of their time in recompense for work we'd done for them, we finally got our bore.

It was good water and shallow – between thirty and forty metres – and less than half a kilometre from the house. We tested the supply by pumping into an enlarged gilgai hole at the side of the track that was cut to allow the rig to reach the site, and watched bemused as twenty or so tiny fish, half the length of a little finger, came out with the first splendid gush of liquid. From pitch darkness forty metres down? And looking indistinguishable from the ordinary fry in Accident Creek – how did that work?

Just another item to store in the *Peculiar* drawer.

Where the wild things were

WHEN I WAS QUITE YOUNG – I HAD STARTED SCHOOL and it was before my mother died, so I must have been about five – our home was a rented farmhouse outside Peterborough, a rural town in South Australia. It was cropping country. I remember paddocks of wheat and a busy fowl-yard with chooks, geese and turkeys. There was a gobbler that terrified my sister, there were big dark outbuildings full of old machines we clambered over, scarlet poppies in the wheat paddock, and somewhere a den of foxes. I never saw the foxes, but we spent a lot of time, my siblings and me, looking for them. There was also a dam and an almond tree that grew behind it, which I remember very clearly as it was there, under the tree, where I accidentally split my eldest brother's head with a tomahawk. The blood terrified me. He screamed and fled for home. I screamed and hid, and Authority, which is to say my parents, never believed my tearful explanation (when I was finally found) that I was trying to chop a green almond off a branch and his head got in the way.

Anyway, the farm had no shortage of cats. Not cuddly indoor pets, but lean, half-wild creatures that lived in the barn, feasting off the mice and rabbit kits, of which there were plenty. This was 1950, pre-myxomatosis days, and rabbits were everywhere, despite all the fur hats the population wore and the rabbit pies they ate. They bred as if they meant to eat themselves off the continent. Every farm had its share of traps and all boys as young as ten knew how to use them.

Occasionally, the traps caught things other than rabbits and one of them was a big tabby tom that hung around the farmhouse we rented. Animals caught in traps will, if they can reach it, chew through their own leg to free themselves and this tom had done just that. Perhaps it was that knowledge, as much as his truncated limb, that so terrified me. Maybe I was just an oversensitive child, or had too busy an imagination. The thought of gnawing one's own flesh was so abhorrent that I would do anything to avoid seeing the big tabby, right up to the day we left the farm and moved away.

Now we jump ahead in time by twenty-odd years to the Gulf Country and the seventies, when my family and I battled on Bowthorn through the worst years the beef industry had known since the days of the Great Depression. Cattle prices were at rock bottom and unlikely to improve for years. Our country was undeveloped, without fences, and most of the herd were scrubbers. The ranges were rife with dingoes, brumbies abounded in their thousands – a hired shooter claimed to have shot four thousand off the neighbouring property of Lawn Hill, but you couldn't tell the difference. We had no roads, no mail service, no airstrip and we worked the country with a packhorse plant, spending up to nine months a year in the saddle.

It was as close to a pioneering life as one could live in the latter years of the twentieth century, with all the disadvantages and drudgery of a (largely) pre-mechanical existence and absolutely none of the misty veils of romance with which history endows the past. The 'good old days' were, in retrospect, merely those when one was young and limber enough that forty miles in the saddle, a bath from a bucket, and a night's sleep on the hard earth weren't an impossible ask of one's body. A hot shower, a decent mattress and a roof when it rained would also have been acceptable, but for us in the seventies that still lay quite a distance in the future.

Places you can only reach on horseback are a naturalist's paradise. Take the areas where easy human access is out of the equation and nature multiplies her children like rabbits on steroids. Every waterhole was brimful of fish back then, their surfaces alive with ducks and magpie geese; fish eagles and wedgetails shared the skies, the barra were enormous and Johnson River crocodiles inhabited the sandbanks and the low, parallel paperbark branches fringeing the river. Larger salties lurked in the depths. Brumbies were a problem, pigs were a pest and the dingoes dominated the nights, their mournful howling ringing from range to range as pack answered pack across the valley. We hadn't brought goats to Bowthorn – those indispensable friends of the battler – because of the dogs.

'Bad enough we've got 'em,' my father said. 'We're not feeding the bastards as well.'

Of course, they ate anyway. The pro-dingo push never tires of telling the world the wild dogs of the bush prefer native game. According to them, dingoes like catching frogs and digging out lizards, and they relish echidna and kangaroo, even if it does take two or three dogs to run one down.

But I never saw a dingo trotting high-mindedly past a calf, weaner or, come to that, a goat. Why would they?

Far easier to collar any of them, with plenty of protein to reward them for the effort, than a high-flying roo. Tennyson thoroughly understood what Sir David Attenborough is always showing us. Nature is ruthless; not Wordsworth's kindly dame with flowers and a delightful frolicking lamb or two in her lap, but her poetic brother's fanged beast, 'red in tooth and claw'. And if the pickings are easy, dingoes go on a killing spree – not because they need the meat, it's just that's the way they're made. It's why they're the top predators on our continent.

The 1970s were also before the 1080 nerve poison program began, when traps and strychnine were used to control dingoes. We had half-a-dozen traps in our gear and, accordingly, when the wild dogs were literally prowling around the fowl house, I took two traps out to the site of our latest killer, some half-mile from the shed we currently inhabited, and set them next to the carcass. Dingoes are cunning and not easily caught. I pre-thought my moves, keeping the traps (and thus my scent at the scene) to a minimum. I buried the traps and spread old sun-bleached newspaper over their jaws, then covered the hole lightly with sand, a sprinkling of dead leaves and old grass stalks. I buried the chains and the wires they led to, which I secured to handy saplings (dogs will drag away a loose trap). Then I got a spadeful of stinking offal that the crows had spread about and layered it over my tracks, feeling hopeful of a good result. The country had not previously been worked over, so the dogs should be ignorant of human wiles. That night I sought my stretcher in hopeful spirits and rose with the dawn to go check what was caught.

It turned out to be a wildcat. Approaching on foot with the little .22 rifle I used to deal with snakes and chicken hawks, I glimpsed a shadowy something blur through the air by the front leg of the carcass and heard a snarling cry. Too small and dark for a dog, I presumed, wrongly, that it was a crow. Damn! Freeing it would overlay everything with my scent. I thought I might as well just pull the traps and reset them somewhere else. Then the creature moved again, growling on a menacing note, and I stared in horror into the face of my childhood nightmare – a spitting mask with flattened ears and a front leg dangling from below its shoulder in the cruel jaws of the trap.

Dingo traps are strong. I had to stand on the springs to open them, my arm muscles alone insufficient for the task. Touch the plate of a set traps and it jumps upwards as it snaps shut so even the quickest reflexes can't save whatever triggers it. The force of its closure, I saw, had all but severed the tom's leg but there was no way I could release it without its co-operation – and that wasn't going to happen. It was wrenching at its bloody limb, snarling, its body a blur of motion as I, in a mixture of pity, horror and gibbering fright, worked the .22's breech to bring a bullet into the chamber, whipped the rifle to my shoulder and fired.

Accidents occur like bolts from the blue and haste is not the same thing as speed. The concussion of the fiery blow to my face momentarily convinced me that, somehow, I had managed to shoot myself, though logic stated this was impossible. I had certainly missed the cat – it gave a demonic howl and fled, leaving its leg behind, while, shocked and blinded, I staggered backwards and my right boot went straight into the second trap. Realisation hit half-a-second later and I didn't know whether to howl or shoot myself for real. Fortunately, perhaps, I'd already dropped the rifle to clutch my burning eyes. I took a second to be grateful I wore riding boots and used my father's favourite oath, *'Jesus, Mary and Joseph!'*

The jaws had caught me across the toes. It was, I thought hysterically, like something out of an Irish comedy – the bomber bombed, the burglar robbed. The pressure on my foot was painful but not acute so I probably hadn't broken anything, even though I was as securely caught as the cat. Through tearing lenses I examined the rifle and worked out the breech was not fully closed when I pulled the trigger. The cap of the cartridge had split so gunpowder blew back into my face when the bullet exited the barrel. I could see, in a fashion, though my eyes hurt worse than my foot, but freeing myself was where it got serious.

I was quite alone. The rest of the mob were out mustering and we were not in daily contact. There's no point in carrying a radio in a pack camp. Bowthorn was on a dead-end road so rough you *really* had to want to get there to even attempt it, and very few people did. Nobody would miss me for two or three weeks, so if I was to get out of this mess I needed to do it myself. There was no use attempting to: a) undo the wire about the tree, because it was Number 8, plus I'd used the fencing pliers to secure it, or b) uproot, break off, or generally remove the sapling. It was coolabah, thicker than my wrist, and trying would be a waste of energy. Which meant I had to open the jaws that held me.

I couldn't do it standing, as the trap was no longer flat. It was too awkward kneeling and half my weight was insufficient for the task anyway. Hands and arms proved too weak, while swearing got one all hot and bothered and achieved nothing. Red ants from the carcass swarmed over my hands and legs, their bites like hot pincers, and the smell was anything but pleasant. I blamed the cat, while remembering all the apocryphal bush tales about those who died in freak accidents that seemed so silly in retrospect. How would this one rate? Just after the nitwit who dropped the bucket down the well *before* the rope was secured, his whole party perishing as a result?

In the end, I remembered my brother saying you could do a lot of things with a lever. He was a master of make-do, so I did, using the severed front leg of the killer wedged beneath the skeletonised hind-quarters to act as a fulcrum for the limb, which I fitted across the spring on one side of the trap. With all my weight balanced on the heavy foreleg

I managed to gain enough leeway in the jaws to wriggle my toes free. My foot was swollen inside the torn boot, but I could still walk, so I did, carrying the rifle and stinking to high heaven of putrid three-day-old meat.

Dirty, in pain and half-blind, I staggered home. The tale was too unbelievable to tell, had there been anyone to hear it, and it wasn't my finest hour anyway. But I have never since been guilty of carelessness with firearms or, come to think of it, grown terribly fond of cats.

Monsoon

THE START OF THE MONSOON ACROSS THE GULF EACH year is an eagerly awaited and frequently prayed-for event. The whole country seems to cry out for surcease from the blistering heat, the bushfires created by the wild dry storms of October, and the daily sight of weakening stock forced to forage ever further from water. In lucky years the storms can start in November, the dry, heat-crazed air replaced by a humidity that wrings sweat from the body even as it conjures the great mass of moisture-bearing cumulus cloud.

November storms are noisy affairs, with lightning, thunder, and a gallop of rain on tin roofs akin to the sound of a thousand bullocks rushing off camp. The air cools dramatically, dust-laden flats become sheeted with water and rivulets tumble and pour into creeks, turning drying holes into muddy cauldrons awash with foam, sticks, old bones – anything that force can move. Then the clouds clear, the sun burns back as fierce as ever and within a week there are green shoots across the land, and limpid waterholes smiling amid the trees. Which is all very nice but it's only a local storm, maybe a paddock or two, while twenty kilometres in the opposite direction it is still as dry as chips.

Get enough storms and the country becomes patchworked with green. Some creeks run, some bits of the road are wet enough to bog the careless traveller, and every day has the exciting feel of an imminent Wet about to break. If the storms continue through December, the stock are granted a good start to the season. Flesh begins to pad bony ribs, starey coats soften, and the weaker cattle are in a better condition to withstand boggy conditions and the hordes of biting insects that will make the succeeding months so difficult for them. And it will stand them in good stead, should the need arise, to fight their way out of rising water, or to survive flash floods.

Very often, as if taking a break from its labours, January produces little more than showers. Providing the early storms have come, this has the advantage of allowing the stock to strengthen in the lull, for the monsoon hasn't yet begun. All that has gone before are the outriders of the army, as it were, that every Gulfite is hoping is near. That's when road travel ceases. Of course, there are no certainties and one should never say as my brother did, in response to the problem of getting out and back home again in the new year, 'What are you worrying about? It never rains in January.'

December was when we made our final trip to town to stock up with rations and everything else the station would need to see it through the Wet. Getting home from the Isa that year proved difficult. We wound up leaving the truck with six tonnes on it (including fuel supplies for six months) in Camooweal and daring a wet road alone in the Toyota. We spent one night camped in the cab of our vehicle, listening to the rain peckle the roof, and the next in a bog halfway through Lawn Hill, but eventually made it home, intending to return for the truck when the roads dried out. Which was bound to happen because it never rains in January, right? Most of the Christmas supplies were on the truck, but even worse was that we were low on fowl feed. I rationed the wheat to make it last and eventually Judith and David set off for Camooweal on New Year's Day of 1974. And within twenty-four hours the monsoon arrived.

I sat alone at the wireless, listening to the chatter as stations called each other. Four inches had fallen at Herbert Vale and the Gregory was running eight feet over the bridge. The Leichhardt River was twenty feet above the crossing at Nardoo, and rising. And after that it just kept raining. As fast as a creek or river dropped, the headwaters rose again with two, four, five inches of rain, all of which had to find its way downstream, swelling crossings and covering the odd causeway and bridge as it did so. Wireless conditions were terrible (these were before single-sideband days) and static ruled the airwaves. For a couple of days my siblings vanished from human sight – they had left Camooweal, been seen at the Gregory, had dinner at Yeldham, then no more was heard of them. Riversleigh's manager sent a light plane on a recce and found them in the hut at Crocodile Yards on Lawn Hill, having abandoned the truck in a shed at the station. From there they battled their way back in the Toyota to Yeldham, where they were stuck for a month.

January or not, it rained and rained. A tropical low was parked above the Gulf and showed no inclination to move. At home, Accident Creek rose and flooded its banks and fell, then rose again. Apart from the night paddock and a strip a few hundred yards in width paralleling the creek bank, the water stretched across the horse paddock to the base of the hills. Meanwhile, the statistics kept coming in. The Georgina River at Camooweal was five feet over the bridge; the Gregory twenty-five feet above its normal level; Undilla Station had nine inches in three days, and Riversleigh four and a half overnight. The mail wouldn't be moving by vehicle or air, for all the airstrips were closed into the foreseeable future.

The fowl feed was finished. I fed the poultry – all sixty of them – on rice, then on cooked vermicelli, then on cooked corned meat, and finally on dough. I was down to three drums of flour and my dog was eating bread and milk when I decided I would have to kill the young steer in the paddock to feed them all. He'd been a milker's calf and went willingly into the yards, but the only way I could get his carcass back to the coldroom was in a wheelbarrow that bogged to the axle the moment it was loaded. To complicate matters, the wood heap was almost spent, and an electrical storm frizzled the battery charger, so I had to crank the Ferguson tractor every day to keep the wireless battery charged. And still it rained.

Mould grew on everything, insects multiplied like maniacs and swarmed the light in the evening. I scavenged half-green wood to cook buckets of meat for the poultry in the rain. Something – a goanna or a wildcat – got into the clucky duck's eggs overnight and broke half of them. I rescued the rest, which were on the point of hatching, and wound up with five extra ducklings to feed and care for. (They did look cute bobbing about in a plastic bowl on the kitchen table, though.) The diesel tank fuelling the generator ran dry and I had to (wo)manhandle a forty-four gallon drum of the stuff across the soaked and yielding sand then stand it up, pumping between downfalls because the rain just kept coming.

Towards the end of January Judith and I began attempting to organise, via the crowded, staticky airways, a charter flight to pick up her, David and the most urgently needed rations from the Lawn Hill airstrip and fly them home. No simple undertaking, as the sky had to be clear enough above the Isa to allow the plane to take off, the road to Lawn Hill had to be traversable so they could get there, and both airstrips dry enough for them to take off and land safely – all on the same day.

The normal test of a dirt airstrip's fitness to receive a plane was made, back then, by loading half a tonne onto a four-wheel drive and screaming the length of it at sixty miles an hour. If the wheels didn't sink in, it would carry a light aircraft. It was patently impossible for me to do this. The best I could manage over succeeding days was to ride the grey gelding Dubloon the six miles to the strip, dodging bog holes and quicksand, then gallop him from one end to the other and try to gauge from the depth of his hoofmarks how safe it would be to land a loaded light plane without killing everyone on board.

I clocked up sixty miles in the saddle riding to and fro. I bogged Dubloon to the hocks and myself to the knees. Day after day we dragged ourselves home covered in mud and insect bites to yell 'no go' into the ether, until a neighbour picked up my voice and relayed the message to Judith. Some days I judged our strip safe, but the Lawn Hill one was out, or the plane was unavailable. We weren't the only ones with problems – the entire Gulf Country was awash in January '74, aviation gas was at a premium and the charter pilots couldn't keep up with demand.

On 4 February, a message was relayed to me via the Doomadgee mission that a Bush Pilots share charter was leaving Burketown for Doomadgee, where they had an all-weather strip, then diverting to Lawn Hill to get Judith and David, who had safely negotiated the road thus far. They should land at Bowthorn by 1.30 p.m. I arranged with Doomadgee to load our mail and the carton of margarine languishing in their cold room for the past six weeks. Then I saddled up again, and rode to the top crossing of the anabranch of the Accident where I tied up the grey to save the labour of hauling him up the boggy far bank, and walked the half mile to the strip.

I waited there while the afternoon passed until finally, with an eye on the lengthening shadows, I started back to my mount. I still had to get home and it was easier to bog a horse in ground you couldn't see properly. And if the gelding floundered into quick-sandy country and sank to his belly I knew I'd never get him out again. I'd made it all the way back to Dubloon when I heard the plane, so was spared the anxiety of watching it land, though I waited fearfully for a crash, or the sight of smoke rising above the turpentine scrub. Neither occurring, I banished images of the wheels sinking, the propeller digging in and snapping off, while the whole aircraft flipped in a mess of fuel and broken struts, and started back up the track to meet my siblings. It was thirty-five days since the pair of them had driven off.

I know I shouldn't have done it, but before I left home that morning I'd written out a message in screaming capitals and stuck it on the fridge door for David to see.

IT NEVER RAINS IN JANUARY!

Unnecessary? Possibly. But satisfying? Oh, very.

Note: The last rain fell in mid April. Total for the Wet, forty-nine and a half inches. We got the loading home in April.

GLOSSARY

Barcoo rot: An ulcerous tropical skin condition linked with a deficiency of vitamin C due to a lack of fresh fruit and vegetables.

Black soil: A grey cracking clay soil that turns to clag after rain.

Boreman: The boreman oversees all stock water on the station, making sure pumps, mills and troughs are in good working order.

Bower shed: A bush-wood frame on which leafy branches are laid to form a shading roof.

Breaker: A horse yet to be broken in.

Bulldogging: A rodeo event where a rider drops from a horse to bring a steer to the ground. Also known as steerwrestling.

Bull roarers: A wooden slat on a cord, whirled to produce a low-pitched roar.

Campdrafting: An Australian sport that involves having a cut-out yard with about nine head of cattle. The competitor cuts out one beast, endeavours to take it outside into an arena, then proceeds to take it around a course of two pegs, then through a gate.

Chinaman's dam: A low bank or barricade built across a watercourse to hold back water, or to form a small barrier over which it can 'dump' as the hole fills. This action shifts the sand and to a degree mitigates the silting up of the waterhole that will be left when the creek stops running.

Coacher mob: The mob of cattle the ringers will walk along with to coax in other cattle being brought in by motorbikes and helicopters.

Condy's crystals: Potassium permanganate. In a weak water solution it is used as a disinfectant for skin conditions such as dermatitis.

Crib: Lunch, usually sandwiches wrapped in plastic wrap or, if money is tight, newspaper.

Crow's nest: An elevated stand in the yards to allow overhead drafting.

Delver: A triangular scooping device driven along bore drains to push debris up onto the banks and keep the water flowing from the bore into the paddocks.

Donga: A demountable building, basic accommodation.

Draught horse: A heavily built carthorse. A dray horse.

Droughtmaster cattle: A hardy, Brahman–Shorthorn cross, first introduced into the Gulf region in the 1930s and 1940s.

Fats: A bullock or other animal that is ready for slaughter.

Galah session: A rather chaotic session of about one hour via channel 5110 on the VHF handheld RFDS radio (after the doctor's session), when people who were physically isolated could send messages, place orders and talk to each other.

Gidgee: A thick, fairly impenetrable, low woodland that grows in many areas of western and north-west Queensland.

Gilgai hole: A hollow where rainwater collects.

Growing-out place: Where calves are grown up to steers for sale.

Hazer: An animal used in steer wrestling or steer undecorating. The beast is let out of a chute with the competitor on one side, and the hazer riding on the other side to keep the beast travelling straight between the two horses.

Jackaroo, Jillaroo: A novice, or first-year ringer on a sheep or cattle station.

Joss house: A Chinese temple.

Killer: An animal killed for food.

Min min: An unusual light phemonemon, usually a ball formation, seen in outback Australia.

Morning Glory: The Gulf's world-famous roll cloud, rolling in from the ocean at about one thousand feet. The wind in front of the roll cloud has a slight roar, and is gusty and energetic. These clouds can roll inland as far as Mount Isa.

The Mrs Potts: A Victorian, cast-iron clothes iron, with a detachable wood handle, heated on a stove top.

Nulla nullas: A wooden hunting stick, a waddy.

Number 8 wire: Wire used for fencing, four millimetres thick.

Pig-rooting: A horse with its head down, kicking up its back legs.

Plant of horses: A small team of mustering horses.

Poddy lambs and calves: Orphaned animals raised by hand.

RFDS: Royal Flying Doctor Service.

Roustabout: In shearing, the labourer who picks up the fleece and throws it onto the skirting table.

Ringers: Stock workers, usually in their second year or beyond.

Siphon pipes: Poly pipe that is submerged one end in water and the other worked by a push–pull action by hand, to create a vacuum to siphon water out of a channel.

Smoko: Morning tea or afternoon tea. Usually a substantial feed, especially morning smoko.

School of the Air (SOTA): a correspondence school that educates children in remote areas via radio or the internet.

Steer and bullock depot: Where young male steers are fattened to a certain weight or size before being sold.

Stock camp: A camp of ringers out from the main station, camping for weeks at a time during mustering.

Stinker: An alpha male goat.

Sugarbag: Honey from native sugarbag bees.

Troopy: A four-wheel drive Toyota troop carrier.

Turkey's nest: A dam (southern) or tank (northern) shaped like a bush turkey's nest or dust bath.

Waddy: A wooden hunting stick.

Walkamaries: Cooking firepits.

Weaners: Calves after weaning.

Weaner cradle: The branding cradle where calves are caught and safely held while they are dehorned and castrated.

hachette
AUSTRALIA

If you would like to find out more about Hachette Australia, our
authors, upcoming events and new releases you can
visit our website or our social media channels:

hachette.com.au

 HachetteAustralia

  HachetteAus